EVERYMAN, *I will go with thee,*
and be thy guide,
In thy most need to go by thy side

Egils Saga

Translated and edited by Christine Fell
Professor of Early English Studies, University of Nottingham

Poems by John Lucas

Dent: London and Melbourne
EVERYMAN'S LIBRARY

© J. M. Dent & Sons Ltd, 1975
© Poems, John Lucas, 1975

All rights reserved
Made in Great Britain by
Guernsey Press Co. Ltd, Guernsey, C.I. for
J. M. Dent & Sons Ltd
Aldine House, 33 Welbeck Street, London W1M 8LX
First published in a hardback edition in
Everyman's Library 1975
First published as an Everyman Classic 1985

This book is set in 9 on 10 pt Times New Roman

No 251 Hardback ISBN 0 460 10251 6
No 1251 Paperback ISBN 0 460 11251 1

Contents

To my mother and the memory of my father

Introduction

Egils saga belongs to a group of sagas known as the *Íslendinga sǫgur*, the sagas of Icelanders. It tells the story of a powerful tenth-century Norwegian family who emigrated to Iceland and settled there in the west at Borg on Borgarfjord. It recounts the family's feud with the kings of Norway, continued even after the emigration, and the hero Egil's exploits in Iceland, in Norway, widely around the Baltic and in Britain. Egil is a distinguished poet as well as a distinguished viking, and the saga also includes many of his poems. Although this is tenth-century material it was not written down in its present form until the thirteenth century, and the manuscripts in which it survives are mostly fourteenth century. The one used as the basis of modern editions is the fourteenth-century *Mǫðruvallabók*, but occasional lacunae and omissions, notably of two major poems, are supplied from the other manuscripts.

The nature of the *Íslendinga sǫgur* is a question that vexes both the historian and the literary historian. The historian dealing with the viking age asks how far he can consider the saga as a historical document. Because the material is deeply concerned with the events of a specific period in Scandinavian history and the style is realistic, many nineteenth-century historians tended to treat the sagas as reliable historical accounts of actual events. Today the pendulum has swung so far the other way that Professor Sawyer, in *The Age of the Vikings* (2nd edition 1971), believes scarcely a word he reads in the sagas, and less iconoclastic assessors of the material treat it with the utmost caution. The literary historian on the other hand is less concerned with the factual or fictional nature of the material. His problem is whether the saga represents the shaped structure of an individual author or the writing down of a tale told by a succession of tellers. If the latter then the shape is imposed by the tradition and the tellers rather than the writer.

However much the scepticism of historians leads us away from reliance on the saga it is not entirely without interest as a historical record. The trouble is that there can be no easy division into fact and fable. The sources are an amalgamation of written authority and oral tradition, but even written authority that precedes the saga is not contemporary with the events. Scaldic poems such as Egil's, when accepted as authentic and contemporary, are still sufficiently obscure to conceal from the eye of the historian more than they reveal. Much has been written about the part Egil and Thorolf played in Æthelstan's battle against the Scots. Although the saga provides a place name Vinheid, the battle in question was almost certainly the battle of Brunanburh. Yet it is impossible to use the saga material to throw light on events at Brunanburh since we cannot be sure that it gives us an actual rather than a conventional picture of a battle. The most that should be said is that the saga preserves Scandinavian knowledge of an actual event in English history.

Egil's visit to York has possibly aroused even more controversy. The poems are valid evidence that it took place, and Alan Binns has demonstrated in an article on 'The navigation of viking ships round the British Isles' that the shipwreck on the Humber is described in terms which accurately represent Humber tides. He suggests further that the description approximates more closely to conditions in the Humber mouth in the tenth century when the shipwreck is supposed to have occurred than in the late twelfth or early thirteenth century in which it was recorded. Someone was conveying to the author details about tenth-century England, and not all the details have been distorted in the telling. The author of the saga clearly assumed that English kings had room for Scandinavian mercenaries in their armies, that trade with England meant export of furs and import of wine and honey, wheat and cloth, that the difference between Christian and pagan presented no barrier to social contact, that the language differences need not prevent an Icelandic poet from offering poems to an English king. These assumptions on the part of the author may not always be valid but at least they merit examination. Occasionally we have documentary evidence to support the saga writer. His account of Thorolf and the Lapp trade is confirmed in many of its details by the account which the Norwegian seaman Ohthere gave to King Alfred in the ninth century, and which was inserted into the Old English translation of Orosius's *Historia*.

The saga also presents a full-scale picture of social and economic conditions, though these may relate more to the author's century than to Egil's. The constant preoccupation with provisioning that we see both in Thorolf's household in Norway and Skalla-Grim's in Iceland presumably reflects tenth-century conditions as well as thirteenth-century. But the intermingling of personal violence with respect for the law, and a dislike of kings combined with an acceptance of the social hierarchy below that level, may well be more characteristic of the later period.

It might be suggested that the genre to which *Egils saga* belongs is that of historical novel rather than historical record, but although there is a superficial aptness about such a description it is misleading. In dealing with historical novels of a later period we know or can hope to find out how much of the material is dictated by the pattern of actual events, and how much by the author's interpretation. We know, or are told, which characters are historical and which are invented by the author. We can be fairly certain that the printed text which reaches us is, save for misprints, the text that the author wrote. With the sagas we have no such certainty. We do not know how closely the scribes who copied the manuscripts felt obliged to follow their exemplars. Differences between manuscripts show variant versions of individual sagas, some shortened, some expanded, some muddled. If we posit a specific author of a written text it does not follow that this text was considered sacrosanct, or that what he wrote is the same as what survives. The alternative hypothesis in its most extreme form rejects the idea of an author, maintaining that the first written text was produced by a scribe copying on to vellum a story which had already attained its form in oral tradition. Yet if we cling to the concept of author responsibility rather than scribal submission we must still accept that traditions formed a large part of the author's source material. We do not know how much independence he was permitted or permitted himself in the handling of these. Certain incidents may be included in the saga not because they are historically true, nor because the writer saw them as part of his structure, but simply because to the immediate audience the saga would have been incomplete without these incidents. This means that we have to be wary in applying modern criteria about structural or thematic relevance. What may seem to us a curious digression might, if left out, have seemed to the first audience an unjustifiable omission of a known, perhaps eagerly anticipated, episode.

In spite of the fact that the term 'author' must be used with
reservations, there has been much discussion about the possible
author of *Egils saga*. A favourite candidate is Snorri Sturluson
who lived at Borg in the early thirteenth century, was the writer
of *Heimskringla*, a history of the kings of Norway, and was
descended from Egil. Snorri is undoubtedly an attractive con-
tender, and the case for accepting this authorship has been
strongly argued by Sigurður Nordal in his edition of the saga.
More recently Peter Hallberg in *Snorri Sturluson och Egils Saga
Skallagrímssonar* (1962), has analysed *Heimskringla* and *Egils
saga* in detail, and produced statistics to show that there is a
more pronounced similarity in the vocabulary of these two
texts than in any of his comparative test material. His con-
clusions have not always been accepted by reviewers and the
case for Snorri's authorship of *Egils saga* cannot be considered
proved. Ólafur Lárusson in *Ætt Egils Halldórssonar og Egils
Saga* (1937) developed a suggestion of Nordal's that Snorri's
source must have been Egil Halldorsson, one of Snorri's
household at Borg and also a descendant of Egil. He concluded
that traditions about Egil Skalla-Grimsson must have been
preserved among his descendants on the family estate at Borg
without interruption from his own time to that of Snorri. In
an article in *Maal og Minne* 1971, Anne Holtsmark takes this
argument a step further and puts forward Egil Halldorsson not
Snorri as the saga's author. Whatever hand wrote the actual
text the saga shows an exact knowledge of the district round
Borg and the traditions relating to Egil's life there, as well as
the political situation in Norway during the preceding generation.
Whether the force behind the saga's creation was writer, teller,
or as some scholars would have us believe, patron, and whether
Egil Halldorsson was first of these or second, and Snorri first or
third, the saga's pattern and purpose suggest that one mind
dominated the material. In discussing this pattern and purpose I
inevitably use the term 'author' for whatever mind gave us
Egils saga in its present form.

Egils saga more than others of the *Íslendinga sǫgur* is closely
bound up with the political history of Norway and shares some
of its material with the sagas of Norwegian kings. For example
certain passages dealing with the activities of King Harald
Finehair who first became sole ruler over the whole of Norway
are almost identical in the saga of Egil and the *Heimskringla*
saga of Harald. Whether or not this material is historically

accurate is arguable, and whether or not Snorri wrote both is also arguable. What is clear is that the historical picture presented by *Egils saga* is consistent with the history on which thirteenth-century Iceland was fed. In a well-known passage in *Sturlunga saga* King Sverrir, entertained by the story of 'the viking Hrongvid and King Olaf Lidsmanna and the grave-breaker Thrain the Berserk', says that such lying sagas are the most amusing. This passage shows an awareness of the difference between history and fiction even where the characters, if not their actions, have some historical validity. There are some passages in *Egils saga* which sound more fictional than others, notably the episode where Egil fights the berserk Ljot the Pale, but for the most part the saga is very closely integrated with ninth- and tenth-century history as known to the thirteenth century. This suggests that the author himself intended his saga to be taken seriously from a historical point of view. The feud of Egil and his family with the kings of Norway is not told purely for entertainment. It is told as part of the history of Iceland, stressing the historical reasons for the settlement of Iceland.

Struggles with the king of Norway in the thirteenth century and the attempts of Iceland to preserve her independence created a climate of thought in which the founders of that independence were highly valued. If at first sight it seems odd that Iceland should in this period be preoccupied with events from so far back, the explanation can be found partly in her isolation and perhaps too in consequent feelings of provincial inferiority. The *Íslendinga sǫgur* frequently describe visits abroad by tenth- or eleventh-century Icelanders who are welcomed at the courts of kings, loved by queens, and return home loaded with gifts and honours. In the late and romantic *Gunnlaugs saga* Gunnlaug recites his poems before three kings and two earls including Ethelred of England and Sigtrygg of Dublin. In the short story of Audun and the bear we have a perfect example of a poor Icelander whose luck and qualities gained him status and substantial rewards from both Svein of Denmark and Harald of Norway. But honoured though these characters may be they are not subservient. Gunnlaug responds to a slighting remark from Earl Eirik of Norway with an insult so telling that he has to get away fast in order to avoid being put to death. The emphasis is dual. On the one hand we are shown how highly valued these men are throughout the aristocratic society of the

northern world. On the other hand we see them asserting their
independence of this society, treating royalty on equal terms,
and not afraid to challenge royal authority. Perhaps the need
for some assertion of this kind can be illuminated by a sentence
in one manuscript of an epilogue to *Landnámabók*, the Book of
the Settlement. Here the reason given for compiling the names
and genealogies of the Icelandic settlers is that an answer is re-
quired to the foreigners who taunt Icelanders with being the
descendants of slaves and robbers.

In *Egils saga* we are shown the relations between three genera-
tions of a single family and two generations of Norwegian kings.
Egil's grandfather Kveld-Ulf lives in Norway at the time when
Harald Finehair is taking it over, and he attempts to preserve
his independence without showing outright hostility to Harald.
He claims that he is too old to serve kings. Thorolf, the elder of
his two sons, is eager to become Harald's man, but Skalla-
Grim, the younger son, shares his father's distrust of royalty.
The pattern is repeated in the next generation. Skalla-Grim also
has two sons, Thorolf and Egil. The second Thorolf becomes
friendly with Harald's son Eirik, but Egil does not emulate his
brother's behaviour. The following arrangement of names
shows the central characters in the conflict. The dates are only
approximations.

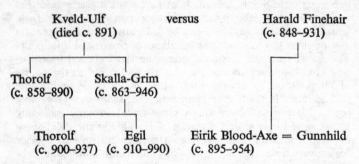

The dealings of Kveld-Ulf and his sons with Harald take up the
first thirty chapters of a saga that is called Egil's. But there is
full justification for this. The pattern of behaviour is being established and Egil's role marked out for him. The author's sym-
pathies are on the side of Kveld-Ulf, but this does not prevent
him from showing how this family gave Harald cause to be

suspicious of it. When Kveld-Ulf and Skalla-Grim so firmly refuse to go and submit to Harald their behaviour contrasts markedly with another father and son, Brynjolf and Bard. It already establishes them in Harald's mind as arrogant men. Thorolf does become his retainer, is valued and ennobled by him, but he too arouses Harald's anger by his tactless display of wealth and force when the king feasts at his house, even before he is slandered to the king by his enemies. Although we see the lies in the reports told by Hildirid's sons to the king, we can also see some ambiguity in Thorolf's actions. When his initial loyalty to the king has been eroded by Harald's belief in the slanders and by the confiscation of his estates, Thorolf quickly turns to overt hostility, and the final combat is fought out on a personal level. It is Harald who gives Thorolf his death-wound, and Thorolf would have killed the king if he could. His dying remark is, 'I've come three feet short'.

After Thorolf's death at Harald's hands there is never much hope of any reconciliation. Harald may be justified in calling the family arrogant, but his behaviour when Skalla-Grim asks compensation for Thorolf's death is not conciliating. Still, other men have put up with Harald's weighted remarks. When Harald told Thorolf he would do as a retainer if he was as good as his appearance, or said to Olvir Hnufa that he could have the king's friendship if he knew how to look after it, there is no flaring of hostility. When he offers Skalla-Grim honours, suggesting that he will need to cope better than his brother did, Skalla-Grim's reply is so brusque and uncomplimentary that it is not surprising Harald's anger should be aroused again. When this is followed by Kveld-Ulf's and Skalla-Grim's vengeance for Thorolf by killing in the king's family, and they make their escape to Iceland, expectations, suspicions and hatreds have been set up ready for the part to be played by the next generation on both sides.

It is emphasized that there are two types in Kveld-Ulf's family. Both the elder and younger Thorolfs are handsome, cheerful men, but Egil is like Skalla-Grim and Skalla-Grim is like Kveld-Ulf. 'Grim was a dark and ugly man, like his father in both appearance and disposition.' 'As he (Egil) grew up it was readily seen that he would be very ugly, like his father, and black-haired.' Along with the looks goes this quality of dogged and ferocious independence, more marked in the saga in Skalla-Grim than in Kveld-Ulf, and at its peak in Egil. It is only the two Thorolfs, the first of whom is explicitly said to be like his mother's people, and the second of whom like his uncle Thorolf, who attempt friendship with kings, and they both fail. The failure of the second Thorolf is not played out for us in detail. After an initial attempt at friendship between Thorolf and Eirik Blood-Axe Egil moves on to the scene. The quarrel is re-opened initially by Egil's behaviour on Atloy when he kills Eirik's servant Bard, but after that it is Eirik's ruthless wife Gunnhild who forces the pace, instructing her brothers to 'get one or other of the sons of Skalla-Grim killed, preferably both'.

There is a fairly recent account of *Egils saga* in Theodore Andersson's *The Icelandic Family Saga* (1967). Andersson praises the depiction of the first Thorolf's conflict, but considers that Egil's 'is handled with less address and considerably less dramatic intensity'. He attacks Egil as contentious and over-assertive, contrasting him with Thorolf who 'conforms to the saga's heroic ideal', and argues that his conflict with Eirik is 'by no stretch of the imagination a result of unjust persecution as in Thorolf's case, but self-inflicted'. This is to misunderstand the whole purpose of the author in giving us Thorolf's conflict. It is also to misrepresent saga pace. Thorolf's conflict is not better handled than Egil's, it is merely handled more swiftly, because it is there not as contrast but as preparation. It would lose impact if it were the whole drama rather than the first act. Almost every facet of Egil's conflict is seen in the light of family history, and it is clear that the author, unlike Andersson, finds Egil's behaviour a natural result of the situation he inherits. Saga writers put their most penetrating observations into the mouths of onlookers, and where Andersson says that Egil's behaviour at Bard's feast is wanton, Thorir more acutely comments, 'Men will say Bard got his deserts in being killed. All the same Egil is following the family tradition overmuch in thinking too little of the king's anger.' Arinbjorn at the famous scene in York admits Egil's offences against the king, but points out also the extent of the king's offences against Egil and Egil's family. An Icelandic audience in the thirteenth century would not, as Andersson does, accuse a man who did not fear the king's anger and was ready to challenge royal injustice, of 'pressing his quarrel quite beyond what a normal sense of tact would allow'.

It is true of course that Egil is not an attractive character, and neither for that matter is his father Skalla-Grim. They are both violent and avaricious men. Andersson describes Egil as 'brutish' without listing the hints of brute in his ancestry. Men were not sure whether Kveld-Ulf was or was not a shape-changer, a man with power to assume animal form. His uncle at any rate was Hallbjorn Halftroll. Skalla-Grim shows the strength and madness normally associated with shape-changers in the ball-game where he kills Thord and nearly kills Egil. Egil himself kills a man in a duel by biting through his windpipe. When Skalla-Grim confronts Harald, foreshadowing the scene where Egil confronts Eirik in York, the vocabulary describing the two men echoes from one episode to the other. The men who see Skalla-Grim arrive report that the newcomers are more like giants than humans in their size and looks. The man in York who tells Arinbjorn that Egil has arrived says that there is a man outside as big as a troll. Olvir speaks fluently to Harald on Skalla-Grim's behalf. The king looks up and sees that a man stands behind Olvir, 'taller by a head than other men, and bald'. Arinbjorn speaks fluently to Eirik on Egil's behalf. The king looks across over men's heads to where Egil stands. In both cases the author implies what he does not state, that the sight alone of the towering, ugly, aggressive figure that was Skalla-Grim or Egil was enough to cancel out all the eloquence of their friends on their behalf, and Harald rightly describes Skalla-Grim as a man 'full of wolf-temper'.

On the other hand in spite of Egil's cruelty and meanness we follow his career with infinitely more interest than we follow that of Thorolf. This is partly because we know that Thorolf's deviation from the family line is not going to work out well. Kveld-Ulf has predicted that it will not, and when the author puts accurate predictions into the mouths of his characters, these characters are Kveld-Ulf, Skalla-Grim and Egil, though Egil himself has further powers—power over runes, power in cursing and power in healing. The two Thorolfs are less wise and less aware and they rush on their fate regardless of the warnings of their kin. We know with the author that when Thorolf Skalla-Grimsson conceals his father's reaction to the axe, the king's gift, and presents Eirik with a nice longship sail, pretending that it is a gift from Skalla-Grim, this tactful action is absurd in its futility. We accept as more reasonable Skalla-Grim's super-ficially unreasonable treatment of the axe, because we have been led by the author to trust Skalla-Grim's judgment. The two Thorolfs are overshadowed by their uglier and cleverer fathers and brothers. The personalities of Kveld-Ulf and Skalla-

Grim linger more in the mind than Thorolf's conventionally heroic behaviour, and from the moment Egil appears in the saga he dominates it. Egil never remotely resembles a conventional hero. We see him in a temper at the age of three because his father has refused to take him to a feast: 'You don't know how to behave among men when there's heavy drinking.' At the age of six his exuberance expresses itself in a childish poem of delight when his mother promises him a warship as soon as he is old enough. One evocative scene follows another from the wild drinking on Atloy to the resentment in Æthelstan's hall where Egil sits, fully-armed, slamming his sword in and out of its sheath, not touching drink until he has been given gold. In York he comments wryly that he has not come prepared for composing panegyrics on Eirik, and back in Iceland he shuts himself in his room to die because his son has been drowned. In his old age he stumbles, blind and arthritic, trying to warm his feet and avoid the sharp-tongued servants. There are few men in the sagas whom we follow from their early childhood to death in old age, and few sagas so dominated by one personality.

Apart from his flamboyance and aggression the main quality that lifts Egil above the common run of vikings is his gift for poetry, a gift inherited along with his looks and temper from father and grandfather. The viking age, like the Elizabethan, valued men who were both poets and fighters, and the Scandinavian kings usually numbered several poets among their retainers. Some kings like Harald Hardradi were accomplished poets themselves. But it is rare for us to have so extensive a corpus of poetry as we have from Egil, and since he is not a king's retainer (except briefly Æthelstan's) most of his poetry is personal rather than official, dealing with the events of his own life, not the battles of kings. Most of the poetry quoted as his is likely to be his genuinely. Even historians are accustomed to accept that scaldic verse quoted in fourteenth-century manuscripts was probably composed by those to whom it is attributed, on the grounds that form and metre are so complex that it had to be remembered accurately. Otherwise distortion of sense or of metre would result. Still there are some of Egil's poems, including even *Hǫfuðlausn*, which at one time or another have been attributed to thirteenth-century interpolators, to saga writer or scribe, not to the poet Egil himself. But even where we assume that the poems are Egil's, it is still not necessary to assume that every poem that Egil composed is precisely what he said on the occasion to which it is attributed. The poems he composed at the age of three are so much more polished than the one at the age of six, that we may assume they were revised later, much as the limericks composed at parties are given a new punch-line before the next party. Yet we need to remember that the art of scaldic verse was an oral not a literate one, and that verses were composed in the emotions and stresses of the moment, not in tranquil recollection afterwards. Some of Egil's best poems are produced on occasions when he is drunk with beer or anger, blood-lust or pride in his achievements. He may have spent the time rowing home from Atloy planning the verse he would speak on arrival, but the ones he spoke during the feasting could not have been prepared beforehand. The last one he speaks on that occasion before running Bard through with his sword is a masterly example of his technical control. In the first line and a half he develops a play on the name *Ǫlvir*, the verb *ǫlva*, 'to grow drunk' and the noun *ǫl*, 'beer'. The poem contains statements on the three subjects of drink, Olvir's condition and poetry. Egil uses the image of rain in each statement, linking the ideas by a different use of the image.

The poems are also our clues to the emotional subtleties of the saga. Egil's verse describing wind and wave in terms of chisel and file as he sails home to Iceland reminds us of his father Skalla-Grim, skilled blacksmith, celebrating the craft in one of his few extant poems. Egil's indignant poems when Berg-Onund calls his wife Asgerd slave-born recall Bjorn and Thora's honeymoon in the broch on Mousa, and Asgerd's birth at Egil's home in Iceland. The irony of empty rhetorical flourish in Egil's poem in praise of Eirik, and the genuine depth of feeling in *Sonatorrek* and *Arinbjarnarkviða* have been remarked on too often to need more than a passing mention. Less often cited is Egil's friendship in his old age with the young poet Einar, and their pleasure in discussing the art of poetry together, or the rueful final poems where Egil sees himself, blind, cold, deaf and impotent, as the man who was honoured by Æthelstan, wrested his life from Eirik, and has grown old without a king's protection, paying the price for his choice of independence.

It is not only in his poems that we see Egil at his best. When we have been most revolted by some example of his cruelty or avarice there are contrasting incidents in the saga that show him to advantage. He behaves like a thug in Armod's house but this is followed by the curing of Helga. Egil repays the help he has received from Arinbjorn by the help he gives Fridgeir. The good terms he is on with Æthelstan are in contrast to the feud with Eirik. The author goes out of his way to emphasize that Egil's behaviour was not outrageous given the circumstances. He was peaceable in Iceland, we are told, but then no-one was trying to deprive him of his rights and property. Andersson seems to think it was unnecessary for Egil to be concerned about his estates in Norway when he was a rich man in Iceland, but concern with property rights is limited neither to Egil nor to the viking age. Egil, the author stresses, is acting within the law. It is the king who breaks the law against him, and Egil finally gets justice from Eirik's brother and antagonist Hakon. Egil is also acting within the viking code. It may seem to us that the Kurlanders who were burned in their house might have preferred Egil not to be so scrupulously honourable. But the code dictates that those who raid or kill claim their deeds, they do not do them in secret. And however much we may feel that Egil might have shown some magnanimity in the quarrel between his son Thorstein and Steinar, the son of his old friend Onund Sjoni, there is no doubt whatsoever that it was Steinar who was the aggressor.

The feud between the families of Kveld-Ulf and Harald, and the adventures of Egil between them occupy most of the saga. But the minor characters cannot be ignored. The feud takes on an extra dimension because of all the interested parties. Friends of the king and friends to Kveld-Ulf and his descendants try continually to cope with the hostilities, to establish temporary settlements if not lasting peace. Olvir does this for the sons of Kveld-Ulf, Thorir and Arinbjorn for Egil.

On the other side are the hostile faction—Hildirid's sons in the first part, Gunnhild in the second. For the most part the women in this saga are shadowy creatures. Bera, Skalla-Grim's wife, is only seen to exist on rare occasions, as when her son kills his first man at the age of six, and she acclaims him as a 'real viking'. Salbjorg, Kveld-Ulf's wife, is introduced to us as a woman of character, but never heard of again. Other women including Asgerd and Gunnhild are conventionally described as the loveliest and cleverest of women. Almost the same words are used of Egil's placid wife as of Eirik's queen. But Eirik's queen already has her character established in Iceland. Whenever she meets us in the sagas she is evil and possessed of magic

powers. In *Egils saga* where other women move silent and un-
noticed in the background Gunnhild's well-known qualities
are superbly displayed. Eirik himself tells her that she, more than
anyone else, taunts him into severity. She shares with Hildirid's
sons a complete mastery of the techniques of persuasion, though
without their obsequiousness. The brothers favour innuendo,
the word that is loaded if not actually a lie, but both they and
Gunnhild play the game of misrepresenting justice as weakness.
King Harald is brought to see Thorolf as a threat by lines like,
'He intends to make himself king over the north there . . . and
it's surprising that you let him do anything he likes.' At the
Gula Assembly Gunnhild says to Eirik about Egil, 'Perhaps
you would not speak against him if he claimed the kingdom at
your hand.' In neither case does the word relate to the fact,
but is directed at the king's fears for his royal power and privi-
lege. In the first part we see these persuaders at work in the
background, and it is not until York that we have the full
confrontation of friend and enemy. The quarrel here may be
between Egil and Eirik but the speakers are Arinbjorn and
Gunnhild. There can be no better example of the build-up of
opposing pressures. Arinbjorn stretches the truth in his stress on
Egil's voluntary submission, Gunnhild demands his immediate
execution. Arinbjorn demonstrates that the king's honour is involved, Gunnhild urges the claims of status. Gunnhild reminds
the king of Egil's offences, Arinbjorn lists the provocations. The
emotional blackmail of Arinbjorn's final bid for Egil's life wins
the game however: 'You will have paid dearly for Egil's life,
Sir, when my men and I are all dead at your feet. I would not
have thought that you would prefer to see me lying dead on the
ground, rather than let me receive the life of a single man that
I ask for.' Neither side relies on rational argument—it is a
conflict of power and pressure, which Arinbjorn wins because
he knows that Eirik in his present precarious kingship cannot
afford to lose the support of such followers as he still has. At
the same time he allows Eirik a graceful way out of the situation.

In this passage we see the rapid thrust of attack and counter-
attack, and we are not deflected from the actual exchange by any
intrusion from the author. The 'Gunnhild said' and 'Arinbjorn
said' are there as stage directions, and we are able to concentrate
all our attention on the subtleties of the actual speech. Neither
here nor elsewhere does the author tell us that men spoke
angrily, or sadly, or cheerfully. Nor does the original vary the

verbs describing conversation. Men do not retort or urge or protest, they say and answer. We are told when King Harald is angry because he expresses his anger by silence, and we are told whether he accepts people's greetings favourably or accepts their greetings. On one momentous occasion the author does give us an adverb. Thorolf closed the conversation with Hildirid's sons 'irritably'. The suggestion is that Thorolf is denying the possibility of further negotiation, with disastrous consequences for himself. But mostly in this as in other things understanding is left to the reader's or hearer's intelligence.

It is a truism that the saga writer expects an intelligent audience, leaving much to be grasped from suggestion and understatement. What is perhaps more difficult for the modern than the medieval audience is that he also assumes good memory. A word or a sentence dropped in an early chapter can illuminate an episode a hundred pages later, if the reader has been alert and his memory retentive. When Egil is trying to compose his poem in praise of Eirik he cannot concentrate because of the swallow chattering outside his window. Arinbjorn arrives there and sees a shape-changer leaving the house. The author had mentioned twenty-three chapters earlier that Gunnhild was skilled in magic, and therefore does not bother to tell us overtly that swallow and shape-changer would be Gunnhild herself. Similarly the author expects his audience to have a clear grasp of the relationships, again an easier matter for medieval than modern thinking. Yet it is important to remember that Olvir Hnufa, who champions Thorolf and Skalla-Grim, is their mother's brother, and that Thorir is linked to both Kveld-Ulf and Eirik by the ties of fostering, scarcely less close than kinship. He himself was foster-son to Kveld-Ulf, foster-brother, therefore, of Skalla-Grim, and in turn he fostered Harald's son Eirik. Egil's closest friend, Arinbjorn, is thus not only retainer but foster-brother of Eirik. The author does not emphasize the pull of loyalties. The relationships speak for themselves, and family loyalties extend far beyond the small unit that we think of as 'family' today. Ketil Hœng who avenges Thorolf is spoken of as a close kinsman, but to us the relationship does not seem particularly close. Ketil's great-grandfather and Thorolf's grandmother were brother and sister.

Sagas often show the men and women torn by conflicting loyalties, but in *Egils saga* we see those who are able to resolve such a situation. Olvir saves Skalla-Grim from Harald, though he could not save Thorolf, and he betrays neither kinsmen nor king. Arinbjorn saves Egil from Eirik, yet stays loyal to Eirik, going into exile with him, and subsequently joining his sons in their exile. If the author of the saga had stressed the tensions underlying the surface relationships he would have thought he was pointing out the obvious. It is important that we should not lose sight of what was obvious to him.

Note on the Translation

One of the first problems in translating *Egils saga* is that it is the saga of a poet, and though many sagas contain poems, few contain so much of the work of a single major poet. The difficulties of translating scaldic verse are sufficiently attested by the fact that no-one has ever done so satisfactorily. The poems are complex in form and vocabulary, relying on a range of cultural allusion that has ceased to have meaning for the modern audience. The translator has either to explain and expand the allusions, sacrificing the taut brevity of the original, or retain them, sacrificing intelligibility.

I quote in the original the verse from chapter 55 where Egil thanks King Æthelstan for the gift of a gold arm-ring. The three long poems and one or two of the shorter ones have a slightly different metrical pattern and I deal with these in the notes, but all poems share the specifically poetic vocabulary. The metrical pattern demonstrated here is usual for the majority of scaldic poems, whether by Egil or anyone else:

> Hrammtangar lætr hanga
> hrynvirgil mér brynju
> Hǫðr á hauki troðnum
> heiðis vingameiði;
> rítmœðis knák reiða
> ræðr gunnvala bræðir,
> gelgju seil á galga
> geirveðrs, lofi at meira.

Each line has six syllables and three stresses. The last line here appears to have seven syllables, but one of the two consecutive vowels in *lofi at* would be elided in pronunciation. In each pair of lines alliteration links two of the stresses in the first line with the first stress of the second. In lines one and two the alliteration falls on *hrammtangar*, *hanga* and *hrynvirgil*; in lines three and four on

Hǫðr, hauki and *heiðis*; in lines five and six on *rítmæðis, reiða*
and *ræðr*; and in lines seven and eight on *gelgju, galga* and *geir-*
veðrs. In addition to this the even lines have internal rhyme; in
line two the syllables *hryn* and *bryn* rhyme; in line four *heið* and
meið; in line six *ræð* and *bræð*; and in line eight *geir* and *meir*.
The odd lines contain an echo of internal consonants. In line
one the *ng* group echoes in *tangar* and *hanga*; in line three *ð*
in *Hǫð* and *troð*; in line five *ð* again in *mæðis* and *reiða*; in line
seven the *lg* group in *gelgju* and *galga*.

They are eight-line poems, but the sense is usually confined
within the two quartets. The word order has no relation to the
normal word-order of prose. In prose the first four lines of this
poem would read: 'Brynju Hǫðr lætr hrammtangar hrynvirgil
hanga mér á hauki troðnum heiðis vingameiði.' The difference
is perhaps best illustrated like this:

4   3   6

Hrammtangar lætr hanga

5   7   1

hrynvirgil mér brynju

2   8

Hǫðr (á hauki troðnum)

9   10

heiðis vingameiði.

A literal translation of the whole poem would run: 'Hod of the
mailcoat lets the halter of the arm hang on my hawk-trodden
hawk-gallows./ I know how to make the pin-string of the shield-
tormentor ride the gallows of the spear-storm. The feeder of the
battle-hawk enjoys the greater praise.' The texture of the poem
is rich with those metaphors beloved of scaldic poets known as
kennings, in which two objects are named and a third object is
understood from the relationship of these two. In the first part
Hǫðr is the name of a god, and the god of the mailcoat is a
kenning for warrior; band or halter of the arm is a kenning for
ring; tree or gallows of the hawk a kenning for arm. In the
second half the kennings are more complicated. In 'pin-string
of the shield-tormentor' there is a double kenning from which
the object to be understood is ring. That which torments shields
is the sword. The pin or nail of the sword is the arm which holds
it. The string round the arm is the ring. The easy way to see how
this works is to remove one kenning at a time:

string of the pin of (the tormentor of the shield)
                              ↓
                            sword
string of (the pin of the sword)
                     ↓
                    arm
string of the arm
      ↓
    ring

The final two kennings of the poem are simple. In 'gallows of the spear-storm' the spear-storm is battle, and its gallows is a sword. 'Feeder of the battle-hawk' is a normal kenning for warrior and here refers to Æthelstan. In a stripped prose version eliminating the kennings we are left with the bare sense: 'The warrior let the ring hang on my arm. I know how to make the ring ride the sword. The warrior (Æthelstan) enjoys the greater praise.' Such a prose version fails to convey anything of the intricate artifice of the poem.

A number of translators of scaldic verse, recognizing the bleakness of a straight prose rendering and the unintelligibility of a literal one, have substituted something almost as complicated as the original in an effort to convey the feeling of highly-wrought, complex poems. This has always seemed to me a mistake. It forces the reader to unravel a crossword-puzzle tangle of ideas, which when unravelled are still not the specific complexities of the original and actual poem. The solution we have arrived at is to put poems in the text and translations in the notes, though even in the notes I have frequently simplified elaborate kennings, and have eliminated a whole range of casual allusion to figures of myth and legend. John Lucas, who claims that a poet must be translated by a poet, has for the entire corpus of poetry in *Egils saga* produced poems which are close to the originals in form, sense and tone, though not in the details of scaldic metaphors. In this way instead of the scaldic poems presenting a barrier to the reader's understanding and enjoyment of the saga, they are an integrated part of the story, adding considerably to its vigour and impact.

The problems of translating the prose are comparatively slight, but there are problems, both stylistic and semantic. Saga style has sometimes been called colloquial, but the colloquialism is more apparent than real. The pattern of writing is formalized and sophisticated, and modern English syntax cannot cope with the interweaving of subordinate clauses and the subtleties of subjunctive conversations, without obvious artifice. The semantic difficulties are largely a matter of trying to avoid anachronism. For example Old Norse distinguishes several kinds of spear. One of them, the *atgeir*, is literally a thrusting-spear, and often translated as 'halberd'. The word halberd, however, describes a weapon which did not exist at the time, and I have not used it, preferring an unqualified 'spear' for the various terms in the original. There are similar difficulties with the hierarchy. To translate *lendr maðr* as 'nobleman' is to impose a concept not precisely in accord with the meaning of the original, but none of the alternative translations seemed an improvement. Most of these specific difficulties I have tried to discuss in the notes.

Any translator is indebted to the editors who provide a competent text from the manuscripts, and also to the earlier translators in the field. Sigurður Nordal's excellent edition of *Egils saga* is the one on which all subsequent scholars, translators and critics must rely, and I have not only used it for the text, but have learned much from Professor Nordal's notes and comments. I share with other readers a debt to Professor Gwyn Jones who produced the first readable English version of *Egils saga* in 1960. It gives me pleasure to acknowledge also those colleagues who, during the past two years, have willingly given me help with many aspects of the translation. Elizabeth Williams has, as always, been generous with her time and constructive in her criticisms. Peter Foote has read through parts of the text and commented, sometimes encouragingly, always pertinently. David Wilson has discussed all the terminology for artefacts in the revealing light of his archæological knowledge, and wherever the saga describes a house or a weapon in complicated technical detail my translation relies on his expertise. For the vocabulary on navigation and the bewildering range of words for different kinds of ship I turned to Alan Binns who combines the knowledge of seaman and scholar, and whose comments I quote in the notes. It is entirely owing to John Lucas that in my translation *Egils saga* remains the saga of a poet. I read through my translation of the saga when it contained my own prose versions of the poems, and read it again when these were replaced by Lucas's work, and I appreciate the full extent of my debt.

Finally I acknowledge my greatest debt which is to Arnold Taylor. He read through my entire text suggesting numerous improvements as well as corrections. For the time he spent on it and for all his help and kindness I am deeply grateful. Whatever merits my translation has, much of the credit goes to the scholarship, co-operation and generosity of these friends and colleagues.

Nottingham   Christine Fell
1974

Note on the 1985 Printing

Small corrections have been made in this edition. I am grateful to reviewers and colleagues for pointing out errors and misprints.

Nottingham   Christine Fell
1985

The Translations of Egil's Poems

Poets have repeatedly argued about the best ways to translate their brother-poets of different languages. The one matter on which there is general agreement is that the form in which the original poem was written has nearly always to be sacrificed. To abide by it is simply to botch the job. For it is a fact that a poet comes much nearer to making a poem worthy of the original if he writes in a manner that feels natural to himself. As W. H. Auden pointed out, Robert Bridges' determined use of hexameters in his Homeric translations often made Homer sound eccentric, which he never was. Pope, on the other hand, put his Homer into couplets; yet although in his version Homer's heroes occasionally sound more like eighteenth-century gentlemen than they perhaps should, Pope's Homer is probably still the best of all English Homeric translations.

Having said this, I need to explain why in my own translations of Egil's poems I have chosen to stay near to the form of the originals. Egil's short poems are composed in eight-line stanzas, in which the six-syllable lines are linked by patterns of alliteration and assonance, and in which there is a major syntactical break at the end of the fourth line. Why keep to this? Well, in the first place, the eight-line stanza is familiar enough to us. English poets are used to thinking in eight-line units. They are still more used to thinking in four-line units, and Egil's eight-line stanza form is very near to being two quatrains. And as to line-length, it is obvious that a six-syllable line can fit one of the great English measures, the iambic trimeter. It sounds natural to English ears. But because it *is* a syllable measure it has the added advantage of being able to accommodate a variable and shifting number of stresses, determined by speech-patterns. Egil's poems are spoken poems: the six-syllable line, clipped and terse though it is, allows the poet a degree of informality—almost a feeling of impromptu delivery—which I think, rightly or wrongly, is an important element of Egil's verse, and against which his un-

doubted formality—those moments when his thoughts compress
to their most rhythmically insistent and densely eloquent—can
be played off. I have retained the patterns of alliteration and
assonance because they seem to me formally beautiful and are
part of Egil's *speaking* of verse. I have not, though, often combined them with stress because to modern ears coincidence of
stress and alliteration—particularly over such a short line—
sounds either hectoring or funny (where I have linked stress and
alliteration it is usually for comic purposes).

There are three long poems attributed to Egil. One of them is a
poem of praise to King Eirik, who is considering whether or not
to lop off Egil's head. The poem is ornate and a bit phoney. It is
in twenty eight-line stanzas. I have followed the stanza form
but have added an extra syllable to what in the original is a four-
syllable line. To try and write a four-syllable line in modern
English is to end up with a silly rocking-horse rhythm, and
whatever Egil may have intended in his poem he certainly
wouldn't have intended to be silly when his neck was at stake. I
have also substituted couplet-rhymes for Egil's rhyme-scheme
(one rhyme for each four-line block). These alterations were made
in the interest of trying to catch the poem's meretricious and
slightly tongue-in-cheek glitter.

The other long poems have twenty-five eight-line stanzas, the
stanzas being made up of alternate four and three-syllable lines.
In my version I have doubled the lines up, so that each stanza
has four seven-syllable lines.

So far then, I could follow Egil reasonably closely and hope to
make poems which with luck would sound satisfying to a modern
audience without being untrue to Egil's shaping powers. But his
language is a very different matter. There is simply no way in which
the language of an Egil poem can be reproduced in a modern
poem. It is a matter for the keenest regret. Like all great poets, Egil
has an insatiable love of words and an unflagging imaginative
intelligence. But no modern poet can hope to rival the way in
which his intelligence *works* through words. To take just one
example: at the end of his long and noble poem to his friend,
Arinbjorn, Egil says that Arinbjorn must not be allowed to think
that he, Egil, is unmindful of his friend's great generosity, that it
has been wasted on him. Now, there is nothing strange about
that. Except that Egil's actual words are: 'It would not be right
if the gold-diminisher had thrown on the mew-path, hard-ridden
by the stud of Rokkvi, the many gains he gave to me.' Mew-

path is the sea, stud of Rokkvi are ships. Is Egil merely finding a roundabout way of describing the sea and the ships? Not at all. He means exactly what he says. He doesn't mean that the mew-path is really the sea. His language isn't imagistic in our sense, it doesn't have to pump life into dead abstractions. Nor is he simply trying to jolly the poem up. On the contrary, for Egil the sea really *is* a mew-path (among other things).

This is so strange to us that we find it difficult to grasp that Egil could have been serious. But once the fact is grasped, it becomes possible to see how staggeringly vital—in a strict sense—such language is. Word and thing penetrate each other, give each other life. Egil's language teems with particular life. By comparison, the corpus of language available to a modern poet feels a shrunken and cadaverous thing.

But Egil is also a great poet because of the range of his interests; and here we can come a little nearer to him. He has nothing to say about sexual love and he is rarely speculative. But how much he gives us. Descriptive poems, caustically funny ones, poems that brood over ill-luck or insult, poems in which he brags of his strength, mourns a brother's death, is derisive, grateful, brutal and friendly by turns, and much else besides:— as we read these poems (aloud, it is to be hoped) we enter and take possession of the world of a quite extraordinary man. And in the poem he makes up to solace himself over the death of a loved son he creates what is by any standards a great work. It is as intensely moving—and exhilarating—as *Lycidas*.

I am well aware of how far short I have fallen from my original aim in undertaking these translations, which was to give a palpable sense to modern readers of Egil's many-sided genius. But I hope at least that my versions of his poems will make readers impatient to read Egil for themselves.

Nottingham   John Lucas
1974

Egils saga

1

There was a man called Ulf, the son of Bjalfi and Hallbera, the daughter of Ulf the Dauntless. She was the sister of Hallbjorn Halftroll in Ramsta, the father of Ketil Hœng. Ulf was such a big and strong man that he had no equals. When he was young he went on viking raids. In partnership with him was Berle-Kari, a man of good birth, distinguished for strength and courage. He was a berserk.[1] He and Ulf shared one purse and were close friends. When they left off raiding Kari went to his farm in Berle; he was a very wealthy man. Kari had three children; his first son was called Eyvind Lambi, a second son Olvir Hnufa, and his daughter was called Salbjorg. She was a beautiful woman and of fine character. Ulf married her. Then he too went to his own estates. Ulf was a rich man, both in land and possessions. He claimed the rank of a nobleman[2] which his ancestors had held, and became a powerful man. It is said that Ulf was very efficient in the management of his estates. He usually got up early and checked the jobs that were being done, or went to the smiths, and looked over his stock and his fields. Sometimes he talked with people who needed his advice. He could give good advice in all matters for he was very wise. But every day when it came to evening he became withdrawn, so that scarcely anyone could get a word across to him. He was sleepy in the evening, and it was rumoured that he must be a great shape-changer. He was called Kveld-Ulf.[3]

Kveld-Ulf and Salbjorg had two sons. The elder was called Thorolf and the younger Grim. When they grew up both of them were big and strong like their father. Thorolf was a handsome and gifted man; he was like his mother's people, cheerful, generous, eager in everything, and a man of great ambition. He was popular with everyone. Grim was a dark and ugly man, like his father both in appearance and disposition. He became a

1

very efficient man, he was clever with wood and iron, and he grew to be an excellent craftsman. He often went out with his boat to net herring during the winters, and many of the servants went with him. When Thorolf was twenty years old he got ready to go raiding. Kveld-Ulf provided him with a longship. Eyvind and Olvir, the sons of Berle-Kari, joined this expedition— they had a big company and a second longship—and they spent the summer in viking raids, gained money for themselves, and made a great profit. There were several summers when they went on viking raids, but in the winters they were at home with their families. Thorolf brought home many treasures which he gave to his father and mother, so that there was no lack at that time of either money or fame. Kveld-Ulf was then getting on in years. His sons were in their prime.

2

The king of Fjordane at that time was called Audbjorn. An earl of his was called Hroald, and the earl's son was called Thorir. At the same time there was an earl called Atli the Slim. He lived at Gaular. His children were Hallstein, Holmstein, Herstein and Solveig the Fair. One year it was very crowded at Gaular for the autumn sacrifice. Olvir Hnufa saw Solveig then, and fell in love with her. Afterwards he asked for her hand, but the earl thought he was not good enough for her, and would not give her to him. Olvir made many love-songs about her. He thought so much of Solveig that he left off raiding, and then Thorolf and Eyvind Lambi went on the raids.

3

Harald, the son of Halfdan the Black, had taken up his father's inheritance east in Vik. He had made a solemn vow that he would not have his hair combed or cut until he was the sole king in Norway. He was called Shaggy Harald.[1] He fought with those kings who were his neighbours and conquered them, and there are long stories about that. Then he took possession of Opland. From there he went north into Trondheim, and fought many battles there before becoming sole ruler of all Trondelag. Then he intended to go north into Namdal against the brothers Herlaug and Hrollaug who were kings over it at that time. But when the brothers learned of his expedition, Herlaug, accompanied by eleven men, entered a mound which they had already been building three years. The mound was closed after them. But King Hrollaug abdicated the kingship,[2] took up the rank of an earl, and submitted afterwards to the rule of King Harald, giving up his sovereignty. In this way King Harald took possession of the district of Namdal and Halogaland, and put men in charge of his kingdom there. Then King Harald prepared to leave Trondheim with a fleet, and went south to More, fought a battle there with King Hunthjof and won the victory. Hunthjof was killed there, and King Harald took possession of Nordmore and Romsdal. But Solvi Klofi, the son of Hunthjof, had escaped, and he went to Sunnmore to King Arnvid, asking him for help. 'Though just now it is we who are in trouble,' he said, 'it will not be long before the same trouble reaches you, for I suppose Harald will be on his way here as soon as he has enslaved and oppressed as much as he wants in Nordmore and Romsdal. You have the same choice as we had. You can defend your property and freedom, and risk for it all the men whose help you can hope for. I am prepared to be on your side together with my people against this tyranny and injustice. On the other hand you may wish to follow the same course as the men of Namdal and go voluntarily into servitude to become Harald's slaves. My father thought it praiseworthy to die in his kingdom with honour, not to become another king's subordinate in his old age. I imagine that you will think like this, and so will all those who have something of pride and courage.' By such arguments the king was persuaded to summon his people and defend his land. He and Solvi bound themselves in fellowship, and sent word to King Audbjorn who ruled over Fjordane, that he should come to their aid. When the messengers came to King Audbjorn with these words he took counsel with his friends. They all advised him to summon his people and go to join the men of More as word had been sent to him. King Audbjorn had the war-arrow despatched, and the summons to war sent out through all his kingdom. He sent men to the most powerful chieftains inviting them to join him. But when the king's messengers came to Kveld-Ulf and told him their errand, and that it was the king's wish that Kveld-Ulf should come to him with all his men, Kveld-Ulf answered, 'The king will think I am under an obligation to be with him if he is attacked in Fjordane and has to defend his land. But I do not see that I have any obligation to go north to More and fight there and defend their land. Tell your king, in short, that Kveld-Ulf is going to sit at home during this plunge into battle, and that he is not going to collect an army, and that he is not going to make a journey from home to fight against Shaggy Harald. I think Harald is loaded with luck,[3] and our king does not have a handful.' The messengers went home to the king and told him the result of their errand, while Kveld-Ulf stayed at home on his farm.

4

King Audbjorn went north to More with the men accompanying him and met King Arnvid and Solvi Klofi there. All together they had a big army. King Harald too had come from the north with his men' and they met beside Solskel. There was a great battle and many men fell on both sides. Of Harald's company there were killed two earls, Asgaut and Asbjorn, and two sons of Earl Hakon of Lade, Grjotgard and Herlaug, and many other great men. On the side of More there fell King Arnvid and King Audbjorn. Solvi Klofi escaped by flight, and was afterwards a great viking. He often inflicted great harm on King Harald's kingdom, and so he got the name Klofi.[1] After that King Harald subjugated Sunnmore. Vemund, the brother of King Audbjorn, held Fjordane and became king over it. That was late in the autumn, and men advised King Harald not to go south round Stadtland during the autumn days. Then King Harald made Rognvald earl over both districts of More and over Romsdal, and he turned back north to Trondheim. He kept a great force of men with him. The same autumn Atli's sons made an attack on the home of Olvir Hnufa and intended to kill him.[2] They had such a large troop that Olvir could offer no resistance and got away by flight. Then he went north to More and met King Harald there. Olvir submitted to him, and went north to Trondheim with the king in the autumn. He became the king's close friend and stayed with him for a long time, and he was the king's poet.[3] That winter Earl Rognvald went by the inner road across Dragseid south to Fjordane. He had reports on the movements of King Vemund and came by night to a place called Naustdal where Vemund was feasting. Earl Rognvald seized the house and burned the king inside it with ninety men. After that Berle-Kari came to Earl Rognvald with a longship and full crew, and they both went north to More. Rognvald took the ships which King Vemund had owned, and all of his posses-

sions he could get. Berle-Kari then went north to Trondheim to
meet King Harald and became his man. The next spring King
Harald went south along the coast with a fleet, and subdued
Fjordane and Fjaler, and put his men in authority there. He
put Earl Hroald over Fjordane.

On taking over those districts which had recently come into
his possession, King Harald took careful stock of the noblemen
and the powerful farmers and all those whom he suspected of
possible revolt. He made each do one of two things, either enter
his service or leave the country. A third choice was to undergo
hardship or loss of life, and some were maimed in hands and
feet. King Harald took possession of all odal rights[4] in every
district, and all the land, inhabited or not, and equally the sea
and the lakes, and all farmers were to be his tenants. Those who
worked in the forests and the salt-burners and all those who hunt
whether by sea or land had to pay his taxes. Many men fled
away from this oppression out of the country, and many waste
lands were then settled, both east in Jamtland and Halsingland,
and in the west lands, the Hebrides, the Dublin area, Ireland,
Normandy in France, Caithness in Scotland, the Orkneys,
Shetland and the Færoes. And at that time Iceland was discovered.[5]

5

King Harald stayed with his army in Fjordane. He sent men
through the land to visit those whom he wanted to contact but
who had not come to him. The king's messengers came to
Kveld-Ulf and received a good welcome there. They told their
errand saying that the king wished Kveld-Ulf to come and meet
him. 'He has heard that you are a distinguished man, of good
family,' they said. 'You will have the chance of great favours
from him. The king sets great store by having men with him
who are, as report tells him, noted for their strength and prow-
ess.' Kveld-Ulf answered that he was old and not fit to be out
in warships. 'I shall stay at home now and cease to serve kings.'
The messenger said, 'Then let your son go to the king. He is
a big man and looks like a fighter. The king will make you a
nobleman, Grim, if you are willing to serve him.' Grim said, 'I do
not wish to be made a nobleman while my father lives. He shall
be my chief while he lives.' The messengers went away and when
they came to the king they reported all that Kveld-Ulf had said

to them. The king was offended at this and had some words
to say about it. He said they must be arrogant men and what
was their idea. Olvir Hnufa was standing near, and asked the
king not to be angry. 'I will go and see Kveld-Ulf. He will want
to come and meet you as soon as he knows that it seems important to you.' Then Olvir went to see Kveld-Ulf telling him
that the king was angry and nothing would help matters unless
one of the family went to the king. He said that they would get
great honour from the king if they were willing to serve him,
and emphasized that Harald was generous to his men both in
money and honours. This was true. Kveld-Ulf said that he had
a presentiment 'that our family will get no luck from this king,
and I will not go to meet him. But if Thorolf comes home in the
summer he will easily be persuaded to go, and to become the
king's man too. Tell this to the king, that I will be his friend,
and I will keep all the men who obey me in friendship with him.
And I will hold the same administration and responsibility
under him as I held before from the previous king, if that is the
king's wish. Later we will see how things turn out between me
and the king.' Then Olvir went back to the king and told him
that Kveld-Ulf would send him his son, saying that the one who
was not at home just then was the better suited for this. The
king then let the matter rest. That summer he went into Sogn,
but when autumn came he prepared to go north to Trondheim.

6

Thorolf Kveld-Ulfsson and Eyvind Lambi came home in the
autumn from their viking raids. Thorolf went home to his
family. Father and sons had a talk together, and Thorolf asked
what those men wanted whom Harald had sent. Kveld-Ulf
answered that the king had sent word that he, Kveld-Ulf, or
one of his sons, should become the king's man. 'How did you
answer?' said Thorolf. 'I said what I thought, that I should
never go into service with King Harald, and neither should
you two if I had my way. I have a feeling it would end in death
at the king's hand.' 'That is very different from my way of
looking at it,' said Thorolf, 'for I think I shall get great advance-
ment from him. I'm determined to go to the king and become
his man. I've been told as a fact that there are only the most
splendid men at his court. I should like more than anything to
be one of them, if they'll accept me. These men have the best

position of any in the country. I have heard this of the king, that he is extremely generous to his men, both in money and in readiness to promote them, and to put those in authority who are fit for it. But I have heard this of the ones who want to turn their backs on him and will not be friendly with him, that they'll get nowhere. Some will leave the country and others become mere tenants. It seems odd to me, Father, that a man as wise as you, and proud, should not have been grateful for the honour the king offered you. But if you think yourself farsighted, saying we shan't be lucky with the king, and he won't want to be our friend, why didn't you fight against him with the king to whom you owed allegiance? It seems to me disgraceful to be neither his friend nor his enemy.' Kveld-Ulf answered, 'It happened as I thought it would. Those who fought Shaggy Harald north in More didn't tread any path of victory. It is also true that Harald will bring great harm on my family. But you will make your own decisions, Thorolf. I am not afraid, even if you do join Harald's court, that you won't be fit for it, and as good as the best of them in any danger. Be careful not to think your abilities greater than they are, and don't fight against men stronger than yourself. But you won't give way to anyone for all that.' When Thorolf was ready to leave, Kveld-Ulf went down to the ship with him, embraced him, and said good-bye, hoping that they would meet again alive and in health.

7

In Halogaland there was a man called Bjorgolf. He lived on Torgoy. He was a rich and powerful nobleman, half a hill-giant[1] in strength, size and ancestry. He had a son called Brynjolf who was like his father. Bjorgolf was old at that time, and his wife was dead, and he had handed over control of everything to his son, and had looked for a wife for him. Brynjolf married Helga, the daughter of Ketil Hœng from Ramsta. Their son was called Bard. At an early age he was big and handsome, and he turned out a very able man. One autumn there was a feast, very well-attended, and Bjorgolf and Brynjolf were the men highest in rank there. They drew lots, according to the custom, over who should drink together for the evening. There was a man called Hogni at the feast. He had a farm on Leka. He was a very rich man, very good-looking and clever. He was a man of poor family who had raised himself by his own efforts. He had a

very pretty daughter who was called Hildirid. She drew as her
lot the place next to Bjorgolf. They talked a lot during the
evening and he found her an attractive girl. A little later the
feast ended. The same autumn old Bjorgolf made a journey
from home on a pinnace[2] which he owned with thirty men on
board. He came to Leka, and went up to the house with nine-
teen men, leaving ten to guard the ship. When they came to the
farm Hogni came to meet Bjorgolf and greeted him, inviting
him and his company to stay there. Bjorgolf accepted that and
they went indoors. When they had taken off their sea-garments
and put on indoor clothing, Hogni had the ale-cask and the
beer brought in. Hildirid, the farmer's daughter, served the
guests. Bjorgolf called the farmer Hogni to him and said, 'My
errand here is to take your daughter back with me, and now we
will have a sort of marriage.' Hogni saw no alternative to letting
this happen as Bjorgolf demanded. Bjorgolf bought her with
an ounce of gold[3] and they went into one bed together. Hildirid
went home with Bjorgolf to Torgoy. Brynjolf expressed dis-
satisfaction with this arrangement. Bjorgolf and Hildirid had
two sons. The first was called Harek and the second Hrœrek.
Then Bjorgolf died. As soon as his body was taken out Brynjolf
made Hildirid and her sons go away. She went to Leka to her
father, and her sons were brought up there. They were handsome
men, small, well-endowed with sense and like their mother's
people. They were known as Hildirid's sons. Brynjolf thought
little of them and did not let them have any of their father's
inheritance. Hildirid was Hogni's heiress, and she and her sons
took the inheritance after him, and they lived on Leka and had
plenty of money. Bard, Brynjolf's son, and Hildirid's sons were
about the same age. Bjorgolf and Brynjolf, father and son, had
for a long time held the responsibility for journeying to Lappland and collecting the Lapp-tribute.[4]

In the north of Halogaland there is a fjord called Vefsnfjord.
In the fjord is an island called Alsten. It is a large island and
fertile, and there is a farm on it at Sandnes. A man called Sigurd
lived there. He was the richest man there in the north, a nobleman, with a keen mind. His daughter was called Sigrid and she
was considered the best match in Halogaland. She was Sigurd's
only child and would inherit after him. Bard Brynjolfsson made
a journey from home taking the pinnace with thirty men on
board. He went north to Alsten and arrived at Sigurd's home at
Sandnes. Bard explained his business and asked for Sigrid's

hand. His proposal was favourably answered, with the result
that the girl was engaged to Bard. The marriage was to take place
the next summer, and Bard to come north for it.

8

That summer King Harald had sent word to the chief men in
Halogaland, summoning those to him who had not been to see
him already. Brynjolf resolved to make this journey, accompanied by his son Bard. In the autumn they went south to
Trondheim and met the king there. He gave them a good welcome. Brynjolf became the king's nobleman. The king provided
him with sources of income in addition to those he already had.
He also allowed him the journey to Lappland, the royal authority
in the mountain district and the trading rights with the Lapps.
Then Brynjolf went away home to his estates, but Bard stayed
behind and became the king's retainer.

The king honoured his poets above his other retainers. They
were assigned to the seat of honour opposite the king. Audun
the Plagiarist[1] sat furthest in. He was the oldest of them and had
been poet to Halfdan the Black, King Harald's father. Thorbjorn
Hornklofi[2] sat next and next to him Olvir Hnufa, and Bard was
placed alongside him. He was called Bard the White or Bard the
Strong. All the men thought well of him. He and Olvir Hnufa
were close companions. The same autumn Thorolf Kveld-
Ulfsson and Eyvind Lambi, the son of Berle-Kari, came to
King Harald and were well received there. They brought a
twenty-oared ship with a good crew, which they used to take on
their viking raids. They and their company were given places in
the guest hall. When they had stayed there until they thought it
time to go and see the king, Berle-Kari and Olvir Hnufa went
with them. They greeted the king. Olvir Hnufa said that Kveld-
Ulf's son had arrived. 'I told you in the summer about this one,
that Kveld-Ulf would be sending him to you. His promises to
you will be fully kept. Since he has sent his son to serve you, you
have the proof that he will be your firm friend. You can see that
Thorolf is a worth-while man. Kveld-Ulf and the rest of us ask
you to welcome him, and appoint him to a good position.'
The king gave a favourable answer and said it should be as he
asked 'if Thorolf turns out to have all the qualities his splendid
appearance suggests'. Then Thorolf went into the king's service
and joined the retainers, while Berle-Kari and his son Eyvind

Lambi went south with the ship Thorolf had brought north, and the two of them went home to Kari's estates. Thorolf stayed with the king who allotted him the seat between Olvir Hnufa and Bard, and all three of them became close comrades. It was commonly said that Thorolf and Bard were each other's equals in looks, size, strength and abilities. The king thought a lot of Thorolf and of Bard as well.

When the winter was over and summer arrived, Bard asked the king for permission to go on the wedding trip that had been planned the summer before. When the king knew that Bard had obligations elsewhere, he gave him leave of absence. When Bard got permission he asked Thorolf to go north with him. He said, and it was true, that Thorolf would be able to meet many of their aristocratic kinsmen, whom he had not met before. Thorolf thought this a good idea and they obtained the king's permission. They made preparations, got a good ship and a crew, and set off when they were ready. When they arrived on Torgoy they sent men to Sigurd to tell him that Bard wanted to carry out the agreement they had made with each other the summer before. Sigurd said he intended to keep to everything they had spoken of. They fixed a day for the wedding, and Bard's party were to come north to Sandnes. When it came to the day Brynjolf and Bard set out, accompanied by many great men—their relatives and in-laws. As Bard had said, Thorolf met many of their kin there whom he had not known before. They went on until they arrived at Sandnes. It was a brilliant wedding, and when it was ended Bard went home with his wife and stayed at home for the summer. Thorolf stayed with them. In the autumn they went south to the king and were with him another winter. That winter Brynjolf died. When Bard heard that the inheritance was waiting for him he asked permission to go home, and the king granted it. Before they separated he made Bard a nobleman as his father had been, and Bard received from the king all the revenues which Brynjolf had had. Bard went home to his estates and soon became a great chieftain. But the sons of Hildirid got no more of the inheritance than before. Bard and his wife had a son whom they called Grim. Thorolf stayed with the king and was highly thought of.

9

King Harald called up a great army, got a fleet together, and

summoned men from all over the country. He left Trondheim
and headed south. He had learned that a huge force had been
drawn together from Agder and Rogaland and Hordaland and
from further afield, down from the country and from the east
from Vik. Many great men had come together intending to
defend their land against King Harald. King Harald and his
men held on their course south. Harald himself had a large
ship manned by his retainers. At the stem were Thorolf Kveld-
Ulfsson, Bard the White and the sons of Berle-Kari, Olvir Hnufa
and Eyvind Lambi. The king's twelve berserks were behind
them on the foredeck.[1] They met south in Havsfjord in Rogaland. That was the heaviest battle King Harald had fought,
and many men fell on both sides. The king brought his ship
up in front, and there the fighting was hardest, but it ended in
King Harald's victory. Thorir Haklang, the king of Agder, fell
there, while Kjotvi the Rich fled with those of his men still on
their feet, not counting the ones who surrendered after the
fight. When Harald's losses were counted many were dead and
many badly wounded. Thorolf had severe wounds, but Bard
worse. There was no-one from the front of the king's ship
without a wound except the berserks, and iron could not touch
them. The king had the wounds of his men bound up, and
thanked them for their courage. He handed out gifts, gave the
most praise where it was deserved and promised an increase of
honours. He named for this the shipmasters, his trusted comrades in the prow, and other foredeck men. That was the last
battle King Harald fought at home, and after that he ruled the
whole country and there was no opposition. The king had his
men looked after if they were destined to live, and to the dead
he granted such ceremonies as were usual at that time. Thorolf
and Bard lay wounded. Thorolf's wounds began to heal but
Bard's turned mortal. Then he asked for the king to be brought
to him, and said to him, 'In case I should die from these wounds,
I want to ask you to let me name my heir.' When the king had
agreed to this he said, 'I wish Thorolf, my comrade and kinsman,
to inherit both land and money after me. I wish also to give him
my wife and the care of my son, since I believe him to be the
best of all men for this.' With the king's permission he confirmed this according to the laws of the time. Then Bard died
and was given burial rites, and he was greatly mourned. Thorolf
was cured of his wounds and accompanied the king during the
summer, and had achieved considerable renown. In the autumn

the king went north to Trondheim. Then Thorolf asked leave to go north to Halogaland to see the bequests which he had received that summer from his kinsman Bard. The king gave permission, and arranged by accompanying messages and tokens for Thorolf to have everything that Bard gave him. He made it clear that the gift was given with the king's consent, and was in accordance with his wishes. Then the king made Thorolf a nobleman, and gave him all the revenues which Bard had previously had, and granted him the Lapp journey with the same stipulations as when Bard had it. The king gave Thorolf a good longship fully equipped, and made the best possible preparations for his journey. Then Thorolf set out on his way, and he and the king parted as good friends. When Thorolf came north to Torgoy he was warmly welcomed. He told of the death of Bard, and that Bard had left to him his land and money, and the wife whom he had married. Then he produced the king's message and tokens. When Sigrid heard this news she thought the death of her husband a great loss, but Thorolf was well-known to her, and she knew that he was an outstanding man, and the match a good one. Also since it was the king's command, she and her friends thought it advisable for her to become engaged to Thorolf, provided it was not against her father's wishes. Then Thorolf took over all the management and also the king's administration. When he was ready Thorolf made a journey from home, taking the longship north along the coast with nearly sixty men on board. One day in the evening he reached Sandnes on Alsten. They brought the ship into harbour. When they had seen to the ship and rigged awnings[2] Thorolf and twenty men went up to the farm. Sigurd greeted him warmly and asked him to stay there, for they knew each other well since Sigurd and Bard had become in-laws. Thorolf and his men went indoors and were hospitably looked after. Sigurd sat and talked with Thorolf and asked for news. Thorolf told him about the battle which had taken place in the south during the summer, and about the deaths of many men whom Sigurd had known. He told him also that Bard his son-in-law had died of the wounds that he got in battle. To both of them it seemed a great loss. Then Thorolf told Sigurd what he and Bard had spoken of in confidence together before Bard died, and he produced the king's message that he wished all of that to be accepted, and he showed the tokens as well. Then Thorolf put forward his marriage proposal, and asked Sigurd for Sigrid his daughter. Sigurd responded favourably to this idea, saying that there was much to be said for it, first that the king wished it, also that Bard had asked for it, and in addition that Thorolf was known to him and he thought it a good marriage for his daughter. It was easy to get Sigurd's consent. Then the two were engaged and the wedding was to be held on Torgoy in the autumn. Then Thorolf and his companions went home to his farm, and made preparations for a great feast, and invited great numbers to it, including many of his well-born relatives. Sigurd also made preparations, and came from the north with a big longship and a chosen company. There was a great crowd of people at the feast. It was soon seen that Thorolf was a generous man and open-handed. He kept a large body of men, which soon became expensive, needing a lot of provisions. It was a good season, and easy to get the necessary supplies. That winter Sigurd died at Sandnes and Thorolf was heir to everything he had. This was a very great inheritance.

The sons of Hildirid went to Thorolf to put forward a claim that they ought to have a share in the property that Bjorgolf their father had owned. Thorolf answered, 'I knew Brynjolf, and knew Bard much better, and they were both such fair-minded men that they would have shared as much of Bjorgolf's inheritance with you as they thought right. I was nearby when you raised the same claim with Bard, and as I understood it he thought there was no truth in it since he called you bastards.' Harek said they could bring witnesses that their mother had been legally married. 'It is true that we did not at first pursue the matter with our brother Brynjolf. It was within the family. From Bard we did hope for full redress, but our dealings did not last long. Still, now that this inheritance has gone out of the family the two of us are not going to stay silent about our loss. But it is possible that just as before the disparity in power will mean that we get no justice from you in this matter, if you will not listen to the witnesses we can bring forward to prove that we are legitimate.' Thorolf answered irritably, 'Why should I think you legitimate, when I've heard that your mother was taken by force, and brought back as loot?' After that they broke off the discussion.

10

During the winter Thorolf made his journey up into the mountains and had a large force with him, no less than ninety men.

Before that the king's officials had usually taken thirty men, sometimes not so many. He took plenty of merchandise with him. He soon organized a meeting with the Lapps, accepted tribute from them, and got a market going. Everything went smoothly and amicably, though the Lapps were slightly suspicious. Thorolf explored great tracts of forest and as he advanced east to the mountains he found that the Kylfings[1] had come from the east and were trading with the Lapps, and in some places pillaging. Thorolf got the Lapps to keep watch on the Kylfings' movements, and followed himself to seek them out. In one camp he found thirty and killed them all so that none escaped. Another time he found fifteen or twenty together. In all they killed over a hundred[2] men and got from them riches beyond count, and in this way they came back in the spring. Thorolf went to his farm at Sandnes and stayed there for a long time. In the spring he had a big longship built, with a dragon prow, had it equipped as splendidly as possible, and brought it down from the north with him. Thorolf collected together most of the catch off Halogaland. He had his men out for the herring and the shoal fishing.[3] There was also plenty of seal-catching and egg-collecting. He had it all brought to himself. He never had fewer than a hundred men in his household. He was a generous man, open-handed, very friendly with all the great men in the neighbourhood. He became powerful and spent a lot of thought on the display of his ships and weapons.

11

King Harald went to Halogaland that summer and feasts were made for him, both on his own estates, and at the homes of noblemen and powerful farmers. Thorolf prepared a feast for the king at great expense. A time was agreed when the king should come there. Thorolf invited great numbers of men and had there all the most distinguished guests possible. The king had nearly three hundred men when he came to the feast but Thorolf had five hundred. Thorolf had made ready an enormous barn which was there, and had benches put in it for the drinking to take place there, since there was no room big enough to take all the guests. Shields were hung round the inside walls. The king took his place in the high seat. But when everyone was seated both above and below, the king looked round, turned red, and said nothing. Men realized that he was angry. It was a

brilliant feast with the best possible provisions. The king was
not very cheerful. He stayed there the three nights that had been
arranged. The day when the king was due to leave, Thorolf
came up to him and asked if they might go down to the shore
together. The king did so. Just off the land the dragon ship was
floating, the one Thorolf had had made, with sails and full
equipment. Thorolf gave the ship to the king, and asked the
king to believe the truth, that his only reason for having so many
men present was to do honour to the king, not to enter into
competition with him. The king was pleased with Thorolf's
words and became good-tempered and cheerful. Many put in a
good word at this point, saying, as was true, that the feast had
been superb, and the farewell present was magnificent, and that
the king drew strength from such followers. They parted on good
terms. The king went north to Halogaland as he had intended,
and turned back south as the summer drew to an end. He still
went to feasts wherever he was invited to them.

12

The sons of Hildirid went to see the king, and asked him to their
house for a three-day feast. The king accepted their invitation
and said when he would come. When the time came the king
arrived there with his company, and there were not many
people present, but the entertaining was excellent. The king was
very cheerful. Harek got into conversation with the king, and
brought the talk round to the king's journeys during that
summer. The king answered his questions, said that everyone
had welcomed him and looked after him in accordance with their
means. 'There will have been a big difference then,' said Harek.
'It would be most crowded on Torgoy.' The king agreed. 'That
was to be expected,' said Harek, 'since great preparations were
made for that feast. You were very fortunate indeed that your
life didn't turn out to be in danger. In the event, as was natural,
you were both lucky and farseeing, for when you saw that great
crowd of men that had been brought together you suspected
straightaway that not everything was as it should be. I heard
that you made all your company keep their weapons or stay on
guard night and day.' The king looked at him and said, 'Why
do you say such things, Harek, and how far do you know what
you're talking about?' He answered, 'Have I your permission,
Sir, to say what I like?' 'Speak,' said the king. 'I think,' said

Harek, 'if you, Sir, heard what people are saying when they
speak their minds in their own homes, about the oppression
which you have imposed on everyone, you would not like it at
all. To tell you the truth, Sir, the people would rise against you if
they only had courage and leadership. Nor is it strange,' he went
on, 'that people like Thorolf think themselves better than everyone else. He lacks neither strength nor looks. He holds court
as if he were a king. He has more than enough money, even if
he only had what he has a right to, but he disposes of other
people's money as freely as his own. Also you have granted him
great revenues, and it is not unlikely that he was on the point
of giving you a poor reward. To tell you the truth, when it was
discovered that you were coming north to Halogaland with no
more troops than you had, three hundred men, they made plans
round here to get an army together and kill you and your whole
company. Thorolf was the prime mover in this because he was
offered the kingship over the regions of Halogaland and Namdal. He went up and down every fjord, and round all the islands,
and got together every man that he could and every weapon.
It was no secret that this army was to be used against King
Harald in battle. But the truth is, Sir, that though you had a
somewhat smaller company, when you met and they saw your
fleet, these peasants were terrified. They adopted the plan of
meeting you peaceably, and inviting you to a feast. They intended if you got drunk and slept to make an assault with fire
and swords. The proof of that, if I've heard correctly, is that you
were taken into a barn, because Thorolf didn't want to burn his
beautiful new house. Another proof is that every building was
full of weapons and armour. But when none of their tricks
against you succeeded, they adopted the plan which seemed
best in the circumstances, and shook free of their designs. I
think that they all have the sense to keep quiet about this, for if
it ever came into the open, I don't think very many would be
sure of their own innocence. My advice, Sir, is that you keep
Thorolf with you, and have him among your retainers, to carry
your standard and be in the front of your ship. He is the best of
all men for this. But if you want him to be a nobleman, then
give him revenues south in Fjordane. All his family are
there. You can then keep an eye on him to see that he doesn't
get too important. But put the administration here into the
hands of moderate-minded men, who will serve you faithfully,
men who have families here, and whose kin have previously held

such appointments. The two of us are ready and willing for this
if you want to make use of us. Our father held the royal administration here for a long time and handled it well. It is difficult for you, Sir, to put men in authority here when you will
scarcely ever be here yourself. The countryside is not capable of
supporting you and an army, and it won't happen again that
you come this way with a small force, for many people here are
unreliable.' The king grew very angry during this talk, but still
spoke calmly as he always did when he learned news of great
significance. Then he asked whether Thorolf was at home on
Torgoy. Harek said that it was not to be expected. 'Thorolf
has enough sense to keep well away from your troops, Sir, because he was bound to realize not everyone would be so discreet
that you wouldn't get to hear of these activities. He went north
to Alsten as soon as he heard that you were away from the
north.' The king did not say much about this to anyone, but it
was noticed that he was prepared to trust implicitly these tales
that were told him. Then the king went on his journey. The
sons of Hildirid gave him an honourable send-off with accompanying gifts, and he promised them his friendship. The brothers
provided themselves with an errand into Namdal, and made
such circles round the king that they were forever running into
him. He was always ready to listen to them.

13

There was a man called Thorgils Gjallandi, one of Thorolf's
retainers and valued by him above the rest of his household. He
had gone on viking raids with Thorolf, was in the prow of his
ship and his standard-bearer. Thorgils had been at Havsfjord
on King Harald's side, and had captained the ship that Thorolf
owned and had taken on viking raids. Thorgils was very strong
and full of courage. After the battle the king had given him
gifts and promised him friendship. Thorgils was in charge of
the farm on Torgoy when Thorolf was not at home, and had full
control. When Thorolf had left home he had got ready all the
tribute of the Lapps which he had brought from the mountains,
and belonged to the king, and he had handed it over to Thorgils
with the instructions to take it to the king, if Thorolf should
not be home before the king left the north for the south. Thorgils
got ready a good big cargo ship of Thorolf's put the tribute on
board, and with about twenty men sailed south after the king

and found him in Namdal. When Thorgils met the king he gave him Thorolf's greeting and said that he brought the Lapp tribute which Thorolf had sent. The king looked at him and said nothing, and people saw that he was angry. Thorgils went away and hoped to find a more favourable day for talking with the king. He went to find Olvir Hnufa and told him everything that had happened, asking if he knew what it meant. 'I don't know,' he answered, 'but since we were in Leka I've seen that the king is silent every time Thorolf is mentioned. I imagine that he has been slandered. I know that the sons of Hildirid are continuously in private conversation with the king, and it is easy to tell from their talk that they are hostile to Thorolf. But I'll soon get to know the truth from the king.' Then Olvir went to find the king and said, 'Your friend, Thorgils Gjallandi, has arrived with the tribute from Lappland belonging to you. There is far more tribute than there has ever been before, and much better skins. He is anxious about his return. Please go and look, Sir, for no-one can have seen such fine grey furs.' The king did not answer but still he went to where the ship was. Thorgils at once produced the goods and showed the king. When the king saw it was true that the tribute was much bigger and better than it had been before, he frowned less, and Thorgils was able to talk to him. He brought the king some beaver skins which Thorolf had sent him, and still more valuable things which he had got in the mountains. The king cheered up and asked what the news was about Thorolf's journey. Thorgils told it all in detail. Then the king said, 'It is a great pity that Thorolf should be disloyal to me and wish to kill me.' Many who were standing near answered, all saying the same thing, that it was the slander of unscrupulous men if the king had been told this, and that Thorolf would be found not guilty. It ended with the king saying that he would prefer to believe this. The king was amiable in the rest of his conversation with Thorgils, and they parted peaceably. But when Thorgils met Thorolf he told him everything that had happened.

14

That winter Thorolf went to Lappland again and had over a hundred men with him. He did as he had done the winter before, arranged trade with the Lapps, and explored large tracts of the forest country. When he had gone a long way east and reports of his journey spread, the Kvens[1] came to him and said that they had been sent to him by command of Faravid, king of Kvenland. They said that the Karelians[2] were raiding his land, and he had sent word that Thorolf was to go there and give him help, and sent also the message that Thorolf would get equal shares with the king, and each of his men as much as three of the Kvens. It was the law among the Kvens for the king to have a third of the share-out (and his men the remainder) but in addition he got all the beaver-skins, sables and martens.[3] Thorolf put this to his men, and gave them the choice of going or not, but most of them chose to risk it since there was so much booty involved, and it was decided that they should go east with the messengers.

Lappland is a very big country. To the west it has the sea with great fjords leading off it, and sea to the north and right round to the east. To the south is Norway, but Lappland extends south in the interior with Halogaland on the seaward side. East of Namdal is Jamtland, then Halsingland, then Kvenland, then Finland then Karelia. But Lappland lies over all these lands and there are hill settlements throughout the country, some in the dales and some alongside the lakes. In Lappland there are incredibly big lakes, and great forests alongside the lakes, and a high mountain range called Kjolen extends the whole length of the country.

When Thorolf came east to Kvenland and met King Faravid they prepared for the expedition. They had three hundred men, with the Norwegians making up a fourth hundred, and they went through the interior of Lappland, and found in the mountains the Karelians who had been raiding the Kvens. When these saw the invaders they organized themselves and attacked, expecting victory as before. But when the battle began, the Norwegians went forward vigorously, and they had better shields than the Kvens. The heavy losses were now on the side of the Karelians: many fell, some fled. King Faravid and Thorolf got riches beyond count, and turned back to Kvenland. Afterwards Thorolf and his men returned to Lappland. He and King Faravid parted good friends. Thorolf came down from the mountains into Vefsnfjord, and first of all went to his farm at Sandnes. He stayed there for a time, and in the spring he and his men left the north for Torgoy. When he arrived he was told that the sons of Hildirid had spent the winter in Trondheim with King Harald, and that they had done everything possible to slander Thorolf to the king. Thorolf was told in detail on what

subjects he had been slandered and he answered: 'The king will
not believe this, even if these lies are being told him. There is no
truth in the report that I would betray him, for he has done a
great many things for me, and nothing against me. Far from
wanting to be a threat to him, had I the choice I would rather
be his nobleman than have the name of king, there being another
king in the same country who could enslave me if he wished.'

15

The sons of Hildirid had spent that winter with King Harald,
keeping with them both the men of their household and their
neighbours. These brothers were often in conversation with the
king, and the tale of Thorolf went on the same way. Harek said,
'Were you pleased, Sir, with the Lapp tribute which Thorolf
sent you?' 'Very pleased,' said the king. 'You would have been
even more pleased,' said Harek, 'if you'd received all your
property, which was far from the case. It was a much bigger
share that Thorolf kept for himself. He sent you three beaver
skins as a gift, but I know for a fact that he kept three tens of
them—your property—and I expect it was the same with the
rest. If you hand over the administration to the two of us, Sir,
you will certainly get more riches brought to you.' Their companions confirmed everything that they said against Thorolf.
As a result the king was furious.

16

In the summer Thorolf went south to Trondheim to meet King
Harald. He had with him all the tribute, much money in addition, and ninety men well turned out. When he came to the
king places were assigned to them in the guest hall, and they
were splendidly looked after. The next day Olvir Hnufa came to
find his kinsman Thorolf and they talked about things. Olvir
said Thorolf had been heavily slandered and the king had
listened. Thorolf asked Olvir to put his case to the king, because
'I,' he said, 'shan't say much to the king if he prefers to believe
the slander of scoundrels rather than my truth and loyalty which
he can test.' The next day Olvir came to see Thorolf and said
that he had put his case to the king. 'I don't know,' he said,
'any more than I did before, what is in his mind.' 'I shall go
and see him myself then,' said Thorolf. He did so. When he

went to the king he was sitting at table, and when he came in he greeted the king. The king accepted the greeting, and gave orders for Thorolf to be served with drink. Thorolf said that he had brought the tribute from Lappland belonging to the king. 'And I have still more things as gifts for you, Sir, which I shall bring you. I know that whatever I have done for your pleasure will prove my best investment.' The king said that he expected nothing but good from Thorolf, 'because I have not deserved anything else. All the same, people give varying reports about how far you are taking care to please me.' 'I have not been reported justly,' said Thorolf, 'if any say that I have been disloyal to you, Sir. Any men who have told you this are less your friends than I am, and one thing is clear, they are very much my enemies. Most likely they will have to pay for it if we have anything to do with each other.' Then Thorolf went away, but the day following he paid out the tribute when the king was present. When it was all paid Thorolf brought forward some beaver skins and sables, saying he wished to give them to the king. There were many standing there who said this was well done and deserved friendship. The king said that Thorolf had seen to it that he had his own reward. Thorolf said that he had loyally done everything he knew of to please the king, 'and if it doesn't please him, there's nothing I can do about it. The king knew what sort of a man I was when I was with him among his retainers. It seems odd if the king now thinks I am a different man from the one he found me to be.' The king said, 'Your behaviour was satisfactory, Thorolf, when you were here. I think it would be best if you joined my household again. Take my standard and be at the head of my retainers. No-one can slander you if I can keep an eye on your behaviour night and day.' Thorolf looked on each side of him where his men were standing. 'I am reluctant to abandon these men. You, Sir, will decide about my titles and the revenues you gave me, but I will not abandon my men so long as my provisions last out, even if I have to manage the cost myself. I ask and hope, Sir, that you will accept an invitation to my home, and hear the talk of men you can trust, and see what evidence they can put forward on my behalf in this. Then you can act in accordance with the truth as you find it.' The king said in answer that he would not again accept Thorolf's hospitality. Then Thorolf went away and got ready to go home. When he had left, the king handed over to Hildirid's sons the royal administration in Halogaland which

Thorolf had previously had, and also the Lapp-trade. The king
seized possession of the farm on Torgoy, and all the property
which had belonged to Brynjolf. He handed it all into the keeping
of Hildirid's sons. The king sent men to see Thorolf telling him
what he had done, and sending tokens. Then Thorolf took what
ships he had and put on board all the possessions he could
travel with, and had all his men with him, both free and slaves,
and went north to his farm at Sandnes. There Thorolf kept as
many men and as much state as before.

17

The sons of Hildirid took over the royal administration in
Halogaland. No-one spoke against it for fear of the king's
power, but the change was very unpopular with those who were
kin or friends of Thorolf. In the winter the brothers went into
the mountains, taking thirty men with them. The Lapps were
much less impressed by these administrators than when it was
Thorolf. The payment due from them, when collected up, was
very much worse. The same winter Thorolf went up into the
mountains with a hundred men. He immediately went east to
Kvenland and met King Faravid. They made plans together,
and agreed to go into the mountains again, as in the winter
before. They had four hundred men, and they came down into
Karelia, swooped down on the settlements which they thought
their numbers could tackle, raided and got great riches. Then,
when the winter was well on, they went back into Lappland. In
the spring Thorolf went home to his farm. He had his men
fishing at Vagar[1] and others in the herring fisheries, and searched
for all kinds of provision for his farm. Thorolf owned a large
ship. It was built for the open sea, as good as it could be in every
respect, with much paint-work above the water-line, and a sail
coloured in blue and red stripes. All the equipment for the ship
was most carefully made. Thorolf had this ship made ready, got
men of his to go with it, and loaded it with dried fish, skins, and
white goods.[2] On top of this he added quantities of grey goods
and other furs which he had brought back from the mountains.
It was a very valuable cargo. He put Thorgils Gjallandi on this
ship to go west to England and buy cloth and other supplies
that he needed. They took the ship south along the coast, and
then to sea, and they reached England. They had a good trade
there, loaded the ship with wheat and honey, wine and cloth,

and came back in the autumn. They had a good wind and came to Hordaland. The same autumn Hildirid's sons brought the tribute to the king. When they paid over the tribute the king himself was there and saw it. He said, 'Is the whole tribute now paid that you two collected in Lappland?' 'Yes,' they said. The king said, 'The tribute paid is both much less and much worse than that which Thorolf collected, and you said that his administration was at fault.' Harek answered, 'It is a good thing that you have considered, Sir, how much treasure reckons to come out of Lappland, because then you'll be all the quicker to know how much you will lose if Thorolf does away with your entire Lapp-tribute. In the winter we went into Lappland, thirty strong, as used to be the custom of your administrators. Then Thorolf came there with a hundred men. We learned this much of his intentions, that he was going to kill the two of us, and all the men with us. His excuse was that you, Sir, had handed over to us the administration that he wanted. Our only choice was to stay as far away from him as possible, and save our lives, and because of this we did not go far from the settlements into the mountains. Thorolf went through the whole of Lappland with an army of men, and took the whole trade. The Lapps paid him tribute, and he bound himself to see that your administrators should not come into Lappland. He intends to make himself king over the north there, both over Lappland and Halogaland, and it's surprising that you let him do anything he likes. Firm proof can be found of Thorolf's haul from Lappland in the cargo ship, the biggest in Halogaland, which was got ready at Sandnes. Thorolf claims that he owns the whole cargo, everything on it. I think it would be nearly full of grey goods, and I think too that more beaver skins and sables would be found there than Thorolf brought to you. It went with Thorgils Gjallandi, and I think he sailed west to England. If you want to know the truth of this, keep an eye on Thorgils' movements when he comes east, for I don't think any cargo ship has arrived in our time with so much wealth on board. I think it only fair to say, Sir, that you own every penny of it.' Harek's companions confirmed all that he said, and no-one knew enough to contradict it.

18

There were two brothers with King Harald called Sigtrygg Snarfari and Hallvard Hardfari. They were men from Vik,

their mother's family came from Vestfold, and they could trace a
kinship with King Harald. Their father had had kin both sides
of the river Gotaalv. He had owned a farm on Hising and was
a very rich man, and they had succeeded to their father's inheritance. There were four brothers all together. The younger
ones were called Thord and Thorgeir, and these stayed at home
to look after the farm. Sigtrygg and Hallvard were sent on all
the king's errands, both at home and abroad. Many of these
had been dangerous, both in putting men to death, and in taking
money from those whom the king wanted attacked in their
homes. They kept a large force of men about them, and were not
friendly with everyone, but the king valued them highly. They
were the most competent of travellers, on foot or on skis, and
they made voyages more quickly than anyone else. They were
big and brave, looking ahead in most matters. They were with
the king when all this was happening. In the autumn the king
went to a feast in Hordaland. One day he had the brothers,
Hallvard and Sigtrygg, called to him. When they came he told
them to take their troops and watch out for the ship which
Thorgils Gjallandi was on, 'which he took west to England in
the summer. Bring me the ship and everything on it except the
crew. Let them go their own way in peace, if they don't try to
defend the ship.' The brothers were all ready for this, and each
took his own longship. They went to look for Thorgils and the
ship, and heard that he had come from the west, and had sailed
north along the coast. They followed him north, and came up
with him in Furusund, soon recognized the ship and brought one
of their ships alongside, while some men went ashore and came
out on to the ship by the gangways. Thorgils and his men were
not expecting anything to be afraid of, and were not keeping
guard. The first thing they knew was that a crowd of men,
fully-armed, was on board, and they were all captured and led
ashore, without their weapons and with nothing but the clothes
they were wearing. Hallvard and his men shoved off the gangways, cut the ropes, and took away the ship, altered course and
sailed south until they came to the king. They brought him the
ship with everything on it. When the cargo was carried from the
ship the king saw that it was very valuable, and that Harek had
not lied to him. Thorgils and his men got a passage for themselves
and went to Kveld-Ulf and his son. They said they had not had a
trouble-free journey, but all the same they were welcomed
there. Kveld-Ulf said it was going the way he prophesied, that

Thorolf would not in the long run get luck from the friendship of King Harald. 'I don't think it would matter much about the loss of money that Thorolf has just suffered, if there were not worse things to follow. I'm afraid now, as I was earlier, that Thorolf won't be able to see the limits of his strength against such overwhelming odds as he will have to deal with.' He told Thorgils to tell Thorolf, 'My advice is that he should leave the country. He can perhaps do better for himself if he goes into service with the king of the English, or the king of the Danes, or the king of the Swedes.' He provided Thorgils with a pinnace, and all its equipment, coverings, food, and everything which they needed for their journey. Then they left, and did not break their journey until they reached Thorolf in the north, and told him the things that had happened. Thorolf accepted his loss calmly and said he would not be short of money, 'It's good to go shares with a king.' Then Thorolf bought meal and malt and what else he needed for the maintenance of his men. He said that for a time his followers would not be so finely dressed as he had intended. Thorolf sold lands and mortgaged others, and kept the same style of living as before. Also he had just as many men with him as in the previous winters, indeed he had rather more. He put more into feasts and hospitality towards his friends than before. He stayed at home all that winter.

19

When spring arrived and the snow and ice melted, Thorolf had a great longship of his brought out, equipped it, supplied a crew from his men, and had more than a hundred on board with him. It was a fine-looking company and very well armed. When the wind was right, Thorolf headed his ship south along the coast, and as soon as they came south to Bjoro they took the outward route the seaward side of all the islands,[1] sometimes so far out that they could only see the top half of the mountains. They kept on south along the coast and heard no news of anyone until they came east to Vik. Then they heard that King Harald was in Vik and intended to go to Opland in the summer. The men ashore had heard nothing about Thorolf's journey. He got a good wind, steered south to Denmark, and from there into the Baltic, and he raided there during the summer, but it was not productive of much. In the autumn he steered west for Denmark at the time when the Skanor fleet dispersed. Numbers of ships from Norway had been there in the summer as usual. Thorolf let them sail past and did not draw attention to himself. One evening he sailed to Mostrarsund. In the harbour was a big cargo ship which had come from Skanor. The captain was called Thorir Tromoy. He was King Harald's representative[2] and was in charge of his farm on Tromoy. It was a big estate where the king stayed for long periods when he was in Vik, and it needed considerable supplies. This was why Thorir had gone to Skanor to buy a load there, malt, wheat, and honey, and paid for it with a lot of the king's money. They attacked the ship, offering Thorir and his men the choice of defending themselves. But since Thorir had not the numbers for defence against Thorolf's crowd, they gave themselves up. Thorolf took the ship with its cargo, and put Thorir ashore on an island. Then Thorolf took both ships north along the coast. When he came to the river Gotaalv, they anchored there and waited for night. When it was dark they rowed the longship up the river, and set course for the farm that Hallvard and Sigtrygg owned. They got there before day and surrounded it, then shouted their battle-cry, waking up those indoors, who at once leapt for their weapons. Thorgeir immediately fled from his room. There was a high fence round the farm. Thorgeir leapt for the fence, gripped the top of a stake, and vaulted over, out of the yard. Thorgils Gjallandi was standing near. He spun round on Thorgeir with his sword, got the hand on the fence, and severed it. Thorgeir ran to the woods, but Thord his brother and more than twenty men were killed there. Then they robbed the house and burned it. After this they went back along the river to the sea. They got a good wind and sailed north to Vik. There they ran into a great trading vessel belonging to the men of Vik, loaded with meal and malt. Thorolf and his men attacked the ship. Those who were on it did not think themselves equipped for defence, and surrendered. They went ashore unarmed. Thorolf and his men took the ship and its cargo and went on their way. Thorolf now had three ships which he sailed west along the Oslo Fjord. Then they took the ordinary route to Lindesnes. They travelled as quickly as possible, but raided the headlands and shores on the way. When they sailed north from Lindesnes they went by the outer route, but wherever they passed land they plundered. When Thorolf came north to Fjordane he turned off his course and went to see his father Kveld-Ulf. He got a good welcome. Thorolf told his father the news of his journeys during the summer.

He stayed there a short time, and was seen off by his father and brother. Before they parted they talked together, and Kveld-Ulf said, 'It has not been very different from what I told you, Thorolf, when you went to King Harald's court, that in the long run there would be no luck in it for you, nor for us, your family. Now you are acting in the way I most warned you against. You are matching your strength against King Harald. You are full of courage and ability, but you do not have the luck needed to hold your own against him. No-one else in the country has done so, even those who used to have both men and power. I believe this will be the last time we meet, and though in the course of things you ought to live longer than me, I think it will be the other way round.' Then Thorolf went on board ship, and went on his way. Nothing is said of his journey worth the telling until he came home to Sandnes, and had all the plunder he had brought carried up to the farm, and the ships drawn ashore. Food for his men was not short that winter. Thorolf stayed at home all the time, and had as many men as in previous winters.

20

There was a rich and powerful man called Yngvar. He had been a nobleman under the previous king, but when Harald came to the throne Yngvar stayed at home and did not serve him. Yngvar was married and had a daughter called Bera. He lived in Fjordane. Bera was his only child and would inherit after him. Grim Kveld-Ulfsson asked for Bera's hand, and this was arranged. Grim married Bera the winter of the year in which he and Thorolf parted. At that time Grim was twenty-five years old, and bald. He was later called Skalla-Grim.[1] He had control of all the estates which he and his father owned and all the provisioning. All the same Kveld-Ulf was still fit and capable. There were many free men in their household, many of whom had grown up there and were of an age with Skalla-Grim. A lot of them were very strong men, because Kveld-Ulf and Skalla-Grim chose men of great strength for their following, and trained them as they wished. Skalla-Grim was like his father in size and strength, in appearance and character.

21

King Harald was in Vik while Thorolf was raiding. In the

autumn he went to Opland, north from there to Trondheim, and spent the winter there, keeping a large body of men with him. Sigtrygg and Hallvard were with the king, and they had heard what Thorolf had done to their home on Hising, and what injuries and robberies he had inflicted. They reminded the king often, both about this, and about Thorolf's robbing of the king and his servants, and raiding in his kingdom. The brothers asked the king for permission to take the men who usually were with them, and to attack Thorolf at his home. The king answered, 'Maybe you think you have reasons for taking Thorolf's life, but I think you don't have nearly enough luck for it. You two are no match for Thorolf, though you think yourselves brave and capable.' The brothers said that could soon be put to the test if the king was willing to give permission, and further that they had often put themselves in jeopardy against men where there was not so much to avenge, and they had usually been lucky enough to win. When it was spring people got ready for their journeys. Hallvard and Sigtrygg still kept on at the king as was said above. Then he said that they had his permission to kill Thorolf, 'and I know that the two of you will bring me his head when you come back, and many treasures along with it. All the same,' went on the king, 'some men are thinking that if you sail north you will row back as well as sail.'[1] At that they got ready as quickly as possible. They had two ships, a hundred and eighty men, and they set off when ready with a north-east wind out along the fjord. That is a head wind for those going north by the coast.

22

King Harald was at Lade when Hallvard and Sigtrygg left, and immediately he made equal haste, getting ready as soon as he could, and going on board ship. They rowed in along the fjord through Skarnssund and across Beitstadfjord into Namdalseid. He left his ship there and went north over the isthmus to Namdal where he took longships owned by the farmers, and went on board with his company. He had retainers with him, in all over three hundred men, and five or six ships, all big ones. There was a strong head wind, and they rowed night and day as hard as they could, the nights being light enough for travel. They arrived at Sandnes late one evening after sunset, and saw floating below the farm a great covered longship. They recognized it as Thorolf's ship. It was made ready for him to leave the country, and he had already had the beer brewed for his farewell feast. The king ordered all his men off the ships, and had his standard raised. It was not far to the farm, and Thorolf's guards were sitting indoors over the drinking, so there was no-one outside. The whole company was sitting indoors drinking. The king surrounded the house with his men. Then they shouted their battle-cry, and the king's horn sounded for battle. When Thorolf's men heard that they seized their weapons, for each man's arms were hanging above his place. The king had it proclaimed at the doors that women and children, old men, slaves and servants[1] might come outside. Then Sigrid, mistress of the house, came out, and with her the women who were indoors and the men who were allowed to. Sigrid asked if Berle-Kari's sons were there. They both came forward and asked what she wanted from them. 'Come with me to the king,' she said. They did so. When she came to the king she asked, 'Is it worth hoping, my lord, for any reconciliation between you and Thorolf?' The king answered, 'If Thorolf is willing to give himself up into my power, and rely on my mercy, he may keep life and limb, but his men will receive punishment according to their offences.' Then Olvir Hnufa went up to the house and sent for Thorolf to talk to him. He told him the alternatives offered by the king. Thorolf answered, 'I won't make a forced agreement with the king. Ask him to let us come out. Then things can go their own way.' Olvir went to the king and told him what Thorolf asked. The king said, 'Set fire to the house. I don't wish to fight them and lose men. I know Thorolf will do us a lot of damage if we fight out here: even indoors he won't be quickly beaten, though his numbers are smaller than ours.' Then the house was set alight, and it burned quickly for the timber was dry, the wood tarred, and the roof lined with birch-bark. Thorolf told his men to break down the partition between the hall and the entrance-lobby, and they attacked the job quickly. When they had got the lengths of wood, as many men as could hold one seized it, and rammed its other end so fiercely at a corner of the house that it gave way and the walls fell apart, so that there was a great rush outwards. Thorolf was out first, and then Thorgils Gjallandi, and the rest on each other's heels. Then the fighting began, and for a time the house shielded the backs of Thorolf's men, but when it began to blaze the fire came at them. Then many of their company fell. Thorolf pressed forward, striking out on both

sides, attacking in the direction of the king's standard. Thorgils
Gjallandi fell. When Thorolf reached the bodyguard[2] he thrust
his sword through the man with the standard. Then Thorolf
said, 'I've come three feet short.' Sword and spear were in him,
but it was the king himself who dealt his death wound, and
Thorolf fell forward at the king's feet. Then the king called out,
telling them not to kill any more men, and they obeyed. He
sent his men down to the ships, and spoke to Olvir and Eyvind,
'Take your kinsman Thorolf, and give him a fitting burial.
Provide graves for the rest who are fallen here, and have the
wounds bound up of any that are expected to live. There will be
no plundering here, for this is all my property.' Then the king
and most of his men went down to the ships, and when they were
on board they began to bandage their wounds. The king went up
and down the ship, looking at the wounded. He noticed a man
binding a flesh wound, and said that Thorolf had not dealt that
one. 'Weapons bit otherwise for him. I don't think many
bandage the wounds that he gave. Such men are a great loss.'
As soon as it was morning the king gave orders to hoist sail,
and he sailed south as fast as possible. As the day went on they
met many rowing ships in every island sound, all of them on
their way to join Thorolf, whose informants had been down
south in Namdal and throughout the islands. They had become
aware that Hallvard and Sigtrygg were on their way north with a
large force aimed at Thorolf. Hallvard and his brother had
faced a continuous head wind, and had delayed in various
harbours till news of them had travelled overland and Thorolf's
reporters had got hold of it. This had caused the rush to do
battle. The king sailed with a good wind until he reached
Namdal. He left his ships there and went overland into Trondheim. He collected the ship which he had left and made his way
out to Lade with his men. The news soon got about and reached
Hallvard and Sigtrygg where they lay at anchor. They turned
back to the king and their journey was thought rather ridiculous.
The brothers Olvir Hnufa and Eyvind Lambi stayed for a time
at Sandnes. They saw to the dead who had fallen there. They
prepared Thorolf's body according to the rites, as the custom
then was with the bodies of men of rank. They put up memorial
stones[3] for him. They had the wounded men cared for; they
arranged everything about the farm with Sigrid. All the stock
remained, but furnishings, table-gear and clothes had mostly
been burned. When the brothers were ready they went south and

joined King Harald in Trondheim and were with him for a time. They were taciturn, not saying much to anyone. One day they went to the king. Olvir said, 'The two of us want your permission, Sir, to go home to our farms. In view of what's happened we are not in a humour for sitting and drinking with the men who used weapons on Thorolf, our kinsman.' The king looked at him and gave a short answer, 'I will not allow it. You will both stay here with me.' The brothers went back to their seats. The next day the king was in his council room. He had Olvir and Eyvind called to him. 'Now you will get the answer to the matter you raised with me, asking to go home,' said the king. 'You have both been with me for a time, and behaved well. You have always been reliable, and everything about you has been satisfactory. Now Eyvind, I want you to go north to Halogaland. I wish you to marry Sigrid of Sandnes who was Thorolf's wife. I will give you all the property which Thorolf owned, and my friendship along with it if you have the sense to keep it. But Olvir is going to stay with me. His gifts make me unwilling to let him go.' The brothers thanked the king for the honour he was doing them, and said that they were very willing to accept it. Then Eyvind prepared for his journey, getting himself a good and suitable ship. The king provided him with tokens in the matter. Eyvind's journey went well, and he came north to Sandnes on Alsten. Sigrid welcomed him. Eyvind put forward the king's tokens and his message to Sigrid, and he proposed marriage to her, saying that it was the king's will that the marriage should take place. Sigrid saw that the way things had turned out her only choice was to accept the king's decision. The marriage went forward and Eyvind wedded Sigrid. He received the farm at Sandnes and all the property which Thorolf had owned. Eyvind was a distinguished man. Their children were Fid Skjalgi, the father of Eyvind Skaldaspillir, and Geirlaug who married Sighvat the Red. Fid Skjalgi married Gunnhild, the daughter of Earl Halfdan. Her mother was Ingibjorg the daughter of King Harald Finehair. Eyvind Lambi stayed on friendly terms with the king while they both lived.

23

There was a man called Ketil Hœng, the son of Earl Thorkel of Namdal, and of Hrafnhild, the daughter of Ketil Hœng from Ramsta. Hœng was a man of rank and fame. He had been a close

friend and near relation[1] of Thorolf Kveld-Ulfsson. He took
part in the rush mentioned earlier when an army was gathering
in Halogaland to go to Thorolf's aid. When King Harald left
the north, and men heard that Thorolf was dead, the army dispersed. Hœng had sixty men with him, and he turned towards
Torgoy. Hildirid's sons were there without many men. When
Hœng arrived at the farm he made an attack on it. Hildirid's
sons fell there with most of their men, and Hœng's troop took
all the property they could. Afterwards Hœng took the two
biggest cargo ships he could get, and had put on board all the
property which he owned and could carry. He had with him
wife and children, and everyone who had gone with him on that
job. Baug, Hœng's foster-brother, a man of money and family,
captained the second ship. When they were ready and the wind
was right, they put out to sea. A few years earlier Ingolf and
Hjorleif had gone to live in Iceland, and everyone was full of
talk about this venture. The land's resources were said to be
excellent. Hœng sailed west out to sea and made for Iceland, and
when they sighted land it was the southern coast. Because the
wind was strong, the sea high, and there was no harbour, they
sailed west along the coast, past the sands. When the wind
decreased, and the sea became calm, a large estuary was in front
of them, and they took their ships up river and anchored off
the east bank. That is now known as Thjorsa river. At that
time it ran narrower and deeper than today. They cleared the
ships, and then began to explore the land east of the river,
taking their stock with them. Hœng spent the first winter beyond
the western Ranga river. In the spring he explored east and took
the land between Thjorsa river and Markarfljot, between hill
and shore, and settled at Hof on the eastern Ranga. Ingun his
wife had a child in the spring after they had been there the first
winter. The boy was called Hrafn, and when the house was taken
down the place was still known as Hrafntoptir. Hœng gave Baug
land in Fljotshlid down from the river Merkia to the river beyond Breidabolstad, and he lived at Hlidarendi. Baug has many
descendants in that district. Hœng gave land to his crew or sold
it to them at a small price, and these are known as the Settlers.[2]
Hœng had a son called Storolf. He owned the Hvall and Storolfsvoll. His son was Orm the Strong. Hœng's next son was called
Herjolf. He had land in Fljotshlid against Baug's and out as far
as Hvalslœk. He lived below Brekkur. His son was called
Sumarlidi, father of the poet Vetrlidi. A third son of Hœng was

called Helgi. He lived at Voll and owned land to the upper Ranga and down towards that of his brothers. Hœng's fourth son was called Vestar. He owned land to the east of Ranga river between Ranga and Thvera, and the lower part of Storolfsvoll. He married Moeid, the daughter of Hildir from Hildisey. Their daughter was Asny whom Ofeig Grettir married. Vestar lived at Moeidarhvall. Hrafn was the fifth son of Hœng. He was the first law-speaker in Iceland. He lived at Hof after his father. Hrafn's daughter was Thorlaug who became the wife of Jorund Godi.[3] Their son was Valgard of Hof. Hrafn was the most notable of Hœng's sons.

24

Kveld-Ulf learned of the death of Thorolf his son. It distressed him so much that grief and old age kept him in bed. Skalla-Grim often came to him and talked to him telling him to rouse himself. He said that anything was preferable to lying bedridden and useless. 'A better plan is to see how we can avenge Thorolf. Perhaps we shall get hold of some men who were at Thorolf's death. If not we can still get men that the king will feel the loss of.' Kveld-Ulf spoke a verse.

> How the Fates claw my heart!
> He's dead, my son, Thorolf.
> Odin snatched him. Too soon
> swordsman, dear son, you're dead.
> These blear eyes and old bones
> ban me from battlefield.
> Poor heart, pounding *Revenge*.
> Patience, impatient heart.[1]

That summer King Harald went to Opland, and in the autumn he went west to Valdres and right on to Voss. Olvir Hnufa was with the king, and often got into talk with him about whether he would be willing to pay compensation for Thorolf, to grant Kveld-Ulf and Skalla-Grim an atonement in money, or some honour which would content them. The king did not entirely reject this, if the two of them would come to see him. Then Olvir started a journey north to Fjordane, and did not stop until he arrived in the evening at the home of Kveld-Ulf and Skalla-Grim. They were delighted to see him, and he stayed there for a

time. Kveld-Ulf asked Olvir in detail about the events at Sandnes
when Thorolf fell, and what Thorolf achieved before he died,
who used weapons against him, where were his greatest wounds,
and what was the manner of his death. Olvir told everything he
knew, that King Harald had given him a wound which alone
would have killed him, and Thorolf fell prone at the king's
feet. Kveld-Ulf answered, 'That is well-said, for old men tell us
that the one who falls forward will be avenged, and that the
vengeance will fall on the man who is in front of him when he
falls. But it is unlikely that we shall have such luck as that.'
Olvir said to them that he was confident that if they would go
and see the king, and ask for recompense, it would turn out to be
a worth-while journey. He asked them to risk it, adding persuasion after persuasion. Kveld-Ulf said he could not go on
account of his age. 'I will stay at home,' he said. 'Will you go,
Grim?' said Olvir. 'I don't think it would be the right errand
for me,' answered Grim. 'The king will not find me eloquent. I
shall not make a long job of asking for recompense.' Olvir said
that it would not be necessary, 'we shall say everything on your
behalf that we can think of.' And because Olvir put so much
stress on it, Grim promised to make the journey as soon as he
felt ready. He and Olvir agreed on a time when he should come
to court. Olvir went off first to see the king.

25

Skalla-Grim got ready for the journey just mentioned. He chose
from his household and his neighbours the strongest men and
the bravest available. There was one man called Ani, a rich
farmer, another called Grani, a third Grimolf with his brother
Grim from Skalla-Grim's own men. There were Thorbjorn
Krum and his brother Thord Beigaldi, who were known as
Thorarna's sons. She lived near Skalla-Grim and had witch's
knowledge. Beigaldi after a lazy childhood had turned out a
champion.[1] There was also Thorir Thurs and his brother Thorgeir Jardlang, a man by name of Odd who lived alone, and a
freedman Gris. All together there were twelve for the journey,[2]
all of them the strongest of men, many of them shape-changers.
They had a rowing-boat of Skalla-Grim's, went south along the
coast, came into the Ostrarfjord and took the land-route up to
Voss as far as a lake which they were obliged to cross. They
obtained a rowing-boat, adequate for what they wanted, rowed

across the lake, and then they were not far from the farm where the king was at a feast. Grim and his men got there when the king was at table. They met men outside to talk to and asked what was happening there. When they had heard, Grim asked if Olvir Hnufa could come and talk with him. The man went indoors to where Olvir was sitting, and told him, 'Outside there are twelve men arrived, if they can be called men. They are more like giants than humans in size and looks.' Olvir stood up at once and went out. He had an idea who had arrived. He greeted his kinsman Grim warmly, and invited him indoors. Grim said to his companions, 'It will be the custom here for men to leave their weapons behind when they go into the king's presence. Six of us will go in, and the other six stay and look after the weapons.' Then they went in. Olvir went to the king and Skalla-Grim stood at his back. Olvir began a speech. 'Grim, the son of Kveld-Ulf, has arrived. We are thankful, Sir, that you are going to make his journey here worth while, as we expect it to be. Many who get great honours from you have less reason for it than he has, and are nowhere near as able as he will be in most ways. You might also consider, Sir, that I think this a matter of great importance, if that counts with you at all.' Olvir, being an eloquent man, spoke long and well. Many others, friends of Olvir, came to the king and pleaded the case. The king looked about him and saw that a man stood behind Olvir, taller than the rest by a head, and bald. 'Is that the man Skalla-Grim,' he asked, 'that big man?' Grim said that he was right. 'If you are asking for recompense for Thorolf,' said the king, 'I want you to become my man and join the retainers here, and serve me. Your service may please me enough for me to give you recompense for your brother, or some other honour equal to what I gave your brother Thorolf. You had better know how to take more care than he did, if I make you a great man such as he was.' Skalla-Grim answered, 'It was known, Sir, how much more able Thorolf was than I am in every way, and he was not lucky in his service to you. I will not take such a course. I will not serve you, because I know that I should not have the luck to give you the kind of service I should wish and that would be right. I think there would be more lacking in me than in Thorolf.' The king was silent and flushed blood-red. Olvir turned away at once and told Grim and his men to get out. They did, they went out and picked up their weapons. Olvir told them to leave as fast as they could. Olvir and many men with him, accompanied them to the lake. Before they parted Olvir said, 'Grim, my cousin, your journey to the king has not gone the way I wanted. I urged you enough to come, but now I'm asking you to get home as fast as you can. And what's more, don't come to see King Harald unless agreement between you looks more hopeful than it does now. Be on your guard against him and his men.' Then Grim and his company went across the lake. Olvir and his men went to where ships were drawn up at the water's edge, and hacked at them till none were usable, for they saw men on their way down from the king's house. There were a lot of them, well-armed and moving fast. King Harald had sent the men after them for the task of killing Grim. He had begun to speak soon after Grim's company left, saying, 'From what I see of that great bald man, he's full of wolf-temper, and if he can, he will be the injury of men whose loss we shall feel. Those of you whom he thinks he has a quarrel with can reckon that he'll spare none of you if he gets in reach. Get after him and kill him.' They went out, came to the lake, and could not find any serviceable ships. They went back and reported to the king, adding that Grim would be over the lake by now. Skalla-Grim and his company went on their way until they reached home. Skalla-Grim told Kveld-Ulf about their journey. Kveld-Ulf expressed approval that Grim had not gone to the king on an errand of submission. He repeated that they would get only harm from the king, not advantages. Kveld-Ulf and Skalla-Grim often discussed plans and they reached full agreement. They argued that they could not remain in the country any more than the others who were on bad terms with the king, and it would be advisable for them to get out of Norway. They thought it a good idea to make for Iceland, because there were good reports of the land and its resources. Ingolf Arnarson and his companions, their friends and acquaintances, had gone there, and made their choice of land and homes in Iceland. People could take land there without paying for it, and choose the site of their farm. The firmest part of their plan was to leave home and get out of the country. Thorir Hroaldsson had been fostered in his childhood by Kveld-Ulf, and he and Skalla-Grim were about the same age. The foster-brothers were close friends. Thorir had become a nobleman of Harald's while all this was going on, but his friendship with Skalla-Grim remained firm. Early in the spring Kveld-Ulf and his people got their ships ready. They had a range of good ships to choose from. They prepared two cargo ships, and had on each thirty able-bodied men, as well as the women and children. They had with them all the possessions they could carry, but no-one dared to buy their lands for fear of the king. When they were ready they set sail, and sailed to the islands called Solundoyar. There are many of these islands, and they are big, with so many bays that it is said no-one can know all the harbours.

26

There was a man called Guttorm, the son of Sigurd Hjort. He was King Harald's maternal uncle, and his foster-father, and had been regent over his lands, because the king was a child when he first succeeded to the throne. Guttorm was leader of King Harald's troops when he conquered the country, and was in all the battles that he fought when he took over Norway. When Harald had become sole king over the whole country and settled down quietly, he gave to his uncle Guttorm Vestfold, Aust-Agder, Ringerike, and all the land which his father Halfdan the Black had ruled. Guttorm had two sons and two daughters. The sons were called Sigurd and Ragnar, and the daughters Ragnhild and Aslaug. Guttorm became ill, and when he grew worse he sent men to King Harald asking him to look after his children and his domains. A little later he died. When the king heard of his death he had Hallvard Hardfari and Sigtrygg called to him, and told them to go east to Vik on an errand for him. The king was then in Trondheim. The brothers made magnificent preparations for their journey, selected men, and took the best ship they could get. It was the one which Thorolf Kveld-Ulfsson had owned, and they had taken from Thorgils Gjallandi. When they were ready for the journey, the king told them that their errand was to go east to Tonsberg. There was a market town there where Guttorm had held court. The king said, 'You will bring the sons of Guttorm to me, but his daughters are to be brought up there until I arrange their marriages. I shall appoint men to take charge of the district and bring up the girls.' When the brothers were ready they went on their way and had a good wind. In the spring they came east to Tonsberg in Vik, and carried out their instructions. Hallvard and Sigtrygg collected the sons of Guttorm and much money. When they were ready they started back. It was some time before they got a good wind, and there was no news of their journey until they sailed north through Sognefjord with a good wind, clear weather, and everyone in good spirits.

27

Throughout the summer Kveld-Ulf, Skalla-Grim and company kept a constant check on the sea-routes. Skalla-Grim had better sight than anyone. He saw Hallvard sailing past, and recognized the ship for he had seen it before when Thorgils was in command. Skalla-Grim kept watch on their voyage, noting where they put into harbour in the evening. Then he went back and told Kveld-Ulf what he had seen, and that he had recognized the ship belonging to Thorolf that Hallvard and crew had taken from Thorgils, and there would be some men on it worth hunting. Then they got ready, prepared both boats, and had twenty men on each. Kveld-Ulf captained one and Skalla-Grim the other. Then they rowed in the direction of the ship, and when they came where it was they put in to land. Hallvard's men had rigged awnings and gone to sleep. When Kveld-Ulf's men approached them, the guards sitting at the end of the jetty leapt to their feet, and called out to the men on the ship to get up, saying that enemies were attacking them. Hallvard's men leapt for their weapons. When the others reached the end of the jetty, Kveld-Ulf went out on the stern-gangway, and Skalla-Grim on the forward one. Kveld-Ulf had a fearsome weapon[1] in his hand. When he came on board he told his men to go round the outer edge and cut the ship's awnings at their fastenings, but he rushed back to the stern[2] and it is said that he went berserk there, and there were others among them who went berserk also. Then they killed everyone before them, and Skalla-Grim did the same, neither father nor son stopping until the ship was cleared. When Kveld-Ulf came back to the stern he swung his weapon and struck at Hallvard so that it penetrated helmet and head, and sank in up to the shaft. He then tugged at it with such vehemence that he pulled Hallvard into the air and threw him overboard. Skalla-Grim cleared the prow and killed Sigtrygg. Many leapt overboard, but Skalla-Grim's men took the boat they had come in, rowed after them and killed everyone in the water. More than fifty of Hallvard's men were killed all together, and Skalla-Grim's men took the ship which Hallvard had brought there, and all the property on board. They seized two or three men who seemed to be least important, let them live, and questioned them. They learned what men had been on the ship and the purpose of their journey. When they knew all the facts they counted the dead on board. They found that more men had jumped overboard and been killed than had fallen on the ship. The sons of Guttorm had jumped overboard and died. One of them was twelve years old, the other ten, and both promising. Then Skalla-Grim set free the men he had let live, and told them to go to King Harald, and inform him in detail about these events which had taken place, and also who had been present. He said, 'You shall carry to the king this little verse: [3]

> On Harald now the chieftain's
> vengeance has done its work.
> Around the Yngling's children
> wolf and the eagle lurk.
> Into bruised seas that broken
> corpse of Hallvard flew.
> Grey eagles tear Snarfari's
> wounds—they bleed anew.

Then Grim and his men moved the ship and its cargo out to their ships. They changed over ships, loaded the one they had just got, and cleared the one they had had before which was smaller. They put stones in, made holes in it, and sank it. Then they sailed out to sea as soon as the wind was right.

It is said of those who were shape-changers, or were taken by the berserk-fury, that while it was on them they were so strong that nothing held out against them, but as soon as it left them they were weaker than usual. Kveld-Ulf was like this, and when the fury left him he was exhausted from his attack, and he felt utterly weak and lay in bed. The wind took them out to sea. Kveld-Ulf captained the ship which they had taken from Hallvard. They had a good wind and kept sailing together, so that most of the time each knew where the other was. But when they had crossed the sea, Kveld-Ulf's illness got worse. When he reached the point where he thought he was dying, he called his crew to him, and told them that he thought it likely that their ways would part. 'I have not been prone to illness,' he said, 'but if it turns out, as I think it almost certainly will, that I should die, then put me in a coffin and throw me overboard. It will be surprising if I don't come to Iceland and take land there. Give my greetings to my son Grim when you meet,

and tell him this. If it turns out that he reaches Iceland, and if it
happens, however unlikely it seems, that I look on it first, then let
him build his house as close as he can to where I have come
ashore.' Soon afterwards Kveld-Ulf died. His crew did as he
had asked, they put him in a coffin and sent it overboard.
There was a man on Kveld-Ulf's ship called Grim, the son of
Thorir, the son of Ketil Kjolfari, a rich man from a good family.
He was an old friend of Kveld-Ulf and Skalla-Grim, and had
been on journeys with them and with Thorolf. Because of this
he too had incurred the king's anger. He took charge of the ship
after Kveld-Ulf's death. When they came to Iceland they approached its south coast. They sailed west along the coast,
because they had heard that Ingolf had made his home on that
side. When they came to Reykjanes and saw the fjord revealed,
both ships turned into the fjord. There were strong winds and
heavy rain and mist, and the ships were separated. They sailed
in along Borgarfjord until they were past the rocks. Then they
cast anchor until the winds were calmer and it became light.
They waited for the high tide, and then moved the ship up into an
estuary. It is the one called Gufua. They took their ship up river
as far as they could. Then they unloaded the cargo and settled
there for the first winter. They explored the land along the coast
in both directions. A short distance away they found Kveld-Ulf's
coffin, drifted ashore in a bay. They carried the coffin up on
to the headland there, set it down, and covered it with stones.

28

Skalla-Grim came ashore where a great headland went out into
the sea, connected by a narrow isthmus. They unloaded their
cargo there and called it Knarrarnes. Then Skalla-Grim explored the land and found extensive marshes, broad woodlands,
a good distance between mountain and shore, and plenty of
seals and fish to catch. When they explored the land south along
the coast there was a big fjord in front of them. They turned up
along the fjord and did not break their journey until they met up
with their fellow-voyagers, Grim from Halogaland and his
crew. That was a happy meeting. They told Skalla-Grim that
Kveld-Ulf had come ashore and they had buried him. Skalla-
Grim went there with them, and he thought only a short distance
away was a good place for building his home. Then he went off,
back to his crew, and each company spent the winter where they

had landed. Then Skalla-Grim took the land between mountain and shore, all Myrar out to Selalon, and in to Borgarhraun,
south to Hafnarfjoll, with river boundaries down to the sea.
The next spring he brought his ship south along the fjord, and
into the bay next to the headland where Kveld-Ulf had come
ashore. He established a farm there, calling it Borg, and the
fjord Borgarfjord, and they called the district round about after
the fjord. To Grim of Halogaland he gave a farm-site on the
south side of Borgarfjord where it was called Hvaneyrr. Not far
from there a small inlet cut into the land where they found lots
of ducks and called it Andakil. The river flowing into it they
called Andakilsa. Grim owned the land between that river and the
river called Grimsa. In the spring when Skalla-Grim had his
cattle brought in from up the coast they came on a little headland
where they caught some swans. They called it Alptanes. Skalla-
Grim gave land to his crew. To Ani he gave land between Langa
river and Hafslœk, and Ani settled at Anabrekka. His son was
Onund Sjoni. Grimolf was the first settler at Grimolfsstadir.
After him are named Grimolfsfit, and Grimolfslœk. He had a
son Grim who lived to the south of the fjord. His son was
Grimar who lived at Grimarsstadir. Thorstein and Tungu-Odd
were to quarrel over it.[1] Grani lived at Granastadir on Digranes.
Thorbjorn Krum was given land up along Gufua river, so was
Thord Beigaldi. Krum settled at Krumsholar, Thord at Beigaldi.
Thorir Thurs and his brother were given land up beyond Ein-
kunnir and the far side of Langa river. Thorir Thurs lived at
Thursstadir. His daughter was Thordis Stong who afterwards
lived at Stangarholt. Thorgeir settled at Jardlangsstadir. Skalla-
Grim explored the countryside. First he went in along Borgarfjord to the end of the fjord, and then along the west bank of a
river which he called Hvita because they had not seen glacier
water before, and thought it an odd colour. They went up along
Hvita until they came to the river which flowed from the north
down from the hills. They called it Nordra, and went up along
it until another river, or little stream, was in front of them.
They crossed that one and continued along Nordra. They soon
saw where the little stream fell from the cliffs and called it
Gljufra. Then they crossed Nordra and went back as far as
Hvita and up along that one. Then they met another river which
came across in front of them into Hvita. They called that one
Thvera. They noticed that all the rivers were full of fish. Then
they went down again to Borg.

29

Skalla-Grim was a very hard worker. He always kept a number of men with him, and had them look for such produce as was available, and could be used as provisions for his people, for at first they had not much stock considering what they needed for all their numbers. What stock they had found its own food in the woods during the winters. Skalla-Grim was a fine ship-builder, and there was no lack of driftwood on the west coast of Myrar. He had a house built on Alptanes, and made a second home there. From there he had men rowing out for fish, catching seals and collecting eggs, all of which were plentiful. There was also driftwood to be brought back. There were frequent stranded whales, and anyone could shoot who wanted. Everything was quiet in the fishing and hunting grounds, for the creatures were not used to men. Skalla-Grim had a third house on the coast in western Myrar. It was an even better place for finding driftwood, and he had crops grown there and called it Akrar. Islands where a whale was found lay opposite, and they called these Hvalseyjar. Skalla-Grim also put men to get the catch on the salmon rivers. He established Odd Einbui on Gljufra for the salmon fishing there. Odd lived below Einbuabrekkur at a place called Einbuanes after him. There was a man called Sigmund whom Skalla-Grim put on Nordra. Where he lived was called Sigmundarstadir, but is now known as Haugar. Sigmundarnes is named after him. Later he moved house to Munodarnes because he thought it easier for the salmon fishing. When Skalla-Grim's stock had much increased it was all sent up into the hills during the summer. He found that there was a great difference in that the sheep on the heaths were better and fatter, and that they throve well over the winter in the mountain valleys even though they were not brought down. Afterwards Skalla-Grim had a house built up under the mountain and owned a farm there. He had his sheep looked after there. Gris was in charge of this farm and from him Grisartunga gets its name. Skalla-Grim had by now more than one leg to stand on.

A little while after Skalla-Grim had come to Iceland, a ship came from the sea into Borgarfjord, owned by a man called Oleif Hjalti. He had with him his wife and children and others of his kin, and the purpose of his journey was to settle in Iceland. Oleif was a rich man from a good family, and with a good brain.

Skalla-Grim invited Oleif and all his people to stay with him. Oleif accepted and was with Skalla-Grim his first winter in Iceland. The following spring Skalla-Grim put Oleif on to the choice of land available south of Hvita beyond Grimsa up to Flokadalsa. Oleif accepted that and moved house there, making his home at the place called Varmalœk. He was a fine man. His sons were Ragi in Laugardal, and Thorarin, Ragi's brother, who became law-speaker in Iceland after Hrafn, the son of Hœng. Thorarin lived at Varmalœk. He married Thordis, the daughter of Olaf Feilan, and sister of Thord Gellir.

30

King Harald Finehair took possession of all the estates that Kveld-Ulf and Skalla-Grim had previously owned in Norway, and any other property he could get. Also he made a thorough search for any men who had been consulted or in their confidence, or had aided Skalla-Grim and his men in those things that they did before leaving the country. The enmity which the king had against this father and son became such that he hated their close kinsmen and other near relations, and anyone he knew who had been friendly with them. Some were punished, many fled and looked for a refuge, some of them in Norway, others escaping right out of the country. Yngvar, Skalla-Grim's father-in-law, was one of these men. He adopted the plan of turning his wealth into money as far as he could, got a seagoing ship, put men on it, and prepared to go to Iceland. He had heard that Skalla-Grim had established himself there, and that there would be no lack of available land where Skalla-Grim was. When they were ready and got a wind they sailed out to sea and had a good voyage. He came to the south coast of Iceland and made west for Reykjanes, sailed into Borgarfjord, and held course in along Langa right up to the waterfall. There they unloaded the cargo. When Skalla-Grim heard of Yngvar's arrival he went to meet him immediately, and invited him to come and stay, bringing as many men as he liked. Yngvar accepted. The ship was put ashore, and Yngvar with many people went to Borg and spent the winter with Skalla-Grim. In the spring Skalla-Grim offered him land. He gave Yngvar his farm on Alptanes and the land in as far as Leirulœk and out as far as Straumfjord. He went to this outlying farm and took it over. He was a most capable man and had plenty of wealth. Skalla-

Grim then built a farm on Knarrarnes and had a house there for a long time afterwards.

Skalla-Grim was an excellent smith and he made many things in the winter. He had a smithy built on the coast at a place called Raufarnes, a long way from Borg. He thought the woods there too far away. But he could find no stone which was so hard and smooth that he thought it adequate for beating iron on. In that place there are no beach boulders, only fine sand all along the coast. One evening when everyone else was asleep Skalla-Grim went down to the sea and pushed out an eight-oared boat of his, and rowed out to Midfjardareyjar islands. There he dropped an anchor over the stem of the boat. Then he stepped overboard, dived, brought up a stone, and put it in the boat. Then he got into the boat himself, rowed ashore, took the stone to his smithy and put it down in front of the entrance. Afterwards he used it as an anvil. The stone lies there still, with a lot of slag by it, and it can be seen that the stone is scored, and that it is sea-worn rock, unlike the other stones that are there. These days four men could not lift a bigger stone than that. Skalla-Grim worked hard at his smithying, but his servants complained about the early rising. Then he composed this verse:

> Look, a smith who wants wealth
> will quit his bed at dawn
> and force awake the fierce
> flames of his slumbering fire.
> Then sledge-hammers will sing,
> slam on red-hot iron,
> and wind-starved bellows will
> whine, suck air, wheeze and squeal.[1]

31

Skalla-Grim and Bera had a great many children, and the first ones all died. Then they had a son. Water was splashed on him and he was named Thorolf. As he grew older he quickly became tall and handsome in appearance. It was generally said that he would be very like Thorolf Kveld-Ulfsson after whom he was named. Thorolf was well ahead of others his own age in strength, and when he was fully grown he excelled at practically every accomplishment usual among men of ability in those days. Thorolf was a man who enjoyed himself. He reached his full

strength at a very early age, and was felt to be quite as capable
as other men. He soon became popular with everyone, and was
deeply loved by his parents. Skalla-Grim and Bera had two
daughters, the first called Sæun and the second Thorun. These
also were promising children. Then they had another son.
Water was splashed on him and a name given to him. He was
called Egil. As he grew up it was readily seen that he would be
very ugly, like his father, and black-haired. When he was three
years old he was as big and strong as other boys of six and seven.
He soon learned to talk and was clever with words. He was
rather obstreperous when playing with other children.

That spring Yngvar went to Borg with the intention of inviting Skalla-Grim to a feast out at his home. He named in the
invitation Bera, his daughter, and Thorolf, her son, and anyone
else whom Skalla-Grim and Bera wanted to bring. Skalla-Grim
promised to go. Then Yngvar went home and got ready for the
feast and had the ale brewed. When the time came for Skalla-
Grim and Bera to go to the feast, Thorolf and the men got
ready for the journey with them, so that there were fifteen of
them in all. Egil told his father that he wanted to go. 'I'm just
as much his friend as Thorolf,' he said. 'You're not going,' said
Skalla-Grim. 'You don't know how to behave among men
when there's heavy drinking. You're not all that easy to deal
with, even though you're sober.' Skalla-Grim got on his horse
and rode away, but Egil was in a temper. He left the house and
found a cart-horse belonging to his father. He got on its back and
rode after Skalla-Grim and the rest. It was an uncomfortable ride
through the marshes, for he did not know the route, but he often
saw Skalla-Grim's company when there were no hills or trees in
the way. The story goes that he arrived at Alptanes late in the
evening, when men were sitting over the drinking. He went indoors. When Yngvar saw Egil he welcomed him warmly and
asked why he had arrived so late. Egil explained what he and
Skalla-Grim had said to each other. Yngvar gave Egil a seat
beside himself. Skalla-Grim and Thorolf sat opposite them.
There was a drinking game going on of inventing verses. Egil
spoke this one:

> Here at last! At the hearth
> he who gives soldiers gold
> owns—Yngvar. Oh, but I'm
> only too pleased I'm here.

> And sir, you who scatter
> such artful gold arm-rings,
> you'll meet no master verse-
> maker of three but me.[1]

Yngvar praised the verse and thanked Egil heartily. The next day Yngvar brought to Egil as a reward for his poetry three sea-snail shells and a duck's egg. The day after, at the drinking, Egil composed another verse about this payment for his poetic skill:

> To pay for his polished
> poem, the skilled sword-smith
> gave Egil three snail-shells
> snatched from the crashing seas.
> But the man who managed
> most to please him could boast
> a duck's egg did the trick.
> Donor? A traveller.[2]

Many men warmly congratulated Egil on his poetry. Nothing else worth telling happened on that excursion. Egil went home with Skalla-Grim.

32

There was a powerful chieftain called Bjorn who lived at Aurland in Sogn. His son Brynjolf took the whole inheritance after his father. Brynjolf's sons were Bjorn and Thord. They were young men when these events were going on. Bjorn was a great traveller, sometimes as viking, sometimes as merchant. He was a very capable man. Bjorn happened to be in Fjordane one summer at a feast where there were a lot of people. He saw a beautiful girl there and was much taken with her. He asked what family she belonged to, and was told that she was a sister of the chieftain Thorir Hroaldsson, and was called Thora Lace-Sleeve. Bjorn put forward a proposal, asking for Thora's hand, but Thorir turned him down and they parted on this note. But the same autumn Bjorn got a crew and went with a fully-manned pinnace north to Fjordane, arriving at Thorir's place when he was not at home. Bjorn took Thora away, and brought her home with him to Aurland. They were there during the winter and Bjorn wanted to marry her. Brynjolf, his father, was not pleased over Bjorn's behaviour. He thought it disgraceful, after the long friendship there had been between Thorir and himself. 'Bjorn,' Brynjolf said, 'you are not going to marry Thora in my house without her brother Thorir's consent; in fact she is going to take her place here as though she were my daughter and your sister.' And it had to be so in Brynjolf's household, exactly as he stipulated, whether it pleased Bjorn or not. Brynjolf sent men to Thorir offering him compensation and atonement for Bjorn's expedition. Thorir told Brynjolf to send Thora home, saying there would be no atonement without that. But Bjorn would not let her go on any account, though Brynjolf wanted this. So the winter passed. One day when spring had arrived Brynjolf and Bjorn had a talk about their plans. Brynjolf asked what he had in mind. Bjorn said he would probably leave the country. 'My dearest wish,' he said, 'is that you would let me have a longship and crew, and I would go on viking raids.' Brynjolf said, 'You cannot expect me to give you a warship and a big crew when I am not sure that you wouldn't get up to all sorts of things that I would disapprove of completely. After all you have caused quite enough trouble as it is. I will provide you with a merchant-ship, and the cargo along with it. Go south then to Dublin. That is the most popular route. I will get you a good crew.' Bjorn said he would have to accept what Brynjolf decided. He had a good merchant-ship made ready and found men for it. Then Bjorn prepared himself for the journey, and he was in no hurry. When Bjorn was quite ready and the wind was favourable, he and twelve men got into a boat, rowed it in to Aurland, and went up to the house to his mother's room. She was sitting inside, and many women were with her. Thora was there. Bjorn said that Thora was to go with him. They took her away, and his mother told the women not to be reckless enough to let the men in the hall know of this. She said that Brynjolf would take it badly if he knew of it, and that father and son might do each other harm. Thora's clothes and jewellery were all laid ready to hand, and Bjorn took the lot with him. Afterwards they went out to their ship by night, hoisted sail at once, and sailed out along Sognefjord and afterwards to sea. They had bad weather and were driven before the wind, storm-tossed for a long time, because they were determined to get as far from Norway as possible. Eventually they sailed west to Shetland with a gale-force wind and damaged the ship in touching land at Mousa. They carried the cargo ashore and went into the nearby broch.[1]

They carried all their goods there, drew the ship ashore and
mended what was broken.

33

A little before winter a ship came north to Shetland from the
Orkneys. They reported that a longship had come to the islands
in the autumn with King Harald's messengers on board, carrying word to Earl Sigurd that the king wanted Bjorn Brynjolfsson
killed wherever he might be taken, and he sent the same message
to the Hebrides, and all the way to Dublin. Bjorn learned this
news and in addition that he had been made an outlaw in
Norway. He had married Thora as soon as he arrived in Shetland. They stayed the winter in the broch on Mousa. But as soon
as it was spring and the sea grew calmer, Bjorn brought out his
ship and got it ready as quickly as possible. When he was ready
and the winds were right he put out to sea. They had good
winds, were on the open sea a little while, and came north to
Iceland. The wind, blowing towards the land, took them west
along the coast and then out to sea, but when they got a return
wind they sailed to land. There was not a man on board who
had been to Iceland before. They sailed into a fjord, an incredibly big one, and approached the western coastline. In
towards the shore they saw only breakers, and nowhere to land.
Then they turned away as far as they could into the wind east-
wards along the coast until a fjord appeared ahead of them,
and they sailed in along the fjord until there was an end of
rocks and breakers. They anchored by a headland. An island
lay to seaward with a deep channel in between, where they made
their ship fast. A creek penetrated west of the headland, and
above the creek stood a huge rock. Bjorn and some of his men
got into a boat. Bjorn told his men to be careful not to say anything about their voyage that might lead to trouble. They rowed
to the farm and met men to talk with. First they asked where
they had landed. They were told that it was called Borgarfjord,
and the farm there called Borg, and the farmer Skalla-Grim.
Bjorn placed him immediately, went to meet Skalla-Grim, and
they had a talk together. Skalla-Grim asked who and what
they were. Bjorn named himself and his father, and Skalla-
Grim, knowing Brynjolf well, offered Bjorn all the assistance he
needed. Bjorn accepted this thankfully. Then Skalla-Grim asked
who else of note was on the ship. Bjorn said that there was

Thora, Hroald's daughter, sister to the chieftain Thorir. Skalla-Grim was very pleased at this, and said that it was right and proper to give such help as was necessary, or as he could, to the sister of his foster-brother Thorir. He invited them both to his house with all their company. Bjorn accepted. Then all the cargo was brought from the ship up to the home-field at Borg. They put up shelters there, and the ship was brought up into a little river close by. Where Bjorn and his men made their quarters is known as Bjarnartodur. Bjorn and the whole ship's crew went to stay with Skalla-Grim. He never had fewer than sixty able men with him.

34

In the autumn when ships had come to Iceland from Norway, the rumour spread that Bjorn had run off with Thora, and did not have her family's approval, and for this the king had made him an outlaw from Norway. When Skalla-Grim got to hear of this he called Bjorn to him and asked what had happened about his marriage, and had it been done by family agreement. 'I did not expect from a son of Brynjolf,' he said, 'that you would not tell me the truth.' Bjorn answered, 'I have told you nothing but the truth, Grim, and you cannot blame me if I told you no more than you asked. Still the facts can be admitted now. You have heard rightly that the match was not made with the consent of her brother Thorir.' Then Skalla-Grim said very angrily, 'Why were you so reckless as to come to me? Didn't you know of my friendship with Thorir?' Bjorn answered, 'I knew you were foster-brothers and close friends. But I came to you for the simple reason that I came ashore here, and I knew that it wouldn't help me to evade you. It's for you to decide my fate, but I hope for good since I am in your household.' Then Thorolf Skalla-Grimsson came forward and spoke at length. He asked his father not to make an issue of this with Bjorn when he had made him welcome. Many other people added their voice to his. It ended with Grim calming down and saying that Thorolf should have his way. 'Take Bjorn and behave to him as generously as you like, if that's what you want.'

35

Thora had a child in the summer, a girl. She was splashed with

water and named with the name Asgerd. Bera found a woman
to look after the girl. Bjorn and his entire crew were there with
Skalla-Grim for the winter. Thorolf made much of Bjorn and
was always with him. One day when spring had come, Thorolf
had a talk with his father asking him what plan he had in mind
for his guest Bjorn, and whether he wanted to give him any
help. Grim asked Thorolf what he thought about it. 'I think
this,' said Thorolf. 'Bjorn would like most of all to go to Norway
if peace could be made for him. It seems to me, Father, that
the right thing is for you to send men to Norway to offer atonement for Bjorn. Thorir will value your word.' Thorolf was so
persuasive that Skalla-Grim was swayed, and he found men for
a journey abroad that summer. The men went with messages and
tokens to Thorir Hroaldsson and they tried for reconciliation
between him and Bjorn. As soon as Brynjolf knew about this
errand he put his whole mind to offering atonement for Bjorn.
The case ended with Thorir accepting atonement for Bjorn
because he saw that Bjorn had no need for fear the way things
had gone. Brynjolf then accepted the terms for Bjorn, and
Grim's messengers spent the winter with Thorir, while Bjorn
spent the winter with Skalla-Grim. The next summer Skalla-
Grim's messengers went back, and when they arrived in the
autumn their news was that terms had been made for Bjorn in
Norway. Bjorn stayed a third winter with Skalla-Grim, and the
following spring he prepared to leave, together with the men
who had accompanied him there. When Bjorn was ready for the
journey, Bera said that she wanted Asgerd, her foster-daughter,
to stay. Bjorn and Thora agreed to this, and the girl was left
and brought up there in Skalla-Grim's family. Thorolf Skalla-
Grimsson planned to go with Bjorn, and Skalla-Grim equipped
him for the journey. He went abroad with Bjorn that summer.
They made good speed and came off the high seas into Sognefjord. Bjorn sailed right up to Sogn and went home to his father.
Thorolf went home with him, and Brynjolf welcomed them
warmly. Then word was sent to Thorir Hroaldsson. He and
Brynjolf arranged a meeting between them. Bjorn also came to
the meeting. He and Thorir confirmed the atonement between
them. Thorir paid out the money which he had of Thora's and
afterwards he and Bjorn established friendship as well as kinship
between them. Bjorn stayed at home with Brynjolf at Aurland.
Thorolf was there too, and made much of by both of them.

36

For a long time King Harald had been in residence in Hordaland or Rogaland at the great farms which he owned at Utstein or Avaldsnes or Fitjar, at Arstad or at Lygra or Seim; but that winter which we are speaking of, he was in the north of the country. When Bjorn and Thorolf had been in Norway for one winter and spring had come, they got ready a ship, found a crew for it, and spent the summer in viking activities in the Baltic. They went home in the winter having made a good haul. When they came home they learned that King Harald was now in Rogaland, and would be there for the winter. King Harald was beginning to age very much, but many of his sons were coming into their strength. Eirik known as Blood-Axe, the son of King Harald, was then a young man. He was fostered by the chieftain Thorir Hroaldsson. The king loved Eirik best of all his sons. Thorir at this time was on very good terms with the king. When Bjorn and Thorolf came home they went first to Aurland, and then began their journey north to Fjordane to visit the home of the chieftain Thorir. They had a cutter[1] rowed by twelve or thirteen men a side, and they had about thirty men. They had taken the ship in the summer on their viking raids. It was painted all above the waterline, and was very splendid. When they reached Thorir they had a good welcome, and stayed there for a time, while the ship floated at anchor below the house. One day when Thorolf and Bjorn went down to the ship they saw that the king's son Eirik was there. Sometimes he went down to the ship, and sometimes back on land where he stood and gazed at it. Then Bjorn said to Thorolf, 'The prince is much taken with your ship. Ask him to accept her from you. I'm certain of this, it will be a great help to us with the king if Eirik is counsel for our defence. I've heard it said that the king has harsh thoughts towards you because of your father.' Thorolf said that this was a good idea. Then they went down to the ship and Thorolf said, 'You're looking carefully at the ship, Prince. How do you like her?' 'Very much,' he said. 'She is a very fine ship.' 'Then if you will accept the ship,' said Thorolf, 'I will give her to you.' 'I do accept her,' said Eirik. 'If I promise you my friendship it will not seem to you much of a reward, but there will be some future in that, if I live.' Thorolf said that the reward seemed to him worth much more than the ship. Then they parted, but from then on the prince was very friendly to Thorolf's party. Bjorn and Thorolf had a discussion with Thorir, asking him if he thought it true that the king was unfriendly towards Thorolf. Thorir did not hide the fact that he had heard this. 'In that case,' said Bjorn, 'I should like you to go and see the king and plead Thorolf's case with him. For I shall hold with Thorolf whatever the outcome. That is how he dealt with me when I was in Iceland.' It ended with Thorir promising to visit the king, and asking them to see if the king's son Eirik would go with him. When Bjorn and Thorolf raised this matter with Eirik he promised them he would intercede with his father. Then Thorolf and Bjorn made their way into Sogn, while Thorir and Prince Eirik got ready the newly-given cutter and went south to see the king. They found him in Hordaland and he welcomed them warmly. They stayed there for a time watching for an opportunity to catch the king in a good mood. Then they brought the matter before him. They said that a man had come there called Thorolf, the son of Skalla-Grim. 'We want to ask you this, Sir, that you should remember the ways in which his kin have behaved well to you, and not make him pay for what his father did, since he was avenging his brother.' Thorir spoke about this humbly in his petition, but the king was slow to answer. He said that no good had ever come to them from Kveld-Ulf and his sons, and it was to be expected that this Thorolf would be of the same temper as the rest of his family. 'They are all,' he said, 'very arrogant men, knowing no moderation, and not caring whom they have to deal with.' Then Eirik began to talk. He said that Thorolf had become friendly with him, and given him a great treasure, the ship which they had there. 'I have promised him my full friendship. No-one will make friends with me if this is not honoured. You will not do that to me, Father, when this man is the first up to now who has given me a great treasure.' In the end the king promised them that Thorolf should be at peace with him. 'But,' he said, 'I do not want him to come and see me. You Eirik can make as much of him as you like, and more of his family as well, but it will result in one of two things. Either they will behave to you more meekly than they did to me, or you will be sorry that you asked this, and sorry too if you keep them with you for any length of time.' Then Eirik Blood-Axe and Thorir went home to Fjordane. They sent word to tell Thorolf how their errand to the king had gone. Thorolf and Bjorn spent the winter with Brynjolf. For many summers they went on viking raids, and they spent the winters with Brynjolf or sometimes with Thorir.

37

Eirik Blood-Axe now assumed power. He took control in Hordaland and throughout Fjordane. He began to have retainers and kept them with him. One spring Eirik Blood-Axe made ready for a journey to Bjarmaland[1] and was careful in his choice of troops for the expedition. Thorolf decided to go with Eirik and was in the prow of his ship and carried his standard. Thorolf was by then bigger and stronger than anyone, being like his father in this. Many things happened on this expedition. Eirik fought a great battle on the Dvina in Bjarmaland, and was victorious as the poems about him record. On the same expedition he obtained Gunnhild, the daughter of Ozur Toti, and brought her home with him. Of all women Gunnhild was the loveliest and the wisest, and she had considerable knowledge of magic. Thorolf and Gunnhild became good friends. At this time Thorolf always spent the winters with Eirik and the summers in viking raids.

The next thing that happened was that Thora, Bjorn's wife, became ill and died, and after a time Bjorn found another wife for himself. She was called Alof, the daughter of Erling the Rich from Osteroy. They had a daughter who was named Gunnhild. There was a man called Thorgeir Thornfoot who lived at a farm on the island Askoy[2] in Hordaland. He had three sons, the first called Hadd, the second Berg-Onund and the third Atli the Short. Berg-Onund was bigger and stronger than anyone, and was an ambitious and overbearing man. Atli the Short was a little man, but square-built and physically strong. Thorgeir was a very rich man. He went in for sacrifices and had knowledge of magic. Hadd went on viking raids and was seldom at home.

38

One summer Thorolf Skalla-Grimsson made ready for a trading-voyage, intending and achieving a journey to Iceland to see his father. By now he had been away a long time and he had won great wealth and many treasures. When he was ready for the journey he went to see King Eirik. When they parted the king put an axe in Thorolf's hand, saying he wished to give it to Skalla-Grim. The axe was a large one decorated with gold, and with a curved blade. The shaft was mounted with silver, and it was a really magnificent treasure. Thorolf went on his journey as soon as he was ready. He made good speed, brought his ship into Borgarfjord and at once went quickly home to his father. There was great joy when they met. Then Skalla-Grim went to the ship to help Thorolf and had it brought ashore, and Thorolf with eleven men came home to Borg. When he arrived home he gave to Skalla-Grim King Eirik's greetings and presented him with the axe which the king had sent. Skalla-Grim received the axe, held it up and looked at it for a while, but said nothing about it. He hung it up over his bed-closet. One day in the autumn at Borg Skalla-Grim had a great number of cattle driven in for slaughter. He had two of them brought up to the wall of the house and placed with their heads crossed. He took a large flat stone and thrust it under their necks. Then he went up to them with the axe, the king's gift, and struck both oxen together, so that both heads were off, and the axe crashed down on to the stone so that the edge was shattered and the blade cracked. Skalla-Grim looked at the edge and said nothing about it. He went into the hall where the fire was, stepped up on a bench and threw the axe up on to the cross-beam. It stayed there for the winter. In the spring Thorolf declared that he intended to go abroad during the summer. Skalla-Grim dissuaded him saying that it was a good thing to drive home with the cart safe. 'You were brilliantly successful,' he said, 'but there's a proverb to the effect that a man's luck changes if he makes too many journeys. Take now whatever amount of property you think you need to establish yourself here as a great man.' Thorolf said that all the same he had a voyage to make. 'I have a compelling reason for it. But when I come back the next time I'll settle down here. Now your foster-daughter Asgerd is to go abroad with me to see her father. He commissioned me to do that when I left Norway.' Skalla-Grim said he must have his way. 'But I have an idea that if we part now we shall not meet again.' Then Thorolf went to his ship and got it ready. When he was quite ready they brought the ship out to Digranes and waited there for a wind. Then Asgerd went with him to the ship. Before Thorolf left Borg Skalla-Grim went in and took down the axe, the king's gift, from the cross-beam and came out with it. The shaft was black with smoke, and the blade rusty. Skalla-Grim looked at the axe's edge, then handed the axe to Thorolf. Skalla-Grim spoke this verse:

> This axe-edge is soft, soon
> snaggle-toothed; and who'd want
> to own a weapon which
> weathered no kind of test?
> Let it go back, this bent
> blade and its smoke-charred shaft.
> I had no need of it.
> No. And it a king's gift![1]

39

One summer while Thorolf had been abroad and Skalla-Grim was at Borg a merchant-ship came from Norway into Borgarfjord. In those days merchant-ships were often moored in rivers, in the mouth of a stream or a cutting. A man called Ketil, known as Ketil Blund, owned that ship. He was Norwegian, rich, and from a good family. His son who was grownup was called Geir and was on the ship with him. Ketil got to Iceland late in the summer, and intended to find a place for himself to live. Skalla-Grim knew all about him and invited him and his entire company to stay. Ketil accepted that and was there with Skalla-Grim for the winter. That winter Geir, the son of Ketil, asked for the hand of Thorun, Skalla-Grim's daughter, and married her, the match being agreed on. Afterwards in the spring Skalla-Grim showed Ketil land up beyond the land of Oleif, along Hvita river from the mouth of Flokadalsa as far as the mouth of Reykjadalsa, and the whole tongue of land in between as far as Raudsgil, and all Flokadal above the slopes. Ketil lived at Thrandarholt and Geir at Geirshlid. He had another farm in Reykjadalr at the upper Reykir and he was known as Geir the Rich. His sons were Blund-Ketil and Thorgeir Blund. A third son was Thorodd Hrisablund who first lived at Hrisar.

40

Skalla-Grim got much pleasure from trials of strength and games, and he enjoyed talking about them. At that time ball-games were

popular. There were plenty of strong men in the district then,
but all the same no-one had the strength of Skalla-Grim. By now
he was beginning to feel his age. The son of Grani at Granastadir
was called Thord, and he showed great promise though still
young, and was very fond of Egil Skalla-Grimsson. Egil spent
much of his time wrestling. He was very impetuous and hot-
tempered, and everyone learned to teach their sons to give way
to Egil. A crowded ball-game was held at Hvitarvellir at the
beginning of the winter. Men came to it from everywhere in the
district. Many of Skalla-Grim's household went to the game
there, and Thord Granason was the best of them. Egil asked
Thord to take him to the game. He was then in his seventh year.
Thord was indulgent and took him up behind him on his horse.
When they reached the sports field men were divided up for the
game. There were a lot of little boys there as well, and they
arranged a second game for themselves. There too they were
divided up. Egil was put to play against a boy called Grim, the
son of Hegg from Heggsstadir. Grim was ten or eleven years
old, and strong for his age. When they played together Egil was
weaker, and Grim made all he could of the difference. Then
Egil got angry, lifted up the bat and struck Grim, but Grim
got hold of him and flung him down hard, dealing rather brutally
with him, and saying that he would do him an injury if he didn't
behave. When Egil got to his feet he left the game and the boys
jeered at him. Egil went to find Thord Granason and told him
what had happened. Thord said, 'I will go with you and the
two of us will take vengeance on him.' Thord put into Egil's
hand a bearded axe he had hold of. Such weapons were common
at the time. They went up to the children's game where Grim
had just got the ball and hit it away, the other boys running
after it. Then Egil ran to Grim and swung the axe into his head
so that it reached the brain. Then Thord and Egil went away to
their own men, and the Myramen reached for their weapons, as
did the others. Then Oleif Hjalti together with those who were
with him ran to join the men from Borg. They were then by far
the bigger party, and in this manner they parted. From this rose
the quarrels between Oleif and Hegg. They fought at Laxfit on
Grimsa river. Seven men fell there, Hegg being fatally wounded
and his brother, Kvig, killed. When Egil came home Skalla-
Grim was not much pleased, but Bera said that Egil was a real
viking, and she said that it would follow that he would get his
war-ships as soon as he was old enough. Egil spoke a verse:

My mother told me men
must and would buy me a good
fast ship and finest oars
to fight with viking men;
to stand tall in the prow,
to steer the vessel well,
to hold for harbour and
hack down man after man.[1]

When Egil was twelve years old he was so tall that there was
scarcely anyone so big or so gifted with strength that Egil could
not beat most of them in the games. That winter, which was his
twelfth, he was at the games continually. Thord Granason was
then twenty and he was physically strong. Often as the winter
passed Egil and Thord together played against Skalla-Grim.
One time when the winter was well on the ball game was at
Borg, south in Sandvik. Thord and Egil were drawn against
Skalla-Grim in the games, and he grew tired against them so that
it was easy for them. But in the evening after sunset then it was
worse for Thord and Egil. Grim then grew so strong that he
seized Thord and threw him down with such force that his bones
were broken and he died immediately. Then he seized Egil. A
servant of Skalla-Grim's was known as Thorgerd Brak. She had
fostered Egil in his childhood. She was a big woman, as strong as
a man, and skilled in magic. Brak said, 'Skalla-Grim, are you
going mad against your son?' Then Skalla-Grim let go of Egil
and reached for her. She got away and ran off, but Skalla-Grim
followed. In this way they went out across Digranes. Then she
ran out over the cliffs into the sea. Skalla-Grim threw after her
a huge stone which struck her between the shoulder blades,
and neither stone nor woman was seen again. The place is now
called Brakarsund. Afterwards when they came home to Borg in
the evening Egil was very angry. When Skalla-Grim and everyone had sat down at table Egil was not in his seat. Then he
marched into the hall, went up to a man whom Skalla-Grim
valued highly; he acted both as his foreman and paymaster.
Egil struck him his death-blow, and then went to his seat.
Skalla-Grim said nothing about this, the matter was not referred to, and neither father nor son ever said a good or bad
word about it. So the winter progressed. The following summer
Thorolf came back as has been said. When he had been one
winter in Iceland the following spring he got his ship ready in

Brakarsund. One day when Thorolf was quite ready Egil went
to find his father and asked him to fit him out for a voyage.
'I want,' he said, 'to go abroad with Thorolf.' Grim asked if he
had discussed the matter at all with Thorolf. Egil said he had
not. Grim told him to do that first. But when Egil broached the
matter with Thorolf he said that there was no likelihood 'that
I will take you abroad with me. If your father doesn't think he
can govern you here in his household, then I have no confidence
in taking you to foreign parts with me. It won't do for you to
show the same temper there as here.' 'Then,' said Egil, 'maybe
neither of us will go.' The next night a raging gale came from the
south-west. During the night when it was dark and the sea at
high tide, Egil came on the scene and went out on to the ship
round the outside of the awning. He cut the ropes on the seaward side. Then he went as quickly as possible across the gang-
plank, shot it out, and cut the ropes on the land side. Then the
ship drifted out into the fjord. As soon as Thorolf and his men
realized that the ship was drifting they jumped into a boat, but
the wind was far too fierce for them to get anything done. The
ship drifted over to Andakil and up on the sandbanks there, and
Egil went home to Borg. When men heard of the trick that Egil
had played most of them blamed him. He said that he was not
going to rest from doing yet more harm and injury to Thorolf,
if he wouldn't take him abroad. Then men intervened between
them, and it ended with Thorolf taking Egil, and he went
abroad with him in the summer.

As soon as Thorolf had got on board he took the axe which
Skalla-Grim had put in his hand, and threw the axe overboard
into the deep so that it never was washed ashore afterwards.
Thorolf made his journey during the summer, made good speed
across the sea, and they reached the Hordaland coast. At once
Thorolf steered north to Sogn. The news there was that Brynjolf
had died of an illness during the winter, and his sons had shared
out the inheritance. Thord had Aurland, the farm where their
father had lived. He had taken service with the king and been
made a nobleman. Thord's daughter was called Rannveig, the
mother of Thord and Helgi. Thord was the father of Rannveig,
the mother of that Ingirid whom King Olaf married. Helgi was
the father of Brynjolf, the father of Serk from Sogn, and of
Svein.

41

Bjorn's share was another estate, a good and imposing one. He did not go into the king's service and for this reason was known as Bjorn the Freeholder. He was a man with plenty of money and very magnificent. Thorolf made haste to see Bjorn as soon as he came ashore, and brought Asgerd his daughter home. That was a joyful meeting. Asgerd was the loveliest and most gifted of women, wise and knowledgeable. Thorolf went to see King Eirik. When they met Thorolf gave Skalla-Grim's greetings to King Eirik, and said that he had gratefully received what the king had sent. Then he brought out a good longship's sail which he said Skalla-Grim had sent to the king. King Eirik accepted this gift favourably, and invited Thorolf to stay with him for the winter. Thorolf thanked the king for his invitation. 'I will go first of all to Thorir. I have pressing business with him.' Then Thorolf went to Thorir as he had said, and got there a very warm welcome. Thorir invited him to stay with him. Thorolf said that he would accept that, 'and there is a man with me who must have lodging where I have it. He is my brother, and he has not been from home before, and he needs me to keep a watch on him.' Thorir said he was welcome to bring more men along with him. 'I consider your brother an addition to the company,' he said, 'if he is anything like you.' Thorolf went to his ship to have it brought ashore and looked after, while he and Egil went to the chieftain Thorir. Thorir had a son who was called Arinbjorn. He was somewhat older than Egil. Arinbjorn while still young became a fine man and a master of every skill. Egil attached himself to Arinbjorn and was continually with him, but the brothers were not on good terms.

42

Thorolf Skalla-Grim's son began a conversation with Thorir about how he would react to the idea should Thorolf ask for his niece Asgerd in marriage. Thorir accepted this cheerfully, saying he would certainly promote the match. Then Thorolf with a good company of men went north into Sogn. He arrived at Bjorn's house and had a warm welcome, Bjorn inviting him to stay there as long as he wished. Thorolf quickly brought up his errand to Bjorn, and put forward a proposal of marriage, asking for the hand of Bjorn's daughter, Asgerd. Bjorn welcomed the match and was easily persuaded, and the conclusion was that they were engaged and a wedding day fixed. The feast was to be at Bjorn's house that autumn. Then Thorolf went back to Thorir and told him what the journey had achieved. Thorir was very pleased that this marriage was to take place. When the time came for Thorolf to go to the feast he invited men to go with him, inviting first of all Thorir and Arinbjorn and the men of their household, and all the more powerful farmers so that there were plenty of good men for that journey. But when they had practically reached the day on which Thorolf was to set out, and the men who were to accompany the bridegroom had arrived, Egil fell ill so that he was unfit to go. Thorolf and his men had a great longship fully manned, and went on their journey as had been arranged.

43

One of Thorir's household was a man called Olvir. He was the manager and controller of the estate, with the job of collecting debts and looking after the money. Olvir was past his youth, but still a very vigorous man. Olvir happened to have a journey to make to claim those of Thorir's ground-rents which were outstanding since the spring. He took a boat with twelve of Thorir's household on board. Then Egil began to get better, and he got up. He found it dull with everyone away, and he had a talk with Olvir saying he wanted to go with him. Olvir did not think the addition of a useful man too much, since the boat was big enough. Egil got ready for the journey. He took his weapons: sword, spear and shield. They went on their way when they were ready, and met hard weather, fierce and unfavourable winds, but they pursued their journey doggedly, using the oars. The voyage resulted in their arrival during the evening on Atloy where they put to land. Not far inland was a large farm belonging to King Eirik. The man in charge of it was called Bard, known as Atloy-Bard, a man with weighty responsibilities, and a hard worker. He was not a man from a great family, but King Eirik and Queen Gunnhild had a high regard for him. Olvir and his men drew their boat up above the flood-tide mark, went to the farm, met Bard outside, and told him about their excursion, and that they wished to stay there for the night. Bard saw that they were very wet, and he took them to an outbuilding with a fire in it, a little way from the main house. He had a big fire made up for them and their clothes were dried there. When they had taken back their clothes, Bard came up. 'Now,' he said, 'we'll put a table for you here. I know you'll be wanting your sleep. You're exhausted with your exertions in the bad weather.' Olvir was pleased with this arrangement. Then a table was put up for them, and food given to them, bread and butter and great bowls of skyr put out. Bard said, 'It's a great shame there's no beer in the house; then I could have entertained you as I should have liked. You will have to manage with what there is.' Olvir's men were very thirsty and finished up the skyr. Then Bard had the whey carried in and they drank that. 'I would be delighted,' said Bard, 'to give you better drink if we had it.' There was no shortage of straw there. He suggested they should lie down and sleep.

44

King Eirik and Gunnhild came to Atloy the same evening. Bard had prepared a feast there for him, and there were to be sacrifices to the spirits. It was the best of feasts and indoors there was plenty of drinking. The king asked where Bard was, 'since I don't see him anywhere.' A man said, 'Bard is outside looking after his guests.' 'Who are these guests,' said the king, 'that he thinks he's more obliged to see to them than to be in here with us?' The man told him that men from the household of the chieftain Thorir had come there. The king said, 'Go for them as quickly as you can and bring them in here,' and it was done, and they were told the king wanted to meet them. Then they came. The king greeted Olvir favourably, and told him to sit in the seat of honour opposite himself, with his companions along from him. They did so. Egil sat next to Olvir. Then beer was brought for them to drink. There were many toasts and the horn had to be emptied at every toast. As the evening wore on, many of Olvir's companions became incapable. Some were vomiting there in the room, and some got themselves out of the door. Bard went on as hard as he could getting drinks to them. Then Egil took that horn which Bard had handed to Olvir and drank it off. Bard said he must be thirsty, and straightway fetched him a full horn and suggested he drain it. Egil took the horn and spoke this verse:

'No drink,' so you said.—And
sacrificed to your fine
gods! Clever, you call it?
Can't say I take that view.
Crafty, yes. To cloak your
cunning from men unknown
to you. But then, Bard, you
badly misjudge your game.[1]

Bard told him to drink and leave off such quibbling. Egil drank
everything which came to him and to Olvir. Then Bard went to
the queen and told her that there was a man there who brought
disgrace on them, never drinking without claiming himself still
thirsty. Then the queen and Bard mixed a poisonous drink and
they carried that in. Bard marked the horn and passed it to the
beer-server. She took it to Egil and asked him to drink it. Then
Egil drew out his knife and stabbed it into the palm of his hand.
He took up the horn, carved runes on it, and rubbed in the
blood. He said:

I hatch runes on the horn,
help seal each spell with blood.
Now, hear the nostrum I've
notched on this wild-ox horn.
Let's booze as we think best
beer those cheerful girls poured.
Bard's marked it. What's that mean?
Mischief? Well, let's find out.[2]

The horn sprang apart and the drink poured down into the straw.
Then Olvir began to feel dizzy. Egil stood up and took Olvir out
to the doors, and he kept a hold on his sword. When they got to
the doors Bard came after them and asked Olvir to drink his
parting draught. Egil took it and drank it and spoke a verse:

I'm half-boozed, Olvir's beer-
blanched. I've drained the horn. Rain
it's like, a long downpour—
lips apart for good swigs.
You're not so steady, old
soldier, my strong old
spearsman. But in me swell
storms of god-sent words.[3]

Egil threw down the horn, grasped his sword and drew it. It was dark in the entrance. He thrust the sword through Bard and the point came out through the back, and he fell down dead with blood running from the wound. Then Olvir fell down, vomit pouring from him. Egil ran out of the hall. It was black-dark outside, and Egil made haste away from the farm. Inside the hall it was seen that Bard and Olvir had both fallen. The king came up and had a light brought. Then it was seen what had happened, that Olvir lay there senseless, and Bard was killed, the whole floor swimming in blood. The king asked where the big man was who had drunk most that evening. They said that he had gone out. 'Search for him,' said the king, 'and have him brought to me.' A search was made for him throughout the house and he was not found anywhere. When they got to the outhouse with the fire in, many of Olvir's men were lying there. The king's men asked if Egil had been there at all. They said that he had run in and taken his weapons 'and went out after that'. This was told to the king. The king told his men to go as quickly as possible and seize all the ships which were on the island. 'In the morning when it is light, we will search the whole island and kill the man.'

45

Egil went on through the night and looked for where there might be boats, but wherever he came to the shore there were men ahead of him. He was on the go the whole night and could not get a boat. But when it became light he was standing on one of the headlands. He could see an island and a channel in between, but it was quite a distance. His plan then was as follows: he put together helmet, sword and spear, broke the spear-shaft off and threw it out to sea, wrapped the weapons in his cloak, making a parcel of them, and tied it on his back. Then he dived into the sea and did not rest until he reached the island. It was called Saudey, and is not a big island, but covered in under-growth. It had animals on it, cattle and sheep belonging to Atloy. When he reached the island he wrung his clothes out. By then it was daylight and the sun had risen. King Eirik had Atloy searched as soon as it was light—a slow process for the island was large, and Egil was not found. They took to ships to look for him on other islands. In the evening twelve men rowed to Saudey to look for Egil, and yet there were many islands around. He saw the boat when it came to the island, and nine men came ashore and arranged the search. Egil had lain down in the undergrowth and hidden himself before the boat came to land. Now three men went in each direction and three stayed in the boat, and when the search-parties were out of sight over a hill, Egil got up and went down to the boat. Those who were guarding it knew nothing before Egil was actually among them. He struck one his death-blow instantly, another rushed off but had to climb a bank. Egil struck after him and took off his foot. One jumped aboard and thrust off with the pole, but Egil pulled the rope towards himself and jumped on to the boat. They were not long exchanging blows before Egil killed him and threw him overboard. Then he took the oars and rowed the boat away. He went on the whole night and the next day and did not stop until he reached the home of the chieftain Thorir. But the king let Olvir and his companions go in peace from these events. The men who were on Saudey were there for a number of nights. They killed the beasts for food, kindled fire and made a fire-pit. They made it big enough to be seen from the farm, lit a fire in it and made a signal. When it was seen, men rowed over to fetch them. The king had gone. He went off to another feast. Olvir and his men got home before Egil, while Thorir and Thorolf had just come home from the wedding. Olvir told the news, the killing of Bard and the circumstances surrounding it, but he did not know of Egil's adventures. Thorolf was very unhappy and Arinbjorn also. They thought he would not return. But the next morning Egil came home, and when Thorolf knew of this he got up and went to meet Egil and asked how he had escaped and what had happened on his journey. Egil spoke a verse:

> I'll tell you the truth, no
> trumpeting name or fame.
> To get clear of Gunnhild's
> grasp took cunning and guts.
> But then three serving-men—
> they were Eirik's—lost heart!
> Now they're dawdling down to
> damned high halls. Lady Hel's.[1]

Arinbjorn made much of these deeds, and said that his father was obliged to reconcile Egil with the king. Thorir said, 'Men will say Bard got his deserts in being killed. All the same, Egil is following the family tradition overmuch, in thinking too little of the king's anger. For most men it is hard to bear. Still, Egil, I will bring you into reconciliation with the king on this occasion.' Thorir went to see the king and Arinbjorn stayed at home. He said it should go the same way for all of them. When Thorir obtained a meeting with the king he made offers on Egil's behalf, pledged himself, and invited the king to decide the terms. King Eirik was furious, and it was difficult to come to terms with him. The king said that it would be proved true what his father had told him, that one should be slow to trust that family. He told Thorir to arrange matters so that 'Egil shall not for long be lodged in my kingdom, though we come to an arrangement of sorts. But for your sake Thorir, I will accept payment for these men.' The king made such charges as he thought and Thorir paid everything. Then he went home.

46

Thorolf and Egil stayed with Thorir in high favour, but in the spring they got ready a great longship, found men for it, and went into the Baltic for the summer, raiding, seizing goods, and fighting frequent battles. They also went as far as Kurland and anchored offshore there for a fortnight's rest and trade. When this was ended they again took to raiding, going ashore at various places. One day they anchored at the mouth of a large river where there was extensive forest. They planned to go ashore there, and were divided into groups of twelve. They went into the wood and it was not long before settlements were located. They plundered and killed people, but the inhabitants ran off and there was no real fighting. When the day was well on, Thorolf had the horn blown for return. Then men turned back into the wood from wherever they found themselves, but the company could not be counted until they reached the shore. When Thorolf arrived Egil had not come there. It began to get dark and they did not think they could search for him. Egil had gone through the wood, twelve men with him, and saw wide plains and buildings. There was one farm a short distance from them, and they headed for that, but when they got there they ran through the house without finding anyone, but taking what property was lying about. There were many buildings and they were delayed there for a long time, and when they came out and away from the farm, a lot of people had gathered between them and the wood, and they attacked the vikings. There was a high fence between them and the wood. Egil said they were to stay with him so that they could not be attacked on all sides. Egil went first, and then one after the other so close that no-one could get between them. The Kurlanders made a vigorous attack, mostly by thrusting and throwing, rather than exchange of blows. As they advanced along the fence Egil and his men did not notice that a second fence joined it from behind them and they could not get out. The Kurlanders penned them in, some attacking from outside, thrusting swords and spears through the fences and some throwing clothes over their weapons. They were wounded and then captured, and all bound and led back to the farm. The man who owned the farm was rich and powerful. He had a grown-up son. They had a talk about what should be done with the prisoners. The farmer said that it seemed to him a good idea to kill each in turn. The farmer's son said that it was getting dark, and they could not amuse themselves with torturing them. He asked that they should wait till morning. They were then thrown into an outbuilding and tightly bound. Egil was bound to a stake by both his hands and his feet. Then the room was securely locked, and the Kurlanders went into their living-room where they ate and drank and were very cheerful. Egil moved himself about and tested the stake until it was loose in the ground. Then it fell down and Egil rid himself of it. Then he freed his hands with his teeth, and when his hands were free he untied the ropes from his feet. Next he freed his companions. When they were all untied they looked around them in the room for where they were most likely to get out. It was built in this fashion; the walls were made of great baulks of timber, but at one end of the room was a thin partition. They hurled themselves at this and broke the partition. Then they had come into another room. There too timber walls were all round. They heard men talking under their feet, looked round, and discovered the floor had a trap-door. They opened this and underneath was a deep pit. It was from there they heard men's voices. Egil asked who was there. The one who answered named himself Aki. Egil asked if he wanted to be out of the pit. Aki said they would like it very much. Then Egil and his companions flung into the pit the ropes they had been bound with and hauled up three men. Aki said they were his two sons, and they were Danes who had been captured the previous summer. 'I was well-treated in the winter,' he said. 'I had a lot to do with looking after the farmer's stock, but the boys were enslaved and they were miserable. In the spring we planned an escape, but we were discovered. Then we were put here in this pit.' 'You will know your way around the buildings,' said Egil. 'Where are we most likely to get out?' Aki said that there was another partition. 'Break that down. Then you will get into the corn store, and from there you can get out as you like.' Egil and his men did so, broke the partition, got into the barn, and then out from there. It was pitch-dark. Egil's men said that now they had better hurry off to the wood. Egil said to Aki, 'If you know your way around the buildings you will be able to direct us to some loot.' Aki said that there was no shortage of movable goods. 'There is a great room upstairs that the farmer sleeps in, with plenty of weapons inside.' Egil said that they were to go to that room, and when they came up the steps they saw that the room was open. There was a light inside and servants were getting the beds ready. Egil told some of his men to stay outside and watch that no-one came out. He ran into the room, seized weapons there of which there were plenty, and killed all who were inside. Then they all took a full set of weapons. Aki went to where there was a trapdoor in the wooden floor and opened it, saying that they should go down into the room below. They took lights with them and went down. There was the farmer's strong-room, fine treasures and much silver. The men loaded themselves and came out. Egil took for himself a good big treasure-chest and carried it under his arm. Then they went to the wood. But when they reached the wood Egil stopped and said, 'This expedition is all wrong and dishonourable. We have stolen the farmer's property in such a way that he does not know of it. We must not be so disgraced. Let's go back now to the farm, and let them know what's going on.' They all spoke against this. They said they wanted to get to the ship. Egil put down his treasure-chest. He rushed off and went to the farm. When he came up to it he saw that servants were going from the kitchen carrying plates and dishes into the living room. Egil saw that in the kitchen there was a huge fire with cauldrons over it. He went up to it. Enormous logs had been brought there and the fire built up, as was usual there, by thrusting one end of the log into the fire, and so letting it burn along the whole. Egil picked up a log and carried it to the living-room, and thrust the blazing end up under the eaves and so into the roofing. The fire took a quick hold of the brushwood.

Those who were sitting drinking knew nothing before the roof
was on fire. Then they ran for the doors but there was no passage because of the flames, and because Egil was guarding the
door. He felled men both in the doorway and outside in front of
the doors. It was only a moment before the living-room was on
fire and collapsing. Everyone in it died and Egil went back to
the wood and found his companions. They all went together to
the ship. Egil said that he wished to have for his own share the
treasure-chest he had brought, and it turned out to be full of
silver. Thorolf and his men were delighted at Egil's reappearance.
They set sail as soon as it was morning. Aki and his sons were
in Egil's band. As the summer drew to a close they sailed for
Denmark, still watching for trading-ships, and plundering
wherever they went.

47

Harald Gormsson had taken over the Danish kingdom and
Gorm his father had died. The country was exposed to raiders,
and vikings anchored freely off Denmark. Aki was well ac-
quainted with the Danish waters as well as the land. Egil had a
lot to ask him about where might be the places for good plundering. When they came into Oresund Aki said that there was a
large market town ashore called Lund. He said there should be
loot for the taking there, but it was likely that the townsmen
would fight. It was put to the ship's company to decide whether
they should plan on going ashore or not. There was no general
agreement. Some were eager, some reluctant. It was then put
to the captain. Thorolf was in favour of landing. Then Egil was
asked what he thought advisable. He spoke a verse:

> Let's go. Let's make our swords
> leap like flame in the air.
> It's when the weather's good
> we need to do fine deeds.
> To Lund, then, swift and sure,
> so that we'll hear the harsh
> song of the spears before
> sunset robs us. Let's go![1]

Then men prepared for landing and went to the market town.
When the townsmen were aware of the invaders they went

against them. There was a palisade round the place and they
set men to defend it. There the battle took place. Egil was first
through the defences and then the townsmen fled and there was
heavy slaughter. They plundered the town and burned it before
they left. Then they went back to their ships.

48

Thorolf took his ship north by Halland, and put in to harbour
where the wind took them. They did not plunder there. An earl
called Arnfid lived a short distance from the coast. When he
knew that vikings had come to land he sent his men to meet them
and discover whether their errand was peace or plunder. When
the messengers reached Thorolf with this question he said they
would not be raiding there. He said that there was no need for
them to raid there or to get their war-shields out, and added
that the countryside was not wealthy. The messengers went back
to the earl and told him the result of their journey. When the
earl realized that he had no need to gather an army on this
account he rode down without a troop to meet the vikings.
When they met the talk between them went very well. The earl
invited Thorolf to come and feast with him bringing such men
as he wished. Thorolf promised to come. When the time came
the earl had horses sent for them to ride. Thorolf and Egil
decided to go and they had thirty men with them. When they
reached the earl he welcomed them cordially. They were taken
indoors, and beer was immediately brought and given to them
to drink. They sat there until evening. But before the tables
were removed the earl said that they should draw lots for the
seating, and a man and woman should drink together as far as
numbers allowed; those who were left over, by themselves. The
lots were cast into a bag[1] and the earl drew them out. The earl
had a very beautiful daughter who was just grown up. The lot
decreed that Egil should sit beside the earl's daughter for the
evening. She was walking about the floor and enjoying herself.
Egil stood up and went to the seat where the earl's daughter had
been sitting during the day. When men took their seats the earl's
daughter came to hers. She said:

> Why take my seat? Tell me
> truthfully now. Have you
> often offered to wolves

> offal of still-hot flesh?
> Have you seen fall-kites hang
> high above corpses? Why,
> you've not heard sword on sword!
> So let me sit alone.[2]

Egil reached for her and pulled her down beside him. He said:

> I've been with sword and spear
> slippery with bright blood
> where kites wheeled. And how well
> we violent vikings clashed!
> Red flames ate up men's roofs,
> raging we killed and killed,
> and skewered bodies sprawled
> sleepy in town gate-ways.[3]

Then they drank together for the evening and were very cheerful. It was the best of feasts, and the day after was too. Then the vikings went to their ships. They and the earl parted in friendship and exchanged gifts. Thorolf and his men held course for the Brenneyjar. At this time it was a real viking lair, for many merchant-ships sailed through the islands. Aki and his sons went home to their estates. He was a very rich man and owned many farms on Jutland. They parted with affection, and promised full friendship to each other. When autumn came Thorolf steered north along Norway and they arrived in Fjordane and went to find the chieftain Thorir. He welcomed them warmly, and Arinbjorn his son more warmly still. He invited Egil to stay there for the winter. Egil accepted that with thanks. But when Thorir knew of Arinbjorn's invitation he said it had been too readily given. 'I do not know,' he said, 'how it will please King Eirik, for he said after Bard's killing that he didn't want Egil in the country.' 'You can easily manage it with the king, Father,' said Arinbjorn, 'so that he doesn't make an issue out of Egil's lodging. You will invite your kinsman Thorolf to stay, and Egil and I will share the same winter-quarters.' From this conversation Thorir saw that Arinbjorn would prevail in the matter. Then father and son offered Thorolf winter-quarters there and he accepted that. They were there with twelve men for the winter. There were two brothers named Thorvald the Proud and Thor-

fid the Strong. They were close kinsmen of Bjorn the Freeholder and had been brought up with him. They were big men
and strong, good fighters and ambitious. They stayed with Bjorn
so long as he went on viking raids, but afterwards when he
settled down quietly, the brothers went over to Thorolf and
joined him on viking raids. They were in the prow of his ship,
and then when Egil became a ship's captain Thorfid was his
second in command. These brothers went everywhere with
Thorolf and he valued them most highly of his crew. The brothers
were in his band that winter, and sat next to Thorolf and Egil.
Thorolf sat in the high seat and drank with Thorir, but Egil sat
with Arinbjorn for the drinking. They went on to the floor for
every toast.[4] In the autumn the chieftain Thorir went to see
King Eirik. The king received him most favourably. When they
began to talk Thorir asked the king not to blame him for the
fact that he had Egil staying with him for the winter. The king
answered this kindly saying that Thorir could receive from him
whatever he wished, 'still it would not go the same way if some
other man had protected Egil.' But when Gunnhild heard what
they were saying she said, 'I think, Eirik, that things go this way
too often. You are very persuadable, and don't remember offences
against you for very long. You'll promote the sons of Skalla-
Grim till they kill some close kinsman of yours yet again. But
though you behave as if you thought Bard's killing of no account, I do not hold it so.' The king said, 'Gunnhild, you more
than anyone else taunt me into severity. But you have been
fonder of Thorolf than you are now. I will not take back my
word to these brothers.' 'Thorolf was well enough,' she said,
'before Egil ruined him. Now I think there's nothing to choose
between them.' Thorir went home when he was ready, and told
the brothers what the king had said, and the queen.

49

The sons of Ozur Toti and brothers of Gunnhild were called
Eyvind the Braggart and Alf the Shipman. They were big men
and strong, and ready fighters. They were at that time highly
favoured by King Eirik and Gunnhild, but not popular with
everyone. They were young in years, but nevertheless come to
their full strength. During that spring there was to be a great
sacrificial feast for the summer at Gaular. That was the most
famous Great Temple. Large numbers of men went there from

Fjordane and Fjaler and from Sogn including nearly all the important people. King Eirik went there. Then Gunnhild said to her brothers, 'I should like it if you could manage in this crowd to get one or other of the sons of Skalla-Grim killed, preferably both.' They said that it should be done. The chieftain Thorir got ready for that journey. He called Arinbjorn to talk with him. 'Now I,' he said, 'will go to the sacrifice, but I do not wish that Egil should go there. I know the persuasions of Gunnhild and the temper of Egil and the power of the king, and it will not be easy to keep watch in all directions. But Egil will not let himself be stopped unless you stay. But,' he continued, 'Thorolf and their other companions shall go with me. Thorolf shall sacrifice and pray for luck on behalf of his brother and himself.' Then Arinbjorn told Egil that he was to stay at home. 'The two of us,' he said. Egil said that it should be so. Thorir and his men went to the sacrifice, and there was a great crowd of men and much drinking. Thorolf stayed with Thorir wherever he went and they did not separate by day or night. Eyvind told Gunnhild that he could not get within reach of Thorolf. She told him then to kill one of his men, 'rather than them all getting away.' One evening when the king had gone to bed and also Thorir and Thorolf, Thorfid and Thorvald happened to be still sitting up. The brothers Eyvind and Alf came up and sat down by them and were very jovial. First they drank in a group.[1] Then it was agreed that they should share a full horn between two, half and half. Eyvind and Thorvald drank together and Alf and Thorfid. But as the evening wore on there was cheating over the drinks, and then quarrelling and abuse. Eyvind jumped up, drew a knife, and thrust it into Thorvald, and that was enough to cause his death. Then men on both sides jumped up, the king's men and Thorir's household, but all the men were unarmed because it was in the temple precinct. Others came in between them and separated those who were most violent. There were no further events that evening. Eyvind had killed in the sanctuary, and he was made an outlaw, and had to go away at once. The king offered compensation for the man, but Thorolf and Thorfid said that they had never taken payment for a man, and they would not accept it. They separated on this note. Thorir and his men went home. King Eirik and Gunnhild sent Eyvind south to Denmark to King Harald Gormsson, for he could not remain in Norwegian territory. The king accepted him and his company favourably. Eyvind took a large longship to Denmark. Afterwards the king put Eyvind to be a look-out against the vikings. Eyvind was the best of fighters.

When spring arrived after that winter Thorolf and Egil got ready to go on further viking raids. When they were ready they made for the Baltic again. When they came into Vik they sailed south for Jutland and made raids there and then they went on to Frisia where they delayed for a long time during the summer, and then turned back again to Denmark. When they came to the land boundary between Denmark and Frisia and anchored off-shore two men came to Egil's ship one evening when those on board were getting ready to go to sleep. They said they had an errand to Egil, and they were taken to him. They told him Aki the Rich had sent them there with this message that, 'Eyvind the Braggart is lying in wait off the Jutland coast, and intends to attack you as you go north. He has assembled a great force so that you will have no chance to resist, if you encounter the whole host. But he himself journeys with a couple of small ships, and is only a little way off from you.' When this news reached Egil they at once took down the covers. He told them to move silently and they did. They came at dawn to where Eyvind's ships lay at anchor. They attacked them immediately hurling both stones and weapons. Many of Eyvind's men fell, but he himself jumped overboard and reached the shore by swimming, as did everyone who escaped. Egil's men took the ships and their baggage and their weapons. Then they went back to their company during the day. They met Thorolf. He asked where Egil had been, and where he had got those ships that were with him. Egil said that Eyvind the Braggart had owned the ships, and they had taken them from him. Then Egil said:

> Off Jutland we hit him—
> hard. And he fought back hard.
> The Danes' guardian gave
> good blows for our best blows.
> But then tricky Eyvind
> tactfully packed it in.
> The loudmouth and his lads
> left ship, slipped away east.[2]

Thorolf said, 'I think that what you have done means that our plans for the autumn will not include Norway.' Egil said that it was all right if they looked now in other directions.

50

Alfred the Great ruled over England. He was the first king of his line to be the sole ruler over the whole of England. This was in the time of Harald Finehair, the king of Norway. After Alfred his son Edward became king of England; he was the father of Æthelstan the Victorious, the foster-father of Hakon the Good. About this time Æthelstan succeeded his father to the English crown. He had several brothers, also the sons of Edward. When Æthelstan succeeded to the throne hostilities began among the chieftains who had lost their power to his ancestors. They thought now would be the easiest time to claim it, while a young king ruled the kingdom. They were from Wales, Scotland and Ireland. But Æthelstan gathered an army and gave pay to all men from home or abroad who were willing to earn such money. The brothers Thorolf and Egil made their way south along Germany and Flanders. When they heard that the king of England thought he had need of help, and there was the prospect of great gain, they decided to go there with their men. They went on through the autumn until they came to meet King Æthelstan. He greeted them well and thought their support would be a great help to him. The subject was quickly brought up in conversation by the English king. He invited them to take pay and become defenders of his land. It was agreed between them that they should become Æthelstan's men. England was Christian, and had been for a long time when this was going on. King Æthelstan was fully Christian, and was known as Æthelstan the Believer. The king asked Thorolf and Egil to let themselves be provisionally baptized. It was a common custom to do so both among merchants and those mercenaries who joined with Christians, since men who received provisional baptism had full contact with Christians and heathens, but kept whatever faith they were inclined to. Thorolf and Egil did this at the king's request, both accepting provisional baptism. They had three hundred of their men there who became the king's mercenaries.

51

There was a king in Scotland called Olaf the Red. He was Scottish on his father's side, Danish on his mother's side, and descended from the family of Ragnar Lodbrok. He was a power-

ful man. Scotland is considered a third of the kingdom of
England. Northumbria is considered a fifth of England, and is
the furthest north next to Scotland on the east side. Danish
kings used to rule there. The chief town is called York. Æthelstan
owned this district and had put two earls in charge, one called
Alfgeir and the other Godrek. They were set to guard the land
against the onslaughts of Scots and Danes or Norwegians who
did a lot of raiding in the land, and thought themselves to have a
claim in the country there, for in Northumbria the only men
who counted for anything were of Danish descent by father or
mother, and there were many of both. Two brothers, Hring and
Adils,¹ ruled over Wales, and they paid tribute to King Æthelstan.
It was part of their service that when they were in the king's
army they and their people should be in the front ranks in the
company with the king's standard. These brothers were fine
warriors and not young men. Alfred the Great had deprived all
tributary kings of name and power. Those who had previously
been kings or princes were now called earls. That had continued
throughout his life and the life of his son Edward, but Æthelstan
came young to the throne, and they stood in less terror of him.
Many became disloyal who earlier had offered good service.

52

Olaf, the king of the Scots, got a great army together and then
went south into England. When he reached Northumbria he
raided continuously. When the earls who ruled there learned of
this, they summoned their people together and marched against
the king. They met and there was a fierce battle which ended in
victory for King Olaf. Earl Godrek fell, Alfgeir fled, and so did
most of their men who survived the battle. Then Alfgeir could
make no resistance, and King Olaf brought the whole of Northumbria under his rule. Alfgeir went to see King Æthelstan and
told him of his defeat. As soon as King Æthelstan knew that
such a large army had invaded his country he immediately
sent off men to summon troops, sending word to his earls and
other leading men. The king started marching immediately with
the army he had collected, moving against the Scots. But when it
was known that Olaf, king of the Scots, had been victorious
and brought much of England under his rule, his army far out-
numbered Æthelstan's and many powerful men joined him.
When Hring and Adils, who had collected a large body of men,

heard of this, they joined forces with King Olaf, who now had men beyond count. When Æthelstan heard of all this he held a meeting with his leaders and statesmen to work out what would be the most expedient thing to do, explaining clearly to the whole gathering what he had learned of the activities of the Scottish king and his great army. They all said the same, that Earl Alfgeir had behaved the worst in this, and it followed that he should be deprived of his rank. But it was resolved that King Æthelstan should go back and work through the south of England, and bring his own army north up` the length of the country. This was because they realized that they would be slow in collecting as many men as they needed if the king himself did not call out the people. The army which had already assembled was put in charge of the chieftains Thorolf and Egil. They were to control that company which the vikings had brought to the king, and Alfgeir himself stayed in charge of his own troops. The king appointed further leaders to divisions as he thought fit. When Egil came home from the meeting to his companions they asked him what he had to say about the news from the king of the Scots. He said:

> Olaf dropped one earl, the
> other one upped and ran.
> A bloody fight! But he's
> bold in battle I'm told.
> Godrek went the fool's wrong
> way in that fight. And right
> now, Olaf—he must hold
> half of Earl Alfgeir's land.[1]

Then they sent a man with a message to King Olaf saying this, that King Æthelstan wished to appoint a battle-field and meet him in fight at Vinheid by Vinuskog wood.[2] He asked that they should not raid in his land, but whichever of them had victory in battle was to rule the kingdom of England. He appointed their encounter for a week ahead, but the one who arrived first should wait a week for the other. It was the custom then that when a king had been challenged to battle he could not raid without dishonour before the battle was ended. King Olaf complied, and halted his army, did not raid, and waited for the fixed day. Then he moved his army to Vinheid. There was a fort to the north of the moor. King Olaf established himself there in that fort and had the greater part of his troops there, for there was good country round, and he thought it better for supplying the provisions needed by the army. He sent men of his up on the moor to the place appointed for battle. They were to find tent sites, and make ready before the army came. When the men reached the place agreed on, hazel stakes were put up indicating the site where the battle was to be. The place needed to be chosen carefully so that it should be level ground where a great host was to be drawn up. As it was, the moor where the battle would be was level, but on one side a river flowed down, and on the other there was a big wood. King Æthelstan's men had pitched their tents where there was the shortest distance between the wood and the river, and even so that was a long stretch. Their tents went the whole length between wood and river. They had organized their tents so that there was no-one in every third tent, and few people in any. When King Olaf's men came up it was crowded in front of all the tents and they could not go into them. King Æthelstan's men said that all the tents were full of men, so that there was barely room for their army. The tents were so high that no-one could see over the top to discover whether their rows were many or few. They thought that an army of men was there. King Olaf's men pitched their tents to the north of the hazels where it sloped downwards a little. Æthelstan's men also said day after day that their king must have arrived or had already arrived at the fort south of the moor. Men came to their support both day and night. When the time had passed that had been specified, King Æthelstan's men sent messengers to King Olaf with these words, that King Æthelstan was ready for battle and had an immense army, but he sent this message to King Olaf, that he did not wish them to engage in so much destruction as was imminent. He suggested rather that Olaf should go home to Scotland, and Æthelstan would give him in friendship a silver shilling for every plough in his kingdom, and he hoped that there would be friendship between them. When the messengers reached King Olaf he was getting his army ready and intending to ride out. But when the messengers put forward their proposals the king stopped movement for that day. He sat in council, the leaders of the army with him. There was no general agreement. Some were very eager to accept this offer. They said that it would have been a splendid expedition if they went home with such payment from Æthelstan. Some held back saying that Æthelstan would offer much more the next time if this were not accepted, and this was the plan adopted. Then the messengers asked King Olaf to give them time to meet King Æthelstan again, and find out whether he was willing to pay out more tribute in the cause of peace. They asked for a truce of one day for riding back, a second day for discussion, and a third for return. The king granted them that. The messengers went back and returned on the third day as had been agreed, saying that King Æthelstan was willing to give everything which he had previously offered, and in addition, for sharing among King Olaf's army, a shilling to every free-born man, a mark to every leader of a company numbering twelve or more, a mark of gold to every leader of the retainers, and five marks of gold to each earl. The king had this put to his army. It was the same as before. Some held back, and some were eager, and it ended with the king making a decision. He said that he would accept this offer if along with it King Æthelstan would let him have the whole of Northumbria with the tributes and dues belonging to it. The messengers asked again for a three-day delay and this also, that King Olaf should send men to hear the words of King Æthelstan, whether he agreed to those terms or not, saying that they thought Æthelstan would not let much stand in the way of peace. King Olaf agreed to that and sent his men to King Æthelstan. Then all the messengers rode together and met King Æthelstan in the fort nearest the moor on the south side. The messengers of King Olaf put their proposals and terms offered before King Æthelstan. King Æthelstan's men also said what proposals they had put before King Olaf, adding that it had been the plan of wise men to delay the battle by these means so long as the king had not come. King Æthelstan quickly gave a decision in the matter, saying this to the messengers, 'Take these words of mine to King Olaf. I will grant him permission to go home to Scotland with his army, and he may pay back all that money which he has unlawfully seized in this realm. Then we will establish peace between our countries, and neither shall make raids on the other. In addition King Olaf shall become my vassal, and hold Scotland from me, and be king under me. Go back now,' he said, 'and tell him how things are.'

The messengers immediately took their way back during the evening, and came to King Olaf about midnight. They woke up the king and told him at once the words of King Æthelstan. The king had all his earls and other chieftains summoned, and

made the messengers join them, and repeat the result of their
errand, including the words of King Æthelstan. When this was
known to the army they were all of the opinion that the only
thing to do was to prepare for battle. The messengers said too
that Æthelstan had a great host of men, and he had reached the
fort on the same day as the messengers did. Then Earl Adils
said, 'Now, Sir, it will be seen to be as I said it would. They show
themselves cunning, these English. We have been sitting here a
long time waiting until they have drawn all their army to them.
Their king cannot have been anywhere near when we arrived.
Now they will have acquired a great force while we sat around.
My advice, Sir, is that we, my brother and myself, ride out immediately with our troops tonight. It is possible that they have
no fear for themselves, since they have learned that their king is
near by with a large army. The two of us will make an attack on
them, and when they are running away they will lose men, and
then not be so brave in attacking us.' The king thought this a
good idea. 'We will get our army ready and join you as soon as it
is light.' They agreed on this plan, and so the meeting ended.

53

Earl Hring and his brother Adils got their troops ready and
went south to the moor immediately during the night. When it
was light Thorolf's guards saw where an army was moving.
Then a warblast was blown and men got their armour on. They
formed into companies and there were two divisions. Earl
Alfgeir commanded one company and his standard was carried
in front of him. In his company were both his own people, and
also the men who had been drawn together from the districts.
This was a bigger company by far than the one with Thorolf.
Thorolf was equipped in the following manner: he had a broad,
solid shield, a very strong helmet on his head, a sword by his
side called Long, a big weapon and a good one. In his hand he
had a spear. The head was three feet long, having a socket with
four facets, the blade was broad at the top and the socket long and
thick; the shaft was no longer than a span, but extremely thick.
An iron spike transversed the socket and the shaft was bound
round with iron. Spears of this kind were called winged spears.
Egil had the same equipment as Thorolf. He had at his side the
sword that he called Adder. He had got that sword in Kurland
and it was the best of weapons. Neither of them had a mailcoat.

They set up their standard and it was carried by Thorfid the
Strong. Their entire troops had Norwegian shields and all
Norwegian armour. In that company were all the Norwegian
men of the army. Thorolf and his company drew up beside the
wood, but Alfgeir's division marched alongside the river. Earl
Adils and his brother realized that they would not take Thorolf's
men unawares. Then they began to draw up their troops under
two standards; the company of Adils against Earl Alfgeir, and
Hring against the vikings. Battle was joined and both sides advanced valiantly. Earl Adils attacked fiercely until Alfgeir drew
back, and then Adils' men attacked twice as boldly. It was not
long before Alfgeir fled, and the story is that he rode away south
over the moor and a body of men with him. He rode until he
came near the fort where the king was. Then the earl said, 'I do
not think we will go up to the fort. We were thoroughly blamed
last time we came to the king after a defeat by King Olaf, and he
is not going to think that we have improved our position by this
episode. It would be idle to hope for honours from his hand.'
Then he rode south through the country and we can say of his
journey that he rode day and night until they came west to
Jarlsnes. There the earl got a passage south over the sea for
himself, and arrived in France. He had half his kin there, and
he never came back to England.

At first Adils pursued those in flight, but it was not long before
he turned back to where the battle was and attacked. When
Thorolf saw that, he turned to meet the earl and commanded
the standard to be brought there, telling his men to follow on
valiantly and stand close. 'Let us move close to the wood,' he
said, 'and let it defend our backs so that they cannot get at us
from all sides.' They did so, skirting the wood. Then there was a
hard battle. Egil attacked Adils and they had a fierce encounter.
The difference in numbers was very great, but yet there fell
more from Adils' company. Thorolf then became so berserk
that he swung his shield round to his back, and took his spear in
both hands. He ran forward, striking or thrusting on both sides.
Men sprang away in all directions, but he killed many. In this
way he cleared a path up to Earl Hring's standard and nothing
stood in his way. He killed the man who carried Earl Hring's
standard and struck down the standard pole. Then he thrust his
spear at the earl's breast through coat of mail and body so that
it came out through the shoulders, and he raised him up on the
spear above his head, then stuck the spear shaft in the ground.

The earl breathed his last there on the spear, and everyone saw it, both his men and his enemies. Then Thorolf drew his sword, striking out on both sides, and his men also joined the attack. Many Welshmen and Scots fell there, and some ran away. When Earl Adils saw the death of his brother and the great slaughter of his troops, some fleeing, while he seemed himself to be hard-pressed, then he turned in flight and ran for the wood. He escaped into the wood and his men with him. Then all the troops who had accompanied them took to flight. There was heavy slaughter of escaping men who by now were scattered widely across the moor. Earl Adils had struck his standard and no-one knew whether he was there or someone else. Night soon began to grow dark and Thorolf and Egil turned back to their tents, and at the same time King Æthelstan came up with the whole army, and they pitched their tents and got them ready. A little later King Olaf came with his army. They pitched their tents and got them ready where their men had put tents before. King Olaf was told that both his earls Hring and Adils had fallen, and great numbers of the rest of his men.

54

King Æthelstan had spent the night before in that fort previously mentioned where he learned that there had been fighting on the moor. Then he got himself and his whole army ready, and came north to the moor where he learned exact news of how the battle had gone. Then the brothers Thorolf and Egil came to meet the king. He thanked them warmly for their exploits and the victory they had won, promising them his full friendship. They remained there all together that night. King Æthelstan woke up his army early in the morning. He had a talk with his leaders and gave instructions how his troops were to be drawn up. He organized his company first and set those troops which he knew to be bravest in the forefront of that company. Then he said that Egil was to be in charge of this division. 'But Thorolf,' he said, 'shall be with his company and those other troops that I put with them. That shall be the second division of our army led by him, because the Scots are always haphazard in their formation, running here and there and appearing in different places. They can often cause damage if people are not watching for them, but they are unstable on the field if attacked in return.' Egil answered the king. 'I do not

wish that Thorolf and myself should be separated in the battle,
though I am glad to be put where the need is greatest and the
fighting hardest.' Thorolf said, 'Shall we let the king decide
where he wants to put us? Let us do as he wishes. If you prefer I
will willingly take the place that has been allotted to you.' Egil
said, 'The decision is yours now, but future regret for these
arrangements will be mine.' Then the men went to their companies as the king had arranged and standards were set up. The
king's company stood on the level ground by the river, and
Thorolf's company went higher by the wood. King Olaf began
to arrange his army when he saw that King Æthelstan was organized. He also formed two companies, and he let his standard
and the company he commanded himself proceed against King
Æthelstan and his company. Both of them had so great an
army that there was no difference of numbers, and the second
company of King Olaf's went by the wood against the troops
which Thorolf commanded. The leaders were Scottish earls.
They were mostly Scots, and in very great numbers. Then
these companies came together and there was soon a fierce
battle. Thorolf attacked vigorously and had his standard carried
forward along the wood, intending to advance so that he reached
the exposed flank of the king's division. They had their shields in
front of them and the forest was on their right where they let it
serve as their protection. Thorolf advanced so that few of his
men were in front of him, when, at the time when he was least
expecting it, Earl Adils and his men with him leapt out of the
wood. They drove at once at Thorolf with many spears, and he
fell there by the forest, and Thorfid who carried the standard,
ran back to where the troops were denser, but Adils attacked
them and there was fierce fighting. The Scots had yelled their
victory cry when they brought down the leader. When Egil heard
that shout and saw that Thorolf's standard was retreating, he
thought it certain that Thorolf would not be with it. Then he ran
up between the companies, and as soon as he found his own
men, was quickly told what had happened. He urged on the
troops in attack, himself at their head, and he had the sword
Adder in his hand. He advanced striking out on both sides,
killing many men. At once Thorfid carried the standard after
him and the rest of the troops followed the standard. Here the
fighting was keenest. Egil pressed on until he met with Earl
Adils. They exchanged only a few blows before Earl Adils fell
and many men round him, but after his fall the people who had

been with him fled, while Egil and his men followed them and
killed all that they could. There was no point in anyone's asking
for peace. The Scottish earls stayed there no longer once they
saw their companions running away. They were off in a hurry.
Egil and his men headed for the king's company, reached their
exposed flank, and inflicted heavy losses. Then the company
wavered and dispersed. Many of Olaf's men fled and the vikings
shouted their victory cry. When King Æthelstan realized that
King Olaf's company was beginning to break up, he urged on his
troops and advanced his standard. Then they attacked fiercely
so that Olaf's troops fell back, and they inflicted heavy slaughter.
King Olaf fell there, and the greater part of Olaf's troops, because all those who tried to escape were killed if caught. King
Æthelstan won a very great victory there.

55

King Æthelstan turned away from the battle, but his men
pursued the stragglers. He rode back to the fort, and did not
stop for night lodging until he reached the fort, but Egil went
after those in flight, pursuing them for a long time, and killing
every man he caught. Then he turned back with his company and
went to where the battle had been, and found Thorolf his brother
there, dead. He took up his body and washed it and prepared it
according to the custom. They dug a grave there and put Thorolf
in it with all his clothes and weapons. Afterwards Egil clasped
a gold ring on each of his arms before he left him. Then they
piled up stones and covered them with soil. Egil spoke this verse:

> Flame-hearted Thorolf, fear's
> foe, Earl-killer, who so
> dared danger in Odin's
> dark wars is dead at last.
> Here, by Vina's bank, my
> brother lies under earth. This
> now's become death-bitter.
> But grief's best laid to rest.[1]

And again he said:

> I filled the English field
> full of corpses. We fought

> savagely and sure, our
> standard tall at my back.
> I attacked Adils with blue
> Adder, young Olaf stormed
> our troops, and Hring fought, too.
> To-day the ravens gorge.[2]

Then Egil went with his men to meet King Æthelstan, and
immediately came to the king where he sat at drinking. It was
all very merry and noisy. When the king saw that Egil had come
in he said that the lower benches[3] should be cleared for them,
and Egil should sit there in the seat of honour opposite the
king. Egil sat down pushing his shield down to his feet. He had
a helmet on his head and put his sword across his knees, and
every now and then half drew it, then thrust it back in the sheath.
He sat upright, head bent down. Egil's features were strongly
marked; a broad forehead, heavy brows, a nose not long but
very wide, lips broad and full, the chin unusually broad and the
whole jawline, a thick neck and shoulders broader than most
men have, harsh-looking and fierce when he was angry. He was
of good size, taller than anyone else, with thick wolfgrey hair,
and he soon became bald. While he sat, as was said above, he
drooped one eyebrow down towards his cheek, raising the other
up to the roots of his hair. Egil had black eyes and dark brows.
He refused to drink though it was served to him, and he moved
his eyebrows alternately up or down. King Æthelstan sat in the
high seat. He too had his sword across his knees, and when they
had sat like this for a time, the king drew his sword from its
sheath, took a gold ring from his arm, a big and good one, put
it on the sword point, stood up, walked across the floor and
reached over the fire to Egil. Egil stood up, drew his sword, and
went on to the floor. He thrust his sword into the circle of the
ring, drew it to him, and went back to his place. The king sat
down in the high seat. When Egil sat down he drew the ring on
to his arm, and then his brows levelled out. He put down sword
and helmet, took up the horn which was brought to him, and
drank it off. Then he said:

> It was the warrior's
> work, to hang this gold band
> round an arm where hawks ride
> ready to do my will.

> And see how I make my sword
> summon the ring to *its*
> arm. There's skill in this. But
> the prince claims greater praise.[4]

After that Egil drank his share and talked with others. Then the king had two chests carried in. Two men carried each, and both were full of silver. The king said, 'You shall have these chests, Egil, and if you return to Iceland you shall take this money to your father. I send it to him as payment for his son. But some of the money you are to distribute among the kin of yourself and Thorolf, those who seem to you of most worth. And you shall take payment for a brother here with me, land or money, what you prefer, and if you are willing to remain with me permanently, I will set you up with such honour and estate as you yourself shall name to me.' Egil accepted the money, and thanked the king for his gifts and words of friendship. From then on Egil began to be cheerful, and he said:

> My great grief had scored deep
> grooves in my brow. But now
> I look up and lose those
> lines that trenched my forehead.
> Murky clouds had dulled my
> mind, but now they've quite gone.
> With your generous gift of
> gold you've lifted my gloom.[5]

Then those men were cared for who were wounded but would live. Egil remained with King Æthelstan the winter after Thorolf's death and he received very great honour from the king. With him were all the men who had previously accompanied both brothers and had survived the battle. Egil composed a long poem in praise of King Æthelstan and this comes in that poem:

> This king's son is supreme.
> Stern in war he towers
> over high lands where he
> has humbled some three princes.
> There's more to tell. Thanks be
> this liberal king is ours
> to praise. And his suave strength
> stirs up our fiercest love.

This is the refrain in the poem:

> The highest reindeer road
> runs under this king's rule.[6]

Then Æthelstan gave further to Egil as a reward for his poetry two gold rings each weighing a mark, and together with them a fine cloak which the king himself had worn. When it was spring Egil explained to the king that he intended to leave in the summer and go to Norway to find out what had happened in the matter of Asgerd, 'the woman whom my brother Thorolf married. There is a lot of money involved, but I do not know whether any of their children are alive. I have to take care of them if they are, but I have the whole inheritance if Thorolf has died childless.' The king said, 'It is for you to decide to go away from here if you think your affairs are urgent, but to me it would seem best for you to establish yourself here with me on whatever terms you wish to ask for.' Egil thanked the king for his words. 'I will go first where I must. But it is very likely that I shall come to you for these promises when I can.' The king told him to do so. Then Egil got ready to go away with his men, but many remained behind with the king. Egil had a great longship, a hundred men or so on board. When he was ready for his journey and the wind was right he put out to sea. He and King Æthelstan parted on the friendliest terms. He told Egil to come back as quickly as possible. Egil said it should be so. Then Egil held course for Norway, and when he came to land he went with all the speed he could into Fjordane. He learned the news that the chieftain Thorir was dead, and Arinbjorn had taken the inheritance and been made a nobleman. Egil went to see Arinbjorn and got a good welcome there. Arinbjorn invited him to stay. Egil accepted. He had the ship brought ashore and the men lodged. Arinbjorn housed Egil with eleven others, and he stayed with him for the winter.

56

Berg-Onund, the son of Thorgeir Thornfoot, had by now married Gunnhild the daughter of Bjorn the Freeholder. She had gone with him to his farm on Askoy, but Asgerd whom Thorolf Skalla-Grimsson had married was with her cousin Arinbjorn. She and Thorolf had one small daughter who was called Thordis and the girl was with her mother. Egil told Asgerd about the loss of Thorolf and offered her his protection. Asgerd was very unhappy at the news, answered Egil's talk courteously and said little more. As the autumn passed Egil became very depressed, often sitting with his head drooping into his cloak. On one occasion Arinbjorn went to him and asked what caused his misery. 'Though you have had such a great loss in your brother, yet a man should bear such things bravely. Men must live on. What are you reciting now? Let me hear it.' Egil said that he had just made up this verse:

> This girl with ash-smooth arms
> already's getting used
> to my bad ways. But I
> bore myself well in youth.
> Now I'm like a nervous
> ninny, sick, out-of-sorts—
> hiding my head when she
> hurries into my thoughts.[1]

Arinbjorn asked who the woman might be that he was making love songs about. 'You have hidden her name in this verse.' Then Egil said:

> To put it plainly, my
> poems rarely conceal
> the woman's name whose love
> kept warm a brother's bed.
> Her sadness will subside
> soon as she'll gird herself
> for love! Secret songs? Well,
> some will glean my meaning.[2]

'Here,' said Egil, 'is the proof of the proverb that one tells all to a friend. I will answer your question about the woman I'm composing poems on. She is your cousin Asgerd, and I should like to have your support so that I can bring about this marriage.' Arinbjorn said that it seemed to him a splendid idea. 'I shall certainly add my voice to bring about the match.' Then Egil took this proposal to Asgerd, but she referred it to the advice of her father and her cousin Arinbjorn. Arinbjorn spoke to Asgerd and she had the same answer for him. Arinbjorn urged the match. Then Arinbjorn and Egil went to see Bjorn, and Egil put

forward his proposal of marriage, asking for Asgerd, Bjorn's
daughter. Bjorn accepted the matter favourably, and said that
Arinbjorn should have the greater say. Arinbjorn urged it
eagerly, and the matter ended with Egil's betrothal to Asgerd,
the wedding to be at Arinbjorn's home. When the time came
there was a grand feast for Egil's marriage. He was then very
cheerful for what was left of the winter.

In the spring Egil got a merchant ship ready for a journey to
Iceland. Arinbjorn advised him not to settle in Norway while
Gunnhild's power was so great, 'for she is very hostile towards
you,' said Arinbjorn, 'and things took a real turn for the worse
when you and Eyvind met off Jutland.' When Egil was ready
and the wind favourable he put out to sea and made good
speed on the journey. He came to Iceland in the autumn and
made for Borgarfjord. By that time he had been abroad twelve
years. Skalla-Grim was becoming an old man now. He was
glad when Egil came home. Egil went to stay at Borg, Thorfid
the Strong with him, and there were very many of them together. They were with Skalla-Grim for the winter. Egil had
uncounted wealth, but it is not recorded that he divided the
silver which King Æthelstan had given him, either with Skalla-
Grim or with anyone else. That winter Thorfid married Sæun
the daughter of Skalla-Grim, and afterwards in the spring
Skalla-Grim gave them a farm at Langarfors, and the land in
from Leiruloek between the Langa and Alpta rivers up to the
hills. The daughter of Thorfid and Sæun was Thordis who
married Arngeir from Holm the son of Bersi the Godless.
Their son was Bjorn Hitdoelakappi, the champion of the Hit-
doela men. Egil stayed with Skalla-Grim for some years. He
took charge of the estate and management no less than Skalla-
Grim. Egil became even more bald. At that time the district
began to be widely settled. Hromund the brother of Grim the
Halogalander and his shipmates lived at Thverarhlid. Hromund
was the father of Gunnlaug, the father of Thurid Dylla, the
mother of Illugi the Black.

By now Egil had been at Borg through the passing of many
winters. Then one summer when ships were travelling from
Norway to Iceland news was brought west that Bjorn the Freeholder was dead. It was told along with this report that all the
property which Bjorn had owned had been taken over by Berg-
Onund his son-in-law. He had taken away to his home all the
movable property, put people on the estates, and reserved all

the rents for himself. He had also taken into possession all the estates which Bjorn had owned. When Egil heard this he asked carefully whether Berg-Onund would have done all this on his own account, or was he relying on the support of someone greater. He was told that Onund had formed a close friendship with King Eirik and an even closer one with Gunnhild. Egil let the matter rest for that autumn, but when the winter had passed and spring arrived, then Egil had a ship that he owned brought out. It had been standing in a boat-shed at Langarfors. He got that ship ready for sea-going, and found men for it. Asgerd his wife decided to go, but Thordis, Thorolf's daughter, stayed. Egil put to sea when he was ready. There is nothing to tell of his journey before he reached Norway. He went at once to see Arinbjorn at the first opportunity. Arinbjorn welcomed him, and invited Egil to stay with him, and he accepted. He and Asgerd both went there, and some of the men with them. Egil soon raised a discussion with Arinbjorn about Egil's idea that he had a claim to property in that country. Arinbjorn said, 'The matter looks unpromising to me. Berg-Onund is hard and overbearing, unjust and avaricious, and he now has full support from the king and queen. Gunnhild is the greatest of your enemies as you already know, and she will not be urging Onund to put matters right.' Egil said, 'The king will let us have law and justice in this matter, and, with your help, to try for legal redress against Berg-Onund won't assume great proportions in my eyes.' They formed this plan, that Egil should man a pinnace. There were nearly twenty on board. They went south to Hordaland and reached Askoy then went up to the house and met Onund. Egil put forward his case and asked Onund for a share of Bjorn's inheritance, saying that the daughters of Bjorn were entitled to equal shares of his inheritance, 'though it would seem to me,' said Egil, 'that Asgerd appears of far higher birth than your wife Gunnhild.' Then Onund answered very swiftly. 'What a very bold man you are, Egil! Outlawed by King Eirik, you come here into his land and try to pick quarrels with his men. You can remember this, Egil, that I've brought down men like you, and for smaller matters than this seems, with you claiming inheritance on your wife's behalf, when everyone knows she is slave-born on her mother's side.' Onund ranted on for a time. When Egil saw that Onund was not willing to do anything in this matter, Egil summoned him to the Assembly and put the case under the laws of the Gula Assembly.[3]

Onund said, 'I will come to the Gula Assembly, and my hope
is that you will not leave it alive.' Egil said that he would risk
coming to the Assembly even so. 'The case will end as it will
end.' Then Egil and his men went away, and when he came home
he told Arinbjorn about his journey and Onund's answer.
Arinbjorn was very angry that Thora, his father's sister, had
been called 'slave'. Arinbjorn went to see King Eirik and put
the case to him. The king took his words rather coldly and said
that Arinbjorn had staunchly upheld Egil's concerns for a long
time. 'He has made use of you in that I have let him stay here in
the land, but I shall think you are pushing matters if you support
him when he picks quarrels with my friends.' Arinbjorn said,
'You will allow us law in the matter.' The king was rather wary
of the case. Arinbjorn found that the queen would be far less
amiable. He went back and said that things did not look too
hopeful. The winter passed and the time came for men to go to
the Gula Assembly. Arinbjorn went to the Assembly with a
very large following. Egil made the journey with him. King
Eirik was there and he had a large following. Berg-Onund and
his brothers were in the king's company and they had a good
body of men. When the Assembly progressed to lawsuits both
sides went to where the court was set up to put forward their
evidence. Onund was full of words. The place where the court
sat was a level plain and hazel poles were set in a circle on the
plain linked by ropes. These were called the sanctuary ropes.
Inside the circle sat the judges, twelve from Fjordane district,
twelve from Sogn district, twelve from Hordaland. These three
twelves should judge the lawsuits. It was in Arinbjorn's control
who the judges were from Fjordane, in Thord's of Aurland who
they were from Sogn. These were all one group. Arinbjorn had
brought great numbers of men to the Assembly. He had a fully-
manned warship, and many small ships, pinnaces and rowing-
boats, captained by the farmers. King Eirik also had a large
company there, six or seven longships. There were also great
numbers of farmers there. Egil put forward his case asking the
judges to decide the law in the matter between himself and
Onund. He related his evidence for claiming the money which
Bjorn Brynjolfsson had owned. He said that Asgerd, Bjorn's
daughter and Egil's legal wife, had a right to the inheritance, and
she was free-born and noble-born in all branches of her family,
and had royal blood in her ancestry. He asked the judges to
award Asgerd half the inheritance of Bjorn in land and money.

But when he stopped speaking Berg-Onund took over. 'My wife, Gunnhild,' he said, 'is the daughter of Bjorn and of Alof, that wife whom Bjorn legally married. Gunnhild is Bjorn's lawful heiress. The reason I took over all the property which Bjorn had owned is that I knew Bjorn's only other daughter was one who had no inheritance due. Her mother was captured on a raid and afterwards taken as a mistress, not with her family's consent, and transported from land to land. You, Egil, think you can behave here as you have in every other place, that is with arrogance and injustice. That will not serve you here, for King Eirik and Queen Gunnhild have promised me that I shall have justice in every case where their authority prevails. I will bring forward valid witnesses before the king and judges that Thora Lace-Sleeve, the mother of Asgerd, was taken in a raid from her home, from her brother Thorir, and a second time from Brynjolf's at Aurland. She left the land with vikings, outlawed by the king, and as outlaws she and Bjorn produced this daughter Asgerd. Now it is a peculiarity of Egil's that he thinks to invalidate all the words of King Eirik. In the first place you, Egil, have come here to the country after King Eirik made you an outlaw, and secondly, though you have married a slave, yet you claim her right to inherit. I wish to ask this of the judges, that they award to me the whole of Bjorn's inheritance, and they sentence Asgerd as the king's slave because she was conceived when her parents were outlawed by the king.' Then Arinbjorn began to speak. 'King Eirik, we will bring forward witnesses and swear oaths to go with them that it was made clear in the reconciliation between Thorir my father and Bjorn the Free-holder, that Asgerd, the daughter of Bjorn and Thora, was to inherit from her father Bjorn. Moreover, Sir, as is known to you, you cancelled Bjorn's outlawry, and the whole case was then ended which had previously prevented the men's reconciliation.' The king was not quick to answer this speech. Then Egil said:

> This crackling son of Thorn's
> thinks it a sharpish point
> to say my wife's slave-born.
> Sir, greed feeds all your words.
> I swear her claim is sound.
> So she's quite entitled
> to what's hers. Sir, you hear
> how true all I vow rings.[4]

Arinbjorn then had twelve men to give witness, and all carefully
chosen for this. They had all heard the reconciliation between
Thorir and Bjorn and they offered to take oath accordingly
before the king and judges. The judges were willing to take
their oaths if the king did not forbid it. The king said that he
would take no action in the matter, neither to praise nor blame.
Then Queen Gunnhild began to speak. She said, 'It is incredible,
Sir, the way you let this big man Egil entangle every matter
for you. Perhaps you would not speak against him if he claimed
the kingdom at your hand. But though you do not wish to make a
decision when it might help Onund, I shall not put up with Egil
treading my friends under his feet and wrongfully taking Onund's
property from him. Alf Shipman, where are you? Take your
men where the judges are, and do not let this injustice be carried
through.' Then Alf the Shipman and his men ran to the court,
cut apart the sanctuary ropes and broke down the poles, driving
away the judges. Then there was a real uproar in the Assembly,
but all the men there were without their weapons. Then Egil
said, 'Can Berg-Onund hear my words?' 'I hear,' he said.
'Then I will challenge you to a duel and we will fight it out here
at the Assembly. Let him who wins have the property, both
land and money. If you dare not, be called coward by everyone.'
Then King Eirik answered, 'If you are eager to fight, Egil, then
we can let you have that.' Egil answered, 'I will not fight against
you nor against overwhelming odds, but I'll not run away from
equal strength of men if this be allowed me. And in that case
I'll make no distinction between opponents.' Then Arinbjorn
said, 'Let us go away. We can't do anything for the moment
that will serve us.' He turned away and all his men with him.
Then Egil turned back and said, 'I call you to witness, Arinbjorn, and you, Thord, and all those men who can now hear my
words, noblemen, lawmen, and everyone, that I lay a curse on
all the estates which Bjorn has owned for living or for working. I
lay a curse on you, Berg-Onund, and on all other men, native or
foreign, noble or commoner, on every man who is involved in
this. I name you breakers of the law of land-rights, breakers of
the peace, incurrers of the gods' anger.' Then Egil went away
with Arinbjorn. They went to their ships over a hill which prevented the ships being seen from the Assembly. When Arinbjorn reached his ship he said, 'Everyone knows how the Assembly has ended, and we have not had a legal settlement, and
the king is so furious that I expect our men will get harsh terms

from him if he can bring it about. Now I want everyone to go to their ships and go home.' Then he said to Egil, 'You and your crew get to your ship and away, and be wary for the king will search for you and try to bring about a confrontation. Come and find me, however things go between you and the king.' Egil did as he said. Thirty men went on board the pinnace and they journeyed as hard as they could. The boat was exceptionally swift. Then there left the harbour numbers of other boats owned by Arinbjorn, pinnaces and rowing-boats. Arinbjorn's longship left last for it was the heaviest under oars. Egil's pinnace got away quickly. Then Egil said this verse:

> This heir of Thornfoot has
> thwarted my golden hopes
> of inheritance. The oaf's
> oaths are all I collect.
> He taunts, threatens, when I
> try to repay his vile
> theft of my land. No love's
> lost between us two men.[5]

King Eirik heard Egil's closing words, those which he spoke last at the Assembly, and he was very angry. But everyone had gone to the Assembly without weapons, and for this reason the king made no attack. He told all his men to go to their ships and they did as he said. Then the king called an assembly of his following and told them his intentions: 'Now we will take down our ships' awnings. I wish to go and find Arinbjorn and Egil. I wish also to make clear to you that I want Egil killed if we have an opportunity, and none of those spared who try to prevent it.' After that they went out to their ships and got them ready as quickly as possible, thrust them out and rowed to where Arinbjorn's ships had been. Then the king made them row north through the straits. When they reached Sognefjord they saw Arinbjorn's men. The longship turned into Saudungssund and the king went that way. There he came upon Arinbjorn's ship, and the king drew up to it at once, and they exchanged words. The king asked if Egil was there on the ship. Arinbjorn answered, 'He is not on my ship. Besides, Sir, you can readily see that. There are only those on board whom you can recognize, and Egil will not be hiding himself below deck if a meeting between you should take place.' The king asked what was the last Arinbjorn knew of him, and he said that Egil and twenty-nine men were in a pinnace, 'and they made their way out to Steinssund.' The king and his men had seen that many ships had been rowing for Steinssund. He said that they would row into the inner strait and so make for a meeting with Egil and his company. There was a man called Ketil, one of King Eirik's retainers. He directed the course of the king's ship though Eirik himself captained it.[6] Ketil was a big man in size and handsome in appearance, and a close kinsman of the king's, and people said that he and the king were alike in looks. Egil had had his ship launched, and the cargo carried on board before he went to the Assembly, and now Egil went to where the merchant-ship was and they went aboard, while the pinnace floated, steering-oar shipped, between the land and the ship, with the oars in their loops. In the morning when it was scarcely light, those who kept watch became aware that great ships were rowing towards them. When Egil knew that, he stood up at once and saw quickly that hostilities were on their way. There were six longships and all making for them. Egil said that they should all get into the pinnace. Egil picked up the two chests which King Æthelstan gave him—he always had those with him. They jumped into the pinnace. He and all of them armed themselves rapidly and they rowed forward between the land and that warship which was passing nearest the land, which was King Eirik's ship. Because things were happening suddenly and there was not much light the ships passed by one another, and when the raised decks were parallel Egil hurled a spear which hit the man who was sitting at the steering full on, and that was Ketil Hod. King Eirik called out telling the men to row after Egil, but when the ships ran alongside the merchant-ship the king's men jumped up on board, and those of Egil's men who had stayed behind and not taken to the pinnace were all killed if they were caught, but some got ashore. Ten men of Egil's company were killed there. Some ships rowed after Egil and his men and some robbed the merchant-ship. All the property was taken that was on board, and they burned the ship. Those who rowed after Egil pursued him vigorously, two men to an oar. There was no lack of people on board, but Egil's crew were short-handed. There were eighteen in the pinnace. The gap between them was closing. But in by the island there was a shallow channel, no more than wading-depth, between it and the next island. The sea was at ebb. Egil and his men took the pinnace in through that shallow strait, but the warships could not clear it, and there they separated. The king turned back south, and Egil went north to find Arinbjorn. Then Egil spoke this verse:

> The brave and bold Eirik's
> brought down ten of my men.
> Ten! Yet truth to tell I'm
> too much to blame myself.
> No need to send my spear
> skewering straight at that
> rib-cage of Ketil's. It
> crashed through, breaking his heart.[7]

Egil went to find Arinbjorn and told him this news. Arinbjorn said that it was no better than he expected of the dealings between him and King Eirik, 'but you will not lack money, Egil. I shall pay you for the ship, and get you another in which you can have a good voyage to Iceland'. Asgerd, Egil's wife, had been at Arinbjorn's while they went to the Assembly. Arinbjorn found for Egil a ship that was fully seaworthy, and provided it with a cargo of wood. Egil prepared the ship for sea, and still had nearly thirty men. He and Arinbjorn parted in friendship. Then Egil said:

> Oh! for Odin to force
> from the land this damned king,
> repay him for his foul
> fleecing me of my wealth.
> Frey and Njord, he's the folk's
> foe. Then rid us of him!
> Thor, you guard our land, then
> thrust out this destroyer.[8]

57

Harald Finehair established his sons in power in Norway, and as he grew old he made Eirik king over all his sons. When Harald had been king for seventy years he gave his kingdom to his son Eirik. At that time Gunnhild gave birth to a son, and King Harald splashed water on him and gave him his name and the assurance that he should be king after his father if he lived. King Harald then lived in retirement, staying most often in

Rogaland or Hordaland. Three years later King Harald died in
Rogaland and a mound was raised for him at Haugesund. After
his death his sons quarrelled a great deal for the Vik men took
Olaf as their king and the men of Trondelag took Sigurd. But
Eirik killed both his brothers at Tonsberg one year after the
death of King Harald. It all happened during the same summer
that King Eirik went with his army from Hordaland east into
Vik to fight with his brothers, and earlier on Egil and Berg-
Onund quarrelled at the Gula Assembly and the other things
happened which have been told. Berg-Onund was at home on
his farm when the king was levying his men for he thought it
risky to leave his farm before Egil had left the country, and his
brother Hadd was with him. There was a man called Frodi,
King Eirik's kinsman and foster-son. He was a most handsome
man, young in years though full-grown. King Eirik left him
behind to support Berg-Onund. Frodi was at Arstad on the king's
estate and had a body of men with him. King Eirik and Queen
Gunnhild had a son called Rognvald. At that time he was ten
or eleven years old and promised to be a fine man. He was with
Frodi when this was going on. Before King Eirik rowed away on
his campaign he made Egil outlaw throughout Norway and any
man might kill him. Arinbjorn was with the king on his campaign but before he left home Egil put to sea in his ship, and
made for that outlying place known as Vitar out beyond Alden.
It is well away from the usual shipping lanes. Fishermen were
there and it was a good place to hear news. There he learned
that the king had made him an outlaw. Egil spoke this verse:

> It's a long road that law-
> less king has set me on,
> Thor! Eirik's been badly
> bamboozled by his wife.
> She's ruthless. But I shall
> shelve my plans for revenge
> till the time's ripe. No rash
> rush now of hot youth's blood.[1]

The winds were light, from the hills at night, and a sea-breeze in
the daytime. One evening Egil and his men sailed out to sea and
the fishermen who had been put there to get news of Egil's
journey rowed ashore. They were able to say that Egil had put
out and sailed to sea and was away. They had this news con-

veyed to Berg-Onund. And when he got this report he sent from him all the men whom he had previously kept there on guard. Then he rowed into Arstad and invited Frodi to his home, for Berg-Onund had a great deal of beer there. Frodi went with him and took some men along. They were given an excellent feast and had a very good time. By then they had completely lost their fear. Rognvald, the king's son, had a cutter rowed by six men a side. It was painted all above the water-line. He had with him ten or twelve men, those who were always at his side. When Frodi had left home Rognvald took the cutter and the twelve of them rowed out to Herdla. There was a big farm of the king's there and in charge of it was the man known as Bearded Thorir. Rognvald had been fostered there in his childhood. Thorir welcomed the king's son warmly. There too any amount of drink was provided. Egil sailed out to sea by night as was told earlier, and when dawn came the wind fell and it became calm. They set the ship to drift and let it drift for several nights. But when a sea-breeze came up Egil said to his seamen, 'We will sail ashore now, for if the sea-winds blow strongly against us we could land anywhere, and the prospect looks hostile in most places.' The oarsmen told Egil to decide their course. Then they used the sail and sailed into Herdluver. They found a good harbour there, covered over the ship, and put up there for the night. They had a little boat on the ship and Egil got into it with two men. During the night he rowed in to Herdla and sent a man up on the island to learn the news. When he came back to the ship he said that Rognvald the king's son and his men were there at the farm. 'They were sitting over the drinking. I met one of the household and he was drunk, and he said that just as much would be drunk here as at Berg-Onund's even though Frodi and four of his men were at that feast.' He said that except for Frodi's party there was no-one else there apart from the men of the household. Then Egil rowed back to the ship and told the men to stand up and get their weapons. They did so. They put the ship out at anchor. Egil put twelve men to look after the ship and he took seventeen men with him in a pinnace which they rowed in along the strait. They went noiselessly until they came to Askoy in the evening and they put into a hidden creek there. Then Egil said, 'Now I will go up on the island alone and see what I can get to know, and you are to wait for me here.' Egil had weapons, those which he usually had, helmet and shield, a sword by his side and a spear in his hand. He went up on the island and on

into a wood. He had pulled his hood over his helmet. He came
to where some boys were, great herd-dogs with them, and when
they fell into talk he asked where they were from and why they
were there with such big dogs. They said, 'You must be stupid.
Haven't you heard that there is a bear here on the island doing
enormous damage, killing men and cattle, and there is a price
set on its head. Every night at Ask we keep watch over our cattle
fastened up in pens. And why are you going about with your
weapons in the night?' He said, 'I am afraid of the bear, and
scarcely anyone seems to travel nowadays without weapons.
The bear has chased me for a long time tonight, don't you see
him now, there he is now at the tip of the wood. Are all the men
at the farm asleep?' The boy answered that Berg-Onund and
Frodi would still be drinking. 'They sit up every night.' 'Tell
them, then,' said Egil, 'where the bear is. I must get home.'
He went away then, and the boy ran up to the farm, and the
living-room in which the drinking took place. As it happened
everyone had gone to sleep except the three, Onund, Frodi and
Hadd. The boy said where the bear was. They took their weapons
which were hanging beside them and ran out at once up to the
wood. There were tongues of woodland projecting from the
forest, and here and there were clumps of bushes. The boy told
them where the bear had been in the bushes. When they saw
that the branches were moving they were convinced that the
bear would be there. Then Berg-Onund said that Hadd and
Frodi should run between it and the main wood, and take care
that the bear did not get away into the forest. Berg-Onund ran
forward into the bushes. He had helmet and shield, a sword by
his side, and a spear in his hand. Egil, not a bear, was there in
the bushes in front of him, and when he saw where Berg-Onund
was he drew his sword. There was a loop round the hilt which he
drew over his right wrist letting the sword hang there. He took
his spear in his hand and ran forward to meet Berg-Onund, and
when Berg-Onund saw that he quickened his pace, and brought
his shield in front of him. Each threw his spear at the other before
they met. Egil thrust the spear off with his shield which he held
slanting, so that it cut past the shield and flew into the earth, but
Egil's spear hit the middle of the shield and the whole length of
the blade went through it, so that the spear was fast in the
shield. This made Onund's shield difficult to carry. Egil quickly
gripped the hilt of his sword. Onund also began to draw his
sword, but while it was not yet half-drawn, Egil thrust into him

with his sword. Onund staggered at the thrust, and Egil pulled
the sword back fiercely and struck at Onund nearly cutting his
head off. Then Egil removed his spear from the shield. Hadd and
Frodi saw the fall of Berg-Onund and they ran up. Egil turned to
meet them. He threw the spear at Frodi through his shield and
his breast so that the point was seen at his back. He fell back
dead at once. Egil then took his sword and turned to meet Hadd
and they exchanged only a few blows before Hadd fell. Then the
boys came up and Egil said to them, 'Look after Onund, your
lord, and his companions here, so that birds and animals don't
tear the bodies.' Then Egil went on his way, and it was not long
before eleven of his companions came to meet him, six having
been left with the boat. They asked what he had done. He said
this:

> We're weak, to have put up
> with this man's unjust ways.
> Time was I took good care
> to guard my hard-earned wealth.
> But I've let Berg-Onund
> become cold in the ground,
> then Hadd, then Frodi. I, who'd
> thickened the earth with blood.[2]

Then Egil said, 'Now we will go back to the farm and behave
like warriors, kill all the men that we take, and seize all the
wealth which we can remove.' They went to the farm and ran
into the house, and killed fifteen or sixteen men there. Some
escaped by running away. They plundered all the wealth, and
destroyed what they could not take away. They drove the cattle
down to the shore, killed them, and put in the boat as much as
it would hold. Then they went on their way and rowed out
through the island channels. Egil was now fighting mad so that
no-one could speak to him. He sat at the tiller on the boat, and
as they rowed out along the fjord to Herdla, Rognvald, the king's
son, rowed to meet them, thirteen all together in the painted
cutter. They had found out that Egil's ship lay at Herdluver and
intended to bring Onund news of Egil's movements. When Egil
saw the boat he knew it at once. He steered straight for it and
when the boats ran together the prow of the pinnace struck the
cutter amidships. The cutter keeled over so that the sea came in
over the side and filled the ship. Egil leaped aboard gripping

his spear calling on his men not to let anyone on the cutter get away alive. That was easy for there was no defence. All who were in the water were killed and no-one got away. Thirteen died there, Rognvald and his companions. Egil and his men rowed to the island of Herdla. Egil spoke this verse:

> We fought well. I don't care
> whether there'll be revenge
> for those we felled. My sword
> flamed and smoked in my hand!
> I bathed it in the bright
> blood-stream of Gunnhild's son.
> Thirteen dead on that boat?
> Then there's a day's fair work.[3]

When Egil and his men arrived on Herdla they at once ran up to the farm with all their weapons. When Thorir and his household saw that, they at once ran from the farm and saved themselves, all who could, both men and women. Egil and his men seized all the money they could lay hands on. Then they went out to their ship. They did not have to wait long before a wind blew off the land. Then they got ready to sail, and when they were on the point of sailing, Egil went up on the island. He took in his hand a hazel pole and climbed on to a rock that jutted out in the direction of the land. Then he took a horse's head and thrust it on the pole. Then he uttered this curse saying, 'Here I erect a Mocking Pole. And I turn this mockery towards King Eirik and Queen Gunnhild'—he turned the horse's head in towards the land—'I turn this mockery against the spirits who guard this land so that they may all wander astray, none reaching nor finding his home until they drive King Eirik and Queen Gunnhild from the land.' Then he thrust the pole into a cleft in the rock and let it stand there. He turned the head towards the land, and he carved runes on the pole and spoke the full curse.[4] After that Egil went to his ship. They hoisted sail and sailed out to sea. Then the wind began to increase and the weather became keen and drove them on. The ship moved fast. Then Egil said:

> This slamming wind's the sail's
> sure enemy. It works,
> cuts and carves the waves which
> curve knife-like out at sea.

It's cold too! And its teeth
tear at the waves that rear
round the planks of our proud-
prowed ship, our uncowed swan.[5]

Then they sailed out in the open sea and they had a swift journey,
and came from the open sea into Borgarfjord. He directed his
ship into the harbour there and carried his goods ashore. Egil
then went home to Borg and his shipmates got themselves
lodgings. Skalla-Grim had now become old and weak with age.
Then Egil took over all the management of the property and
responsibility for the household.

58

There was a man called Thorgeir whose wife was Thordis, the
daughter of Yngvar and sister of Bera, Egil's mother. Thorgeir
lived at Lambastadir near Alptanes. He had come to Iceland
with Yngvar. He was wealthy and men thought well of him.
The son of Thorgeir and his wife was Thord and he was living
at Lambastadir after his father when Egil came back to Iceland.
In the autumn, before winter, Thord rode into Borg to see his
cousin Egil, and invited him back to a feast. He had been having
beer brewed out there. Egil promised to go and it was arranged
for about a week ahead. When the time came Egil got ready for
the journey and his wife Asgerd with him. There were ten or
twelve in the party. When Egil was ready Skalla-Grim went out
with him and turned to him before Egil mounted and said,
'You seem to me, Egil, to have been slow in paying over the
money that King Æthelstan sent me. What are you thinking of
doing with it?' Egil said, 'Are you very short of money now,
Father? I did not know that. I will let you have silver the moment I realize you need it, but I feel sure you still have a chest or
two filled with silver to keep an eye on.' 'It seems to me,' said
Skalla-Grim, 'that you think you've made a fair division of our
money. You won't mind what I do with the stuff I'm keeping
an eye on?' Egil said, 'You don't think you need ask my permission for that. You will want to have your own way no matter
what I say.' Then Egil rode away until he reached Lambastadir.
He was received there warmly and well and was to stay there
three nights. The same evening on which Egil left home, Skalla-
Grim had a horse saddled for himself. He rode away from home

while other men were asleep. When he went away he was carrying a very large chest on his knees and a bronze cauldron under his arm. Afterwards men held it as a fact that he had let one or both of them drop into Krumskelda swamp and had let a great flat stone fall on top. Skalla-Grim came home about the time of midnight and went to his bed and lay down in his clothes. In the morning when it was light and men were getting dressed Skalla-Grim was sitting on the edge of the bed and he was dead and so stiff that no-one could get him raised or straightened, though everything was tried. They found a horse and a man for it who galloped as hard as he could until he reached Lambastadir. He went immediately to find Egil and told him this news. Egil found his weapons and clothes and rode home to Borg in the evening, and as soon as he had dismounted he went in and into a passage which went behind the hall. There were doors off this passage to the back of the bed-closets.[1] Egil went forward into the bed-place and took Skalla-Grim by the shoulders and bent him backwards, laid him down on the bed and paid him the last rites. Then Egil told them to take their tools and break the wall to the south. When that was done Egil raised Skalla-Grim's head and others took his feet and they carried him across the house and out through the wall where it was broken.[2] They carried him immediately down to Naustanes. He was covered there for the night. In the morning at high tide Skalla-Grim was placed in a ship and they rowed with him out to Digranes. Egil had a mound made there on the end of the headland. Skalla-Grim was placed in it with his horse and his weapons and his smith's tools. There is no record that money was put into the mound with him. Egil then took over the inheritance, lands and wealth. He had control over the farm. Thordis the daughter of Thorolf and Asgerd was there in Egil's home.

59

King Eirik ruled over Norway for one year after the death of his father King Harald, before Hakon, Æthelstan's foster-son, another of King Harald's sons, came east to Norway from England the same summer that Egil Skalla-Grimsson went to Iceland. Hakon went north to Trondheim and was received there as king. He and Eirik were both kings in Norway for the winter. The next spring each collected an army. Hakon had by far the greater numbers. Eirik then saw no other choice than to flee the country. He went away with Gunnhild his wife and their children. The chieftain Arinbjorn was Eirik's foster-brother and the foster-father of his child. He was the dearest to the king of all his noblemen. The king had made him chieftain over all Fjordane. Arinbjorn left the country with the king. First they went west across the sea to the Orkneys where Eirik married Ragnhild his daughter to Earl Arnfid. Then he went south to Scotland with his troops and raided there. From there he went south to England and raided there. When King Æthelstan heard of this he gathered his people and marched against Eirik. When they met a treaty was established between them, the terms being that King Æthelstan put Eirik in control of Northumbria and he was to guard the land of King Æthelstan against the Scots and the Irish.[1] King Æthelstan had made Scotland pay tribute to him after the death of King Olaf but the people were always disloyal to him. King Eirik always kept his residence at York. It is said that Gunnhild worked spells[2] and spelled out this, that Egil Skalla-Grimsson should never know peace in Iceland until she had set eyes on him. That summer when Hakon and Eirik had come up against each other and quarrelled over Norway, there was a ban on travel anywhere from Norway and that summer no ships came to Iceland and no news out of Norway. Egil Skalla-Grimsson was at home. The winter after the death of Skalla-Grim while he was living at Borg Egil became moody, and his misery grew worse as the winter passed. When summer came Egil declared that he intended to get his ship ready for a voyage during the summer. He chose a crew and intended to sail for England. There were thirty men on the ship. Asgerd stayed behind and looked after the farm, and Egil intended to go and find King Æthelstan and see about the promises which he had made to Egil at their parting. Egil was not ready early, and when he put to sea he was slow to get a wind, and it drew into autumn with harsh weather. They sailed north of Orkney but Egil did not wish to land there since he thought that King Eirik's authority would hold right through the islands. Then they sailed south off Scotland and endured severe storm with the wind against them. They weathered the Scottish coast and the north of England. But towards the end of the day when it became dark the wind was at its height. They noticed nothing until there were breakers both on the seaward side and in front of them. There was no other choice than to make for the land. They did this. They sailed in to wreck the ship at the Humber mouth. All the men were saved and most of the cargo, but not the ship. It was broken to bits. When they found men to talk to they learned this news, which Egil thought threatening, that King Eirik Blood-Axe was there and Gunnhild, and they had control of the district, and he was not far away in the town of York. Egil also learned that the chieftain Arinbjorn was with the king, and on terms of the greatest friendship with him. When Egil had become convinced by this report he made his plans. He did not think there was any hope for an escape even if he tried it, hiding and disguising himself for so long a journey as it would be before he got out of Eirik's kingdom. He was easy to recognize, whoever spotted him. He thought it humiliating to be seized when escaping. So he made a firm resolve and came to a decision on the very night of his arrival. He got himself a horse and rode immediately to the town. He arrived there in the evening and rode straight into the town. He had a hood covering his helmet and was fully armed. Egil asked where in the town would be the place which Arinbjorn owned. He was told and he rode there at once. When he came to the house he dismounted and found a man to talk to. He was told that Arinbjorn was sitting over his food. Egil said, 'Listen, my friend, will you go into the house and ask Arinbjorn whether he prefers to talk to Egil Skalla-Grimsson outdoors or indoors.' The man said, 'That won't give me much trouble.' He went into the room and said very loudly, 'There is a man arrived here out in the yard, and he's as big as a troll. He asked me to come in and find out whether you prefer to talk to Egil Skalla-Grimsson outdoors or indoors.' Arinbjorn said, 'Go and ask him to wait outside and he will not have to wait long.' He did as Arinbjorn said, went out and repeated what he had been told. Arinbjorn ordered the tables to be removed, then went out and the men of his household with him. When Arinbjorn saw Egil he greeted him and asked him why he had come there. Egil gave an account of his journey in a few clear words. 'If you wish to give me any help you shall now decide what plan I am to follow.' 'Before you reached my house did you meet anyone in the town who will have recognized you?' said Arinbjorn. 'No-one,' said Egil. 'Men, get your weapons,' said Arinbjorn. They did so, and when they were fully armed including all the men of Arinbjorn's house, he went to the king's house. When they reached the hall Arinbjorn knocked on the doors demanding entry and saying who was there. The guards at once opened the doors. The king was sitting at table. Arinbjorn said that twelve of them should go in, naming Egil and ten others. 'Now, Egil, you are to offer King Eirik your head, and embrace his feet, and I will do the talking.' Then they went in. Arinbjorn went to the king and greeted him. The king welcomed him and asked what he wanted. Arinbjorn said, 'I have come here in the company of a man who has travelled a long way to find you and be reconciled with you. It is great honour for you, Sir, when your enemies come of their own free will from other countries, and do not think that they can bear your anger, though you are not near. Behave chivalrously towards this man. Let him get a real reconciliation since he has increased your honour so much, as anyone can see, travelling over many seas and difficult ways from his own home. No obligation forced him on this journey, only goodwill towards you.' Then the king looked across and saw over the heads of men where Egil was, and he glared at him and said, 'Why were you so bold, Egil, daring to come and see me? You left in such a manner last time that there could be no hope of your life from me.' Then Egil went up to the table and embraced the king's feet. He said this:

> I have weathered huge waves
> willingly and fought winds
> through many sea-miles to
> make this visit to you.
> I'm rash in strength, rash so
> roughly to kneel to you,
> I know. But I hold here
> Harald's dearest-loved son.[3]

King Eirik said, 'I do not need to count up your crimes against me. They are so many and so great that any one of them could result in your not leaving here alive. You have no hope of anything except that you must die here. You could have known beforehand that you would get no reconciliation with me.' Gunnhild said, 'Why shouldn't Egil be killed at once? Is it that you don't remember any longer, Sir, what Egil has done— killed your friends and your kinsmen, and above all else, your son, and mocked yourself. Where has anyone heard of such actions against a king?' Arinbjorn said, 'If Egil has spoken ill of the king he can compensate for it in those words of praise which will live for ever.' Gunnhild said, 'We do not want to

listen to his praise. Sir, have Egil taken out and killed. I do not
wish to hear his words nor to see him.' Then Arinbjorn said,
'The king will not let himself be egged on to all your shameful
suggestions. He will not have Egil killed tonight because night-
killings are murders.'⁴ The king said, 'It shall be as you ask,
Arinbjorn. Egil shall live tonight. Take him home with you and
bring him to me in the morning.' Arinbjorn thanked the king
for his words. 'We expect, my lord, that from here the case
between you and Egil will take a turn for the better. Though Egil
has done much in the way of crimes against you, yet take this
into account, that he has had great losses at the hands of your
kin. King Harald, your father, took the life of a fine man,
Thorolf, Egil's uncle, because of the slander of evil men, not for
any crime. And you, Sir, broke the law against Egil in the matter
of Berg-Onund, and in addition to that you wanted Egil to be
put to death, and killed men of his, and robbed him of all his
property, and beyond that you made him an outlaw and drove
him from the land, and Egil is not a man to accept provocation
meekly. A man ought to consider the circumstances in whatever case he has to judge. I will now,' concluded Arinbjorn,
'take Egil home to my house with me tonight.' So it was done.
When they came into the yard the two of them went into
a little first floor room and talked about the matter. Arinbjorn
said this, 'The king was furious just now, but I thought his
temper softened slightly towards the end. Now luck will decide
the event. I know Gunnhild will put all her mind to destroying
your case. Now I am going to give you advice. Stay awake tonight and compose a poem of praise about King Eirik. It would
seem to me a good idea if it were a formal poem of twenty
stanzas,⁵ and you could recite it in the morning when we come
before the king. Bragi my kinsman did this when he was facing
the anger of Bjorn, the Swedish king. He made up a twenty-
stanza poem in one night and received his head in exchange. It
could be that we might be lucky with the king, and that this
would make your peace with him.' Egil said, 'I will try your
advice since you wish it, but I have not come prepared for thinking up praise of King Eirik.' Arinbjorn told him to try it.
Then he went away to his men. They sat at the drinking till
midnight. Then Arinbjorn and the company went to their
sleeping-quarters, but before he undressed he went upstairs to
Egil and asked how the poem was going. Egil said nothing was
composed. 'A swallow has been perching here by the window,

and it chattered the whole night so that I never got any peace from it.' Then Arinbjorn went away and out through the doors to where he could go up outside, and he sat by the window of the room upstairs where the bird had previously been perching. He saw where some shape-changer⁶ left the house by another way. Arinbjorn sat there by the window the whole night until it was dawn, and after Arinbjorn had come there Egil composed the whole poem and had it by heart so that he could recite it in the morning when he met Arinbjorn. They kept watch until it was time to go to the king.

60

King Eirik went to table as usual and there were very many men with him. When Arinbjorn got to know of this he went with his whole company fully armed to the king's house, while the king was at table. Arinbjorn asked admittance to the hall. It was readily granted him. He and Egil went in with half the company. The other half stood outside in front of the doors. Arinbjorn greeted the king, and the king replied favourably. Arinbjorn said, 'Now Egil has come here. He has not tried to escape in the night. Now we wish to know, Sir, what his fate is to be. I expect generosity from you. I have, as was fitting, spared no exertion in word or action that your honour might be greater than before. I have also lost all the wealth and family and friends that I had in Norway, and accompanied you when all your other noblemen left you. This was right, for you have in many ways been very generous to me.' Then Gunnhild said, 'Do be quiet, Arinbjorn, and don't go on so long about this. You have done much and done it well for King Eirik, and he has repaid you in full. You have a greater obligation by far to King Eirik than to Egil. This ought not to be asked by you, that Egil should go unpunished from this meeting with King Eirik, considering all his offences.' Then Arinbjorn said, 'If you, Sir, and you, Gunnhild, have decided between you that Egil is to get no reconciliation here, then the decent thing to do is to allow him truce and permission to travel for the length of a week, so that he may save himself. Yet he has of his own free will come here to meet you, and hoped for peace for himself from this. Your dealings from then on can go as they will.' Gunnhild said, 'I can see from this, Arinbjorn, that you are more loyal to Egil than to King Eirik. If Egil is to ride from here in peace for a week

he will reach King Æthelstan in that time. King Eirik does not
need to hide from himself the fact that all kings now are men of
more power than he is. Yet only a short time ago it would have
seemed very unlikely that King Eirik would not have had both
will and energy to avenge injuries against any such man as Egil.'
Arinbjorn said, 'No-one will call Eirik the greater man because
he killed one foreign farmer's son who was in his power. But if
he wishes to augment himself from this, I shall let him do so.
These events will seem well worth the telling since Egil and I
will hold together now, and you must deal with the two of us
together. You will have paid dearly for Egil's life, Sir, when my
men and I are all dead at your feet. I would not have thought
that you would prefer to see me lying dead on the ground,
rather than let me receive the life of a single man that I ask for.'
Then the king said, 'You are bringing great pressure to bear,
Arinbjorn, in order to help Egil. I would be reluctant to do you
injury, if it should come to that, if you prefer to give your life
rather than let him be killed. But there are matters enough
counting against Egil, whatever I have done with him.' When the
king had said this Egil went before him, began his poem, spoke
loudly and at once had silence.

> I crossed the deep sea,
> My cargo, poetry,
> Odin's boundless gift,
> On board my sleek ship.
> Soon as the ice broke
> I'd the ship afloat,
> Cabin crammed with praise
> For King Eirik's ways.
>
> The prince has shown me
> Hospitality.
> Praise is my duty,
> Praise in poetry.
> I have brought my praise
> To England, bright praise,
> And ask a hearing
> To laud this great king.
>
> Prince, consider this:
> If I have my wish

Of silence you'll long
Recollect my song.
Few men but have heard
What battles occurred
With you at their head:
Odin saw the dead.

Clang of shield and sword!
Like an angry word
War swirled round Eirik,
Caused him to attack.
Vast rivers of sound!
Sword on sword, rebound-
Ing like wide echoes
Where huge waters flow.

Always there'd appear
A tight fence of spears
Before the bright fields-
Full of the king's shields.
Blood brindled the seal-
Haunted, wave-blue sea.
Loud waves of violence
Broke its long silence.

Arrows cut the air
Like butcher-birds. Where
They struck flesh they killed.
Men fell or were felled.
A clever tactic
That. And King Eirik
Rightly had much fame
Added to his name.

If folk keep silent
I've more to recount.
When the princes met
Wounds ran redder yet.
Sword fractured on sword,
Men died as they fought—
Bravely. They taught us
All that's courageous.

Sword on sword again.
Men advanced on pain

Or death. Sword-points drew
Blood or ran flesh through.
The swords bit so deep
(Wolf-fangs tearing sheep)
In that harsh battle
That many men fell.

Men were spitted on
Spear-points. Dull swords shone
Redly, edges fresh-
Honed to razor flesh.
A clever tactic
That. And King Eirik
Rightly had much fame
Added to his name.

The king's sword dripped blood,
Saucing raven-food.
Arrows made their kill,
Spears helped blood to spill.
The Scots-killer made
Meat for wolves. Death strayed
Here and there. Men fell.
Eagles would feed well.

Eagles flew where those
Corpses lay in rows.
Ravens' jabbing beaks
Gleamed with bloody streaks.
The wolves tore open
New wounds in dead men.
In a thousand rills
Blood ran for birds' bills.

Even the wolves grew
Fat. They couldn't chew
Much more flesh. They crept
Some way off and slept.
By that blood-drenched shore
Eirik threw down more
Corpses than the wolves
Could stomach themselves.

Valkyries woke the
Warrior. Sword spoke

To sword, shield crashed
On shield, spears flashed.
Metal splintered, bit:
Men hit and were hit:
Slim waspish arrows
Flew from well-strung bows.

Those arrows' deadly
Sting killed off peace. The
Coming of war meant
Wolves would find content.
Though the dead grew thick,
Men's guardian Eirik,
Fought death off, while strong-
Bows sang their war-song.

Eirik drew the yew-
Bow. The arrows flew,
Stinging men to death.
They slumped out of breath.
By that blood-drenched shore
Eirik threw down more
Corpses than the wolves
Could stomach themselves.

Yet let me make clear
Eirik's character.
I'll hasten my praise
Speaking of his ways.
He scatters much gold
But will not loose hold
Of his land. Such ways
Must have the best praise.

Eirik presses gold
Into men's palms. Cold
Thrift is not for such
As him. He spends much.
Always he gives well.
All seafarers tell
How he warms their hearts
With his generous arts.

As he fights he gives—
Hugely. What man lives

Anywhere but knows
How the king's fame grows?
Rightly, too. I say
What I think. Norway
Knows about this king's
Aptness in all things.

Prince, consider now
This poem, and how
Silence served me well.
There was much to tell.
Odin's gift of words
Gushed from me. All heard
What my mind could store
Of your gifts at war.

I broke the silence
To praise this great prince.
Poetry's my art.
I address man's heart.
And from my heart I've
Made praise come alive
And tell of this king.
Most men heard me sing.[1]

61

King Eirik sat upright while Egil spoke the poem, and glared at him. When the poem was ended the king said, 'The poem has been very well spoken. Now Arinbjorn I have thought what to do in the case between myself and Egil. You have pleaded Egil's cause with great energy in that you were willing to set yourself against me. For your sake things shall be as you ask, Egil shall leave here alive and uninjured. But you, Egil, arrange your journeys after you have left my house so that you never come into my sight, nor my sons' sight, and never approach me or my men. Still I give you your head on this occasion. Because you came into my power I will commit no shaming act of violence against you, but you are to know this for a fact, that this is no reconciliation neither with me nor with my sons nor with any of our kinsmen who wish to take rightful vengeance.' Then Egil said:

> I'll gladly have
> this princely gift
> of my head, though
> it's an eyesore.
> What man has had
> greater gift from
> a kind son of
> a king of kings?[1]

Arinbjorn thanked the king gracefully for the honour and friendship which the king had shown him. Then Arinbjorn and Egil went home to Arinbjorn's house. Arinbjorn had horses saddled for his men. He rode away with Egil, keeping a hundred fully-armed men with him. Arinbjorn rode with the troop until they reached King Æthelstan, and received a warm welcome there. The king invited Egil to stay with him, and asked how things had gone between him and King Eirik. Then Egil said:

> That killer-king is the
> kind who're better off dead.
> No love's lost there, though he
> left my neck in one piece!
> All praise to Arinbjorn.
> A brave man that. He helped
> me to make sure I'd keep
> my head at Eirik's court.[2]

At the parting between Arinbjorn and Egil, Egil gave to Arinbjorn those two gold rings which King Æthelstan had given him, each weighing a mark, and Arinbjorn gave to Egil that sword which is called Dragvandil. Thorolf Skalla-Grimsson had given that to Arinbjorn, but before that Skalla-Grim had received it from his brother Thorolf and Thorolf was given the sword by Grim the Hairy, the son of Ketil Hœng. Ketil Hœng had owned the sword and used it in duels, and it was the sharpest of all swords. They parted in the greatest friendship. Arinbjorn went home to York, to King Eirik. Egil's companions and crew were in full safety there and with Arinbjorn's support they traded their wares. But as the winter drew on they moved south to England and went to find Egil.

62

Eirik the Wise was the name of a nobleman in Norway. He married Thora, the daughter of the chieftain Thorir, and the sister of Arinbjorn. He owned property east in Vik. He was very rich, and a man of immense distinction, full of wisdom. His son was called Thorstein. He was brought up with Arinbjorn and at that time was fully-grown, though still a young man. He had gone west to England with Arinbjorn. But the same autumn that Egil went to England they heard the news from Norway that Eirik the Wise was dead, and the king's representatives had seized the inheritance and put it into the king's possession. When Arinbjorn and Thorstein heard this news they decided that Thorstein should go east and see about his inheritance. As the spring passed and men intending to travel between lands got their ships ready, Thorstein went south to London and met King Æthelstan there. He presented to the king and also to Egil the tokens and message of Arinbjorn, stating that he was sent to plead with the king that King Æthelstan might send word to his foster-son King Hakon in order that Thorstein might obtain his inheritance and possessions in Norway. King Æthelstan was easily persuaded to this because he knew only good of Arinbjorn. Then Egil also came to talk with King Æthelstan and told him his intentions. 'This summer,' he said, 'I will go east to Norway to see about the property which King Eirik and Berg-Onund stole from me. Atli the Short, Berg-Onund's brother, is sitting on it now. I know that if your words come there I will get law in the matter.' The king said that Egil should decide his own movements, 'but it would seem best to me if you stayed here and guarded my land for me, and ruled over my troops. I will give you large revenues.' Egil said, 'This offer seems to me most attractive. I should wish to accept, not refuse it. Nevertheless I must first go to Iceland and visit my wife and property there.' King Æthelstan gave Egil a good merchant-ship and a cargo with it. The ship was loaded with wheat and honey and still more wealth in other goods. When Egil had his ship ready for the sea Thorstein Eiriksson (mentioned before, known afterwards as Thoruson) planned on going. They sailed when they were ready. King Æthelstan and Egil parted in great friendship. Egil and his men had a swift journey, arrived in Norway east in Vik and took the ship right up the Oslo fjord.

Thorstein owned an estate in the district extending right to Romerike. When Thorstein came ashore there he put in a claim concerning his inheritance from his father to those king's men who were in control of his estate. Many people gave Thorstein support in this. Meetings were arranged and Thorstein had many powerful kinsmen there. It ended with being transferred to the decision of the king, Thorstein in the meantime taking charge of the property which his father had owned. Egil took lodgings for the winter with Thorstein and there were twelve of them together. The wheat and honey were brought to Thorstein's home. There was great merriment there during the winter, and Thorstein lived magnificently since there were provisions enough for it.

63

At that time, as was said above, King Hakon, Æthelstan's foster-son, ruled over Norway. The king spent that winter north in Trondheim. When the winter was well on Thorstein prepared for his journey and Egil with him. They had nearly thirty men. When they were ready they went first to Opland, from there north by Dovrefjell to Trondheim, and there they went to see King Hakon. They put forward their errand to the king. Thorstein explained his case and brought forward witnesses that he owned all that inheritance which he claimed. The king responded favourably. He let Thorstein obtain his possessions and in addition made him a king's nobleman as his father had been. Egil went to see King Hakon and put forward his errand, and in addition the words of King Æthelstan and his tokens. Egil spoke of the property which Bjorn the Freeholder had owned, the lands and the wealth. He claimed for himself and his wife Asgerd a half of this property, he produced witnesses and oaths for his case, and said also that he had put all that to King Eirik, and went on to add that he had not obtained law because of Eirik's power and Gunnhild's malice. Egil alluded to the whole state of the case as it had been at the Gula Assembly. He then asked the king to grant him law in the matter. King Hakon said, 'I have heard that my brother Eirik and Gunnhild too would claim that you, Egil, have thrown a heavier stone than you could handle in this conflict. It would seem to me, Egil, that you are well off if I keep out of this matter, even though Eirik and I don't have luck in our dealings.'

Egil said, 'Sir, you cannot be silent about such important matters. Everyone here in the land, Norwegians and foreigners, will obey your orders. I have heard that you have established laws here in the land and justice for every man. Now I know that you will let me have that equally with other men. I think I have the strength and support of kin here in the land to cope with Atli the Short. But in the affair between Eirik and myself I have this to say to you, that I have met him and we parted with his telling me to go in peace wherever I wished. I should like, my lord, to offer you my support and service. I know that there will be no-one here with you who will prove to be a better warrior in battle than I am. It is my conviction that not much time will pass before there is a meeting between you and King Eirik if you both live. It will astonish me if it doesn't turn out to be your impression that Gunnhild has raised a full family of sons.' The king said, 'Egil, you will not take service with me. Your family has struck too hard at mine for you to establish yourself here in this country. Go to Iceland, and live there on your father's estate. Then you will be in no danger from our line. Here in this land it can be expected that our kin will be the stronger throughout your life. But for the sake of King Æthelstan my foster-father, you shall have peace here in Norway and obtain law and land-rights, because I know that King Æthelstan has a great affection for you.' Egil thanked the king for his words, and asked this, that the king should let him have firm proof for Thord in Aurland or other noblemen in Sogn and in Hordaland. The king said that it should be so.

64

As soon as they had completed their errands Thorstein and Egil got ready for their journey. Then they took their road back, but when they came south by Dovrefjell Egil said that he wished to go down to Romsdal and then south by the sea-road. 'I want,' he said, 'to finish matters in Sogn and in Hordaland, since I wish to get my ship ready for Iceland this summer.' Thorstein said that he should plan his own movements. Thorstein and Egil parted. Thorstein went south through Dalane and the rest of the way until he reached his farm. He brought the king's tokens and message to the attention of his representatives. They were to hand back all the property which they had taken over and which Thorstein claimed. Egil and his eleven men went their

own way and reached Romsdal. They got transport for themselves and then went south to More. Nothing is told of their
journey before their arrival on the island called Vigra,[1] and they
went to lodge at a farm called Blindheim. It was a fine place. A
nobleman lived there called Fridgeir. He was a young man who
had just taken up his father's inheritance. His mother was
called Gyda. She was sister to the chieftain Arinbjorn, a woman
of good birth and fine character. She ran the place together with
her son Fridgeir, and they had a very great estate there. Egil
and his men were warmly welcomed. Egil sat next to Fridgeir
for the evening, and his companions along from him. There was
plenty of drink and lavish hospitality. The mistress of the
house, Gyda, went to talk to Egil during the evening. She asked
after her brother Arinbjorn, and about others of their kin and
friends who had gone with Arinbjorn to England. Egil told
her what she asked. She wanted to know the news about Egil's
travels. He gave her a graphic description. Then he said:

> I resented the rough
> rage of that grab-land king.
> No wren will rest from flight
> when the hawk hangs above.
> And so I again used
> Arinbjorn. And as so
> often he helped. No man's
> helpless who boasts his help.[2]

Egil was very cheerful during the evening, but Fridgeir and his
household were rather quiet. Egil saw a pretty girl there, well-
dressed. He was told that she was Fridgeir's sister. She was
unhappy and cried throughout the evening. They thought this
odd. They were there for the night, and in the morning the
weather was fierce and not fit for sea-travel. They needed conveying from the island. Then Fridgeir, and Gyda also, went up
to Egil. They invited him to wait there with his companions
until the weather was fit for travel, and to receive from there the
help they needed for their journey. Egil accepted this. They
stayed there, weatherbound, for three nights, and there was the
most excellent entertainment. After that the weather became
calm. Egil and his men got up early in the morning and made
ready. They went to their food, and were given beer to drink,

and sat for a while. Then they picked up their clothes. Egil stood up and thanked Fridgeir and Gyda for their help, and then they went out. Fridgeir and his mother went out with them. Then Gyda began to talk quietly to her son Fridgeir. Egil stood meanwhile, waiting for them. Egil said to the girl, 'Why are you crying, girl? I never see you cheerful.' She could not answer and cried all the more. Fridgeir answered his mother aloud. 'I do not wish to ask this now. They are all ready for their journey.' Then Gyda went to Egil and said, 'Egil, I will tell you the thing that has happened to us here. There is a man called Ljot the Pale.[3] He is a berserk, a duellist, a hated man. He came here and asked for my daughter, but we answered him at once, refusing the match. Then he challenged my son Fridgeir to a duel, and in the morning they are meeting to fight on the island called Valderoy. Egil, I should like you to go to the duel with Fridgeir. It is a fact that if Arinbjorn were here in the country we would not suffer the arrogance of such a man as Ljot.' 'Lady, for the sake of your kinsman, Arinbjorn, I am obliged to go with your son, if he thinks that will be any use to him.' 'Then you will do well,' said Gyda. 'We will go back into the living-room and stay together all day.' Egil and his men went back to the living-room and the drink. They were there for the day, and in the evening friends of Fridgeir arrived, who were committed to the journey with him. It was crowded there that night and there was a fine feast. The next day Fridgeir and many men with him got ready for the journey. Egil was in the company. The weather was good for travelling. They set off and they reached the island Valderoy. A pleasant meadow a short way from the sea was the place for the duel. The duelling area was marked out and stones placed round it. Then Ljot turned up with his men, and made his preparations for the duel. He had a shield and a sword. Ljot was a very big man and strong. When he went forward to the duelling area in the field the berserk temper came on him so that he began to bellow violently, and to bite at his shield. Fridgeir was not a big man. He was slender of build, handsome in looks, but not strong. He was not used to fighting. When Egil saw Ljot he spoke this verse:

> Let's get on with it, lads.
> Ljot mustn't win this girl.
> But Fridgeir can't be left
> battling with this madman.

> How he bites the rim of
> his shield, and mouths vows to
> his gods! And how he glowers,
> glares with a doomed man's stare![4]

Ljot saw where Egil stood and heard his words and said, 'Come here to the duel, big man, and fight with me if you're so eager for it, and we'll try ourselves against each other. That is fairer than fighting with Fridgeir, since I shouldn't think my reputation any greater from bringing him to the ground.' Then Egil said:

> It would be rude to refuse
> requests—however less
> than important they seem.
> There'll be fun in a fight.
> Let's buckle to. Ljot don't
> look for hope of mercy
> from me. This fight in More's
> fashioned to Egil's needs.[5]

Then Egil prepared himself for the duel with Ljot. Egil had the shield which he usually had, and by his side the sword which he called Adder, but he kept Dragvandil in his hand. He went in over the boundary to where the duel was to be, but Ljot was still not ready. Egil swung his sword and spoke a verse:

> I'll go to work with my
> willing sword, test his shield,
> thrust out that iron tongue
> thirsting to taste his blood.
> And Ljot won't have much life
> left when I end my game.
> Cool metal will calm him.
> Carrion he'll be then.[6]

Then Ljot came on to the field and they rushed together. Egil struck at Ljot, but Ljot fended it off with his shield. Egil struck blow after blow so that Ljot could get no blow struck in return. He moved back in order to give himself room to strike, but Egil followed him just as quickly and struck as hard as he could. Ljot went out through the boundary stones and round the field.

That was the first bout. Ljot asked for a rest. Egil allowed that.
They stopped and rested themselves. Then Egil said:

> I have a hunch that Ljot
> hasn't the guts for much
> battling. He backs away
> briskly, won't risk a fight.
> He hasn't hit me and
> has no wish to be hit.
> So he scurries in wide
> sweeps before my sure feet.[7]

It was duelling law at that time that if a man challenged another
in any matter and the one who issued the challenge won the
victory, then his due as victor was whatever the challenge had
been made for. If he were defeated, he was obliged to ransom
himself by an agreed sum. But if he fell in the duel, the fight lost
him all his possessions, and the one who had killed him in the
duel inherited from him. It was also the law that if a foreigner
died who had no heir in the country, the property went into the
king's possession. Egil told Ljot to get ready. 'I want us to fight
this duel now.' Then Egil leapt at him and struck at him. He
went so close to him that Ljot fell back and the shield was swept
from him. Then Egil struck at Ljot, and it got him below the
knee and took his leg off. Ljot fell then, and was lifeless. Then
Egil went up to Fridgeir and his companions and he was warmly
thanked for his work. Then Egil said:

> This most errant of men
> must lie still now. I killed
> him, sliced off his leg, and
> have gained Fridgeir his peace.
> I don't want paying, don't
> desire Fridgeir's bright gold,
> for it was fun enough
> fighting that white-faced Ljot.[8]

Few men grieved for Ljot since he had been the most ruthless
of men. He was Swedish by race and had no kin there in the
country. He had come there to get money for himself by duelling.
He had killed many fine farmers, having challenged them for
their lands and ownership rights, and had become extremely rich

both in land and money. Egil went home with Fridgeir from the duelling field, and remained there for a little time before he went south to More. Egil and Fridgeir parted with great affection. Egil invited Fridgeir to claim the estates which Ljot had owned. Egil went on his way and reached Fjordane. From there he went into Sogn to a meeting with Thord in Aurland. He welcomed him, and Egil put forward his business together with King Hakon's message. Thord received Egil's words well and promised him his help in the matter. Egil stayed there with Thord for a long time in the spring.

65

Egil made his way south into Hordaland. He had a rowing boat for the journey and thirty men on it. They arrived one day at Ask on Askoy. Egil went up there with twenty men, leaving ten to look after the ship. Atli the Short was there with some men. Egil had him called out, saying that Egil Skalla-Grimsson had business with him. Atli took his weapons, as did all the men of his household who could fight, and they went outside. Egil said, 'Atli, I have been told that you have in your charge that property which is by right mine, and my wife Asgerd's. You will have heard it spoken of earlier that I claimed my inheritance from Bjorn the Freeholder which your brother Berg-Onund withheld from me. I have now come to see to this property, lands and money, and to ask that you let go of it and hand it over to me.' Atli said, 'Egil, we have heard for a long time that you are an overbearing man. Now I see the proof of it if you think to claim at my hands this property which King Eirik judged to my brother Onund. Command and prohibition were in Eirik's power at that date in this land. I thought, Egil, that you would have come here in order to offer me payment for my brothers whom you killed, and you would wish to recompense that robbery which you committed here at Ask. I would then have been able to answer you if you had come on that business, but in this matter I have no answer.' 'I wish to offer you,' said Egil, 'the same as I offered Onund, that the law of the Gula Assembly shall decide our case. I count your brothers beyond atonement through their own actions, since they had previously robbed me of law and land-right, and taken my property by looting. I have the king's permission to take you to law in the matter. I intend to summon you to the Gula Assembly, and receive there a legal decision in the case.' 'I will come to the Gula Assembly,' said Atli, 'and the two of us will contest the case there.' Then Egil went away with his company. He went north to Sogn and into Aurland to his kinsman Thord, and stayed there until the Gula Assembly. When men came to the Assembly Egil was one of them. Atli the Short had arrived too. They began to discuss their case and present it to the men who should judge it. Egil put forward his claim to the property, and Atli offered a legal defence in opposition, the oaths of twelve men that he did not have in his keeping property which Egil owned. When Atli went to the courts with his oath-swearers Egil went to meet him and said that he was not willing to let these oaths be set against the property. 'I wish to offer you different law, namely that we meet in a duel here at the Assembly, and let the one who gets the victory have the property.' It was valid law that Egil cited, and an ancient custom that any man had the right to challenge another to a duel whether he was defender or prosecutor. Atli said that he would not refuse to meet Egil in a duel. 'You are saying what I should say for I have injuries enough to avenge against you. You have brought down my two brothers, and I should fall very far short of maintaining my rights if I preferred to lose my property to you illegally, rather than fight you when you make me the offer.' Then Egil and Atli shook hands and confirmed between them that they would fight a duel and whoever got the victory should have the estates over which they were quarrelling. After that they prepared for the duel. Egil advanced with a helmet on his head, a shield in front of him, a spear in his hand, and the sword Dragvandil fastened to his right wrist. Men taking part in duels usually let the sword be easily at hand so that it could be used immediately it was needed, and so that they did not have to draw their swords on the spot. Atli had the same equipment as Egil. He was used to duels. He was a strong man and full of courage. A large and old bull was led forward. This was known as the sacrificial beast. The one who won the victory was to kill it. Sometimes it was one animal, sometimes each man in the duel had one brought up. When they were ready to fight they ran at each other, and first threw their spears, but neither spear hit a shield, both landed in the earth. Then both of them took to their swords. They went at each other fiercely exchanging blows. Atli did not retreat. They struck quickly and hard and the shields were soon useless. When Atli's shield was no good at all he threw it from him, gripped his sword with both hands, and struck as fiercely as he could. Egil struck at his shoulder but the sword did not bite. He struck a second and a third time. It was easy for him to find places to strike Atli for he had no protection. Egil swung the sword with all his strength, but it did not bite wherever he struck with it. Then Egil saw that nothing could be done as things were, for by now his shield was becoming useless. Egil let go his sword and his shield and leapt at Atli seizing him with his hands. Then the difference in strength was felt and Atli fell back to the ground. Egil crouched down and bit through his windpipe. There Atli lost his life. Egil jumped up quickly and went to where the sacrificial beast stood, gripped jaw in one hand, horn in the other, and jerked it so that the legs pointed upwards and the neck bone cracked. Then Egil went to where his companions were standing. Egil said:

> No matter how hard I
> hacked at his shield, my sword
> couldn't cut through at all.
> Curse him! He'd blunted it.
> So I used strength on that
> sword-swinging loudmouth and
> bated his breath. Then I
> broke the bull's helpless neck.[1]

Then Egil took possession of all the estates that the feud had been about and that he claimed his wife Asgerd ought to have inherited from her father. It is not reported that anything else happened at the Assembly. Egil then went straight to Sogn and put into order the estates which he had taken into his possession. He stayed there for a long time during the spring. Then he went east to Vik with his companions. He went to see Thorstein and was there for a time.

66

Egil got his ship ready during the summer and travelled as soon as he was ready. He made for Iceland and had a good journey. He directed the ship into Borgarfjord and brought it close up to his farm. He had his cargo unloaded and brought the ship ashore. Egil spent that winter on his farm, and had brought great riches home with him. He was an extremely wealthy man with a great and splendid estate. Egil was not meddlesome in

the affairs of others and most people found him unaggressive
when he was in this country. On the other hand no-one made
any attempt to interfere with his affairs. Egil was at his farm while
a good many winters passed. Egil and Asgerd had children whose
names were as follows. Their first son was called Bodvar, the
second Gunnar, the daughters Thorgerd and Bera. The youngest
was Thorstein. All Egil's children were promising and had
plenty of intelligence. Thorgerd was the eldest child, Bera the
next.

67

From east across the sea Egil learned the news that Eirik Blood-
Axe had died west in viking raids, and Gunnhild with their sons
had gone south to Denmark, and all the people who had accompanied Eirik and his family to England had left. Arinbjorn
had gone back to Norway. He had obtained the revenues and
possessions which he had formerly owned, and was on very
friendly terms with the king. Egil again decided it would be a
very good idea to go to Norway. A second piece of news accompanying the first was that King Æthelstan was dead[1] and his
brother Edmund now ruled over England. Egil prepared his
ship and got a crew for it. Onund Sjoni, the son of Ani from
Anabrekka, decided to go with him. Onund was big and the
strongest of the men in the district. It was not everyone who
agreed that he was not a shape-changer. Onund had often made
journeys from land to land. He was somewhat older than Egil.
They had been friends for a long time. When Egil was ready he
put to sea and they had a swift journey. They reached the middle
of the Norwegian coast and when they saw land they steered in
for Fjordane. When they had news from ashore they were told
that Arinbjorn was at home on his farm. Egil directed his ship
to the harbour nearest Arinbjorn's home. Then Egil went to find
Arinbjorn and there was a very happy meeting between them.
Arinbjorn offered lodging to Egil and those of his crew whom
he wished to bring. Egil accepted that and had his ship brought
ashore. The crew found quarters for themselves, Egil and eleven
men going to Arinbjorn's. Egil had had a longship sail made
and elaborately worked. He gave the sail to Arinbjorn and still
more gifts which were worth the giving. Egil was there for the
winter and in high favour. During the winter Egil went south
into Sogn for the rents from his estates. He stayed there a very

long time. Then he went north into Fjordane. Arinbjorn had a great Yule feast, inviting to it his friends and the farmers in the area. It was very crowded and a good feast. He gave Egil as a Yule-gift a robe made of silk, thickly embroidered with gold, and with gold clasps all the way down. Arinbjorn had had this garment made for Egil's size. Arinbjorn gave Egil a full set of garments newly made for Yule. They were cut from English cloth in many colours. Arinbjorn gave many kinds of friendship gifts during Yule to those men who were visiting his home, because of all men Arinbjorn was the most generous and princely. Then Egil composed this verse:

> I, the poet Egil, swear
> That the gifts of this great man
> And the gold-trimmed coat I wear
> Testify, if mere things can,
> To the friendship which he gave
> Unsparingly. Friend, Arinbjorn,
> Many years will pass before
> Another such as you is born.[2]

68

Egil became very depressed after Yule and did not talk. When Arinbjorn observed this he opened a conversation with Egil asking what his depression signified. 'I wish,' he said, 'that you would let me know whether you are ill or something else is wrong. Then we can look for a cure.' Egil said, 'I am not ill. I am much troubled about how to obtain the money that I won when I killed Ljot the Pale north in More. I have been told that the king's representatives have taken over all that wealth and put it into the king's possession. I should like to have your help now in claiming this property.' Arinbjorn said, 'It is not against the law of the land for you to have that property. Still it seems to me firmly anchored elsewhere. A king's court has a wide entrance and a narrow exit.[1] We have undertaken many difficult property claims against overbearing men, and then we had a better relationship with the king than we have now. The foundations of the friendship between King Hakon and myself are only shallow, though I am obliged to do as the old proverb says, cultivate the oak I have to live under.' 'All the same,' said Egil, 'my thought runs on these lines. If we have a lawful case we should put it to the test. It is possible that the king will let us have our rights, for I have heard that the king is a just man and holds fully to the laws which he has established in the land. I am convinced that I should go and see the king and put the matter to him.' Arinbjorn said that he was not happy about this. 'It seems to me, Egil, that it will be an uneasy alliance between your boldness and vehemence and the temper and power of the king. I do not think he is your friend, and he considers he has no cause to be. I would rather let this case drop and not drag it up. But if you wish, Egil, I had better go to the king on this business.' Egil said that he was very pleased and grateful, and willingly accepted this offer. Hakon was in Rogaland at that time, sometimes in Hordaland. This was not long after their talk, and it was not difficult to visit him. Arinbjorn got ready for the journey. Everyone could see that he intended to go to the king. He manned with men of his household a twenty-benched ship that he owned. Egil was to stay at home. Arinbjorn did not wish him to go. Arinbjorn set off when he was ready and had a good journey. He found King Hakon and was welcomed. When he had been there for a little time he brought up his errand to the king, saying that Egil Skalla-Grimsson had arrived in the country and thought that he owned all the money which Ljot the Pale had had. 'We are told, Sir, that Egil has a legal claim, but your representatives have taken over the property and put it in your possession. I want to ask, my lord, that Egil should have justice in this.' The king answered his case, but was slow of speech. 'I do not know why you are here on Egil's behalf in such a matter. He came to see me once, and I told him that I did not want him lodging here in the land, for reasons which are already known to you. Egil need not bring up such a claim against me as he did against my brother Eirik. As for you, Arinbjorn, there is this to be said. You may stay here in this country so long as you do not value foreigners more highly than myself and my words. I know that your thoughts turn in the direction of your foster-son Harald Eiriksson, and your best course is to go and find the brothers and stay with them. I have a strong suspicion that men such as you will be a poor support for me if it comes to the test in dealings between myself and the sons of Eirik.' When the king reacted so strongly against the suit Arinbjorn saw that it would not help to pursue the matter with him. He prepared to go home. The king was rather remote and ungracious towards Arinbjorn, once he knew his errand. Arinbjorn was in no mood to humble himself to the king in this matter, and in this way they parted. Arinbjorn went home and told Egil the result of his errand. 'I will not open such matters with the king again.' Egil frowned heavily at this tale, for it seemed to him the loss of a great deal of money, and unjustly at that. Early in the morning a few days later when Arinbjorn was in his room and there were not many men about, he had Egil called to him. When he came there Arinbjorn had a chest opened and took from it forty marks of silver and said this: 'I will pay you this money, Egil, for those estates owned by Ljot the Pale. It seems fair to me that you should have this payment from Fridgeir and myself, for you saved his life from Ljot, and I know you did it on my account. I am therefore obliged not to let you be cheated in this suit.' Egil accepted the money and thanked Arinbjorn. Then Egil became cheerful again.

69

Arinbjorn stayed at home on his farm that winter, but afterwards in the spring he announced that he intended to go on a viking raid. Arinbjorn had a fine range of ships. In the spring he got three longships ready, all big ones. He had three hundred men, with the men of his household on his own ship which was very well manned. He also had many farmers' sons along with him. Egil planned to go on the voyage with him. He captained a ship, and with him went many of the company that he had brought with him from Iceland. Egil had the merchant ship which he had brought from Iceland moved east to Vik. He put men on it to see to the cargo. Arinbjorn and Egil took the longships south along the coast. Then they laid course with their men for Germany and raided there during the summer, getting money for themselves. When it came to autumn they turned back north and were lying off Frisia. One night when the weather was calm they turned up into a large river which was badly off for harbourage, with the water ebbing fast. Ashore there were broad level fields, and a short way off there were woods. The fields were swampy for there had been heavy rains. They decided to go ashore, and left a third of the men to look after the ships. They went up along the river, between it and the woods. Soon there was a village ahead of them, many farmers living there. The people ran from the village into the hinterland, those who could do so, as soon as they were aware of the raiders, but the vikings pursued the attack. Afterwards there was a second village and a third. All the people who could manage it ran off. The land was flat there with big level fields. Ditches had been dug everywhere through the land, and there was water in them. They had enclosed the arable and grazing land, but in some places palings were set up above the ditches at crossing places. They acted as bridges and planks were placed across them. The inhabitants ran off into the wood. But when the vikings had penetrated some distance into the inhabited country the Frisians gathered together in the wood, and when they had assembled three hundred men they went towards the vikings, planning to fight against them. That was a hard battle, but it ended with the Frisians running away, and the vikings took up the chase. The people from the farms scattered in all directions, those who were running off, and so did the pursuers. So it happened that few on either side kept together. Egil was pursuing vigorously, not many with him, but very many running away from him. The Frisians came to where there was a ditch ahead and they crossed it. Then they removed the bridge-planks. Egil and his men came up on the other side. Egil rushed on immediately, jumping over the ditch, but that was no jump for anyone else, and no-one attempted it. When the Frisians saw this they attacked him but he defended himself. Eleven men came at him, but their fight ended with his bringing them all down. After that Egil pushed the bridge across and went back over the ditch. He saw then that all their troops had turned to the ships. He was standing near the wood. Then Egil went along by the wood and on to the ships in this way, so that he had the wood there if he needed it. The vikings had brought a great deal of loot and cattle down, and when they reached the ships some were slaughtering the cattle, some were lifting their gains aboard ship, and some stood beyond them with a shield-wall, for the Frisians had come down with a great force and were shooting at them. The Frisians had by then had reinforcements. When Egil came down and saw what was going on he ran as quickly as possible to where the crowd stood. He had his spear with him and he took it in both hands, swinging his shield round to his back. He thrust forward with the spear and everyone sprang back who was in its way, and in this manner he cleared his way through the host. So he got down to his men, and they thought they had got him back from the dead. Then they went aboard and held course away from the land.

They sailed to Denmark. When they came to Limfjord and were lying off Hals, Arinbjorn had a meeting with his men, telling them his intentions. He said, 'Now I am going to find the sons of Eirik, with whatever company will go with me. I have just heard that the brothers are here in Denmark, and keep a large body of men, spending the summers in raiding, and spending the winters here in Denmark. I am willing to give permission to go to Norway to all those who would rather do that than come with me. It would seem to me a good idea, Egil, if you went back to Norway, and then made for Iceland as quickly as possible, once we part.' Then the men organized themselves on the ships. Those who wished to go back to Norway went with Egil, but it was by far the larger part of the company that went with Arinbjorn. The parting between Arinbjorn and Egil was cheerful and friendly. Arinbjorn went to find the sons of Eirik and to join his foster-son Harald Greycloak, and he stayed with him as long as they both lived. Egil went north to Vik and made his way into the Oslo fjord. His merchant ship was there, the one he had moved south in the spring. His cargo was there too, and the men who had gone with the ship. Thorstein Thoruson came to find Egil, and invited him to stay during the winter, together with those men that he wished to have with him. Egil accepted that and had the ship brought ashore and the cargo put up. Some of the men who were with him took lodging there, and some went north in the country to their own people. Egil went to stay with Thorstein and there were ten or twelve of them all together. Egil was there for the winter, and well looked after.

70

King Harald Finehair had brought east Varmland under his control. Olaf the Wood-Carver had been the first to conquer Varmland. He was the father of Halfdan Whiteleg who was the first of his race to be king of Norway, and from whom King Harald was descended on his father's side. All Harald's paternal ancestors had ruled over Varmland, taken tribute from it, and put men there to defend the country. When King Harald had grown old the earl who ruled over Varmland was called Arnvid. The tribute there as elsewhere proved to be worse than it was when King Harald was in his prime. It was the same when the sons of Harald quarrelled over the kingdom of Norway. Little notice was taken of the tributary countries which lay furthest off.

But when Hakon ruled without opposition, he looked for the full power which his father Harald had had. King Hakon sent twelve men east to Varmland. They had received tribute from the earl. When they came back through Eidskog forest footpads attacked them and killed them all. The result was the same when King Hakon sent other messengers east to Varmland: the men were killed and the tribute did not get through. It was rumoured in some circles that Earl Arnvid must have set his men to kill the king's men and recapture the money for return to the earl. Then King Hakon sent the third lot of men. He was in Trondheim at the time, and they were to go east into Vik to find Thorstein Thoruson with the message that he was to go east to Varmland to collect the king's tribute. The alternative was that Thorstein should leave the country, for the king had learned that his uncle Arinbjorn had gone south to Denmark and was with the sons of Eirik; also that they had many men and went raiding during the summers. King Hakon thought that none of them was to be trusted, for he expected hostile action from the sons of Eirik if they should win sufficient support for a rising against him. He took action against all the kin and connections and friends of Arinbjorn, driving many from the land or making things difficult for them in other ways, and this was also the reason why the king made his proposal to Thorstein. The man who brought the message was a man of all countries. He had been in Denmark for a long time and in Sweden. He knew everything about the roads and the inhabitants. He had travelled widely in Norway too. When he put the matter to Thorstein Thoruson, Thorstein told Egil on what errand these men had come, and asked what the answer should be. Egil said, 'It seems to me very clear from this message that the king wants you out of the country like the rest of Arinbjorn's kin. I consider this no errand for a man as well-born as you are. My advice is that you call the king's messengers to talk with you, and I want to be in on your discussion. Then let us see what this is about.' Thorstein did as he said and brought them into talk. Then the messengers told the whole truth about their errand and the king's words that Thorstein was to go on this mission or, as an alternative, be outlawed. Then Egil said, 'I see this errand of yours clearly. If Thorstein does not wish to go, then you will have to go and claim the tribute.' The messengers agreed that this was so. 'Thorstein will not go on this journey, because no man of his birth is under any obligation to go on such paltry matters. But Thorstein will act where he has obligation, and he will accompany the king in the country or out of it, if the king wishes to ask this. Also if you want any men provided for the journey from here you will be allowed that, as well as everything for the journey that you wish to suggest to Thorstein.' Then the messengers talked among themselves, and agreed that they would accept this alternative if Egil would go on the expedition. 'The king,' they said, 'is ill-disposed towards him, and he will think our journey an excellent one if we bring it about that Egil gets killed. Then he can drive Thorstein from the land if he wants to.' So they said to Thorstein that they would be ready to agree if Egil went and Thorstein stayed at home. 'Then it shall be so,' said Egil. 'I will free Thorstein from this undertaking. How many men do you think you need from here?' 'There are eight of us,' they said. 'We should like four men from here. We are then twelve.' Egil said it should be so. Onund Sjoni and some others of Egil's company had gone down to the sea to look to their ship and other goods which they had put into custody for the autumn, and they were not back. Egil thought this a great annoyance, for the king's men were in a hurry to start and did not wish to wait.

71

Egil and three of his companions prepared for the journey. They had horses and sledges the same as the king's men. There were heavy snows and the routes had all had to be changed. They went on their journey when they were ready, and drove up through the country, and as they headed east in the direction of Eidskog there came such a heavy snowfall in one night that the way could not be seen clearly. Travelling was slow the next day, for there were deep drifts as soon as they were off the road. As the day wore on they stopped and fed the horses. Nearby was a ridge covered with trees. Then they said to Egil, 'We will go different ways now. Below the ridge here lives a friend of ours, a farmer called Arnald. Our party will seek lodging there. You go up on the ridge and when you reach it there will soon be a big farm ahead of you. You will certainly get a lodging there. It is the home of a very rich farmer called Bearded Armod. We will meet early in the morning and travel to Eidskog by the evening. An excellent man called Thorfinn lives there.' Then they separated. Egil and his men went up the ridge, and we can say of the king's men that as soon as they were out of Egil's sight

they took the skis which they had brought with them and put
them on. Then they went back as fast as they could. They
went day and night, making for Opland, and from there north
by Dovrefjell, and they did not stop until they found King
Hakon and told him how their journey had gone. Egil and his
companions crossed the ridge during the evening. The quickest
way to tell this is to say that they immediately lost the road.
There was heavy snow. The horses kept sinking into drifts and
had to be dragged out. There were uphill climbs, undergrowth
in places, and the climbs and the undergrowth were very difficult
to cope with. The horses delayed them greatly and it was very
difficult for the men to move forward. They were very tired,
but nevertheless they managed to get over the pass. They saw
in front of them a big farm, and went up to it. When they came
into the yard they saw that there were men standing outside,
Armod and his servants. They spoke to each other and asked
what news there was. When Armod understood that they were
the king's messengers he offered them lodging there. They accepted that. Men of Armod's household took their horses and
tack, while the farmer invited Egil indoors, and they went in.
Armod put Egil in the high seat on the bench opposite himself,
and his companions along from him. They talked a great deal
about their difficulties in getting through that evening, and to the
men in that household it seemed incredible that they had made it,
for they said it was no fit route for men even without the snow.
Then Armod said, 'Doesn't it seem best to you that the table
should be set for you, and you have your meal, and then go to
bed. That way you will get the most rest.' 'That would be very
satisfactory,' said Egil. Then Armod had a table put up for them,
and big bowls full of skyr. Armod pretended he was sorry that
he had no good beer to give them. Egil and his men were very
thirsty from weariness. They picked the bowls up and drank the
contents eagerly, Egil by far the most. No other food was produced. Many of the household were there. The farmer's wife sat
on the cross-bench at the end of the room, and the rest of the
women beside her. The farmer's daughter, ten or twelve years
old, was in the room. Her mother called her to her side and
whispered to her. Then the girl came in front of the table where
Egil was sitting. She said:

> My mother sends me with this
> message for Egil's ears:

> don't fill up with food
> forced down in such great haste.
> She wants to warn you, be
> wary of what you take.
> Eat less and less so that
> later you're better fed.[1]

Armod struck the girl and told her to be quiet. 'You always say the wrong thing.' The girl went off but Egil put down the skyr bowl, and by then it was nearly empty. Then the bowls were taken away from them. The men of the household went to their places, tables were set up right through the room and food set on them. Then choice meats came in and were put before Egil as before others. Beer was carried in and it was a strong and excellent brew. The drinking soon became one man one horn, the horn to be drained at each toast. The greatest attention was given to Egil and his company. They had to drink as hard as they could. At first Egil drank for a while unstintingly. When his companions were becoming incapable he drank for them whatever they could not cope with. It went on like this until the tables were taken away. Then everyone inside was very drunk, and at every cup that Armod drained he said, 'I drink to you, Egil,' and the men of his house drank to Egil's companions, using the same formula. A man was set to this job of carrying every drink to Egil and his company, and he warmly urged them to drink up quickly. Egil said to his companions that they should not drink any more, and he drank for them whatever they could not avoid in any other way. Egil then found that he could not manage in this way. He stood up and went across the floor to where Armod sat. He got hold of him by the shoulders and pushed him back to the wall. Then Egil brought vomit up out of his mouth, and it gushed over Armod's face, into his eyes and nostrils and mouth and ran down over his breast, and Armod was at the point of suffocation. When he got his breath, then his vomit gushed out. Everyone, all the household of Armod who were there, said that Egil should be blamed as the worst of men, and it was disgusting behaviour for a man not to go outside when he wanted to vomit, but to make a spectacle of himself in the drinking room. Egil said, 'Don't blame me for that. I do as the host does. He's spewing with all his might no less than I am.' Then Egil went to his place and sat down, asking them to give him drink. Then Egil said at the top of his voice:

What comes out of my mouth
makes plain that I approve
your food. And full in your
face I've placed all the facts.
Some might serve you better.
So? You'd serve *them* better.
Thank God we don't meet much.
Mind! your beard drips beer-spew![2]

Armod jumped up and went out, but Egil asked to be given drink. The wife said to the man who had been pouring out for the evening that he should provide drink, and it was not to run short so long as they wanted it. He took a great aurochs' horn, filled it and carried it to Egil. Egil drained the horn at one go. Then he said:

No matter that this man
may bring beer-brimming horns
throughout the night, I'll give
thanks and empty them all.
I'll leave no last horn nor
least drop go unswallowed
though I'm brought beer until
break of day or beyond.[3]

Egil drank for a time and drained every horn which came to him, but there was little merriment in the room though some men were drinking. Then Egil and his companions stood up and took their weapons from the walls where they had fastened them. They went out to the barns where their horses were. They lay down in the straw there and slept during the night.

72

Egil got up in the morning as soon as it was daylight. The companions got themselves ready and as soon as they were up went back at once to the farm to look for Armod. When they reached the room in which Armod and his wife and daughter slept, Egil pushed open the door and went to Armod's bed. He drew his sword and with one hand he seized Armod's beard pulling him forward to the edge of the bed. But Armod's wife and daughter ran up and asked Egil not to kill Armod. Egil said he

would consent for their sakes, 'for that is right. But he deserves
to be killed.' Then Egil said:

> This sneaky sly-boots should
> say thankyou to his wife
> and sweet girl. They saved me,
> so I won't spill his blood.
> But don't think you deserve
> decent treatment from me.
> I don't take kindly to
> tainted beer! I'll be off![1]

Then Egil cut off his beard at the chin. Then he hooked a finger
into his eye so that it lay on his cheek. After that Egil went off
to join his companions. They went on their way and came to
Thorfinn's farm at breakfast time. He lived by Eidskog forest.
Egil and his men asked for breakfast, and to rest their horses.
The farmer Thorfinn willingly agreed to that. Egil and his men
went indoors. Egil asked if Thorfinn had had any sign of his
companions, 'We had agreed to meet here.' Thorfinn said, 'Six
men together passed here sometime before dawn and they were
heavily armed.' Then one of Thorfinn's men said, 'I drove out
for wood last night, and I met six men on the road. They were
of Armod's household, and that was a very long time before
daybreak. I do not know whether these and the men you speak
of were all the same group.' Thorfinn said that the men he had
seen had gone past after the other had come home with his
cartload of wood. While Egil and the others sat eating, Egil
saw that a woman who was ill was lying on the cross-bench at
the end of the room. Egil asked Thorfinn who this woman was
that suffered so much. Thorfinn said that she was called Helga
and was his daughter. 'She has had a long illness and is wasting
away. She never sleeps at night, and is not in her right mind.'
'Has anything been done for her illness?' said Egil. Thorfinn
said, 'Runes have been carved. The man who did that was a
farmer's son from not far away. After that it was much worse
than before. Do you, Egil, know anything about such illnesses?'
Egil said, 'Perhaps it won't get worse if I take a look.' When
Egil had finished eating he went to where the woman lay and
spoke to her. He told them to take her from the bed and to
spread clean sheets under her which was done. Then he went
through the bed on which she had been lying and he found a

piece of whalebone with runes carved on it. Egil read these and
then he erased the runes, scraping them into the fire. He burned
the entire piece of whalebone, and had all the bedclothes she
had used carried out into the wind. Then Egil said:

> No man should notch a rune—
> not without knowing how
> to control it. Carved lines
> can muddle meddling men.
> I counted ten crude runes
> cut in that piece of bone.
> They've done damage to your
> daughter's health all this time.[2]

Egil carved runes and placed them under the pillow in the bed
where she lay. It seemed to her as though she woke from sleep,
and then she said that she was well, though she was still weak.
Her father and mother were overjoyed. Thorfinn said that Egil
should receive all the aid that he thought he needed.

73

Egil said to his companions that he wished to get off on his
journey and not delay longer. Thorfinn had a son who was
called Helgi. He was a brave man. Both father and son offered
Egil their company on his journey through the wood. They said
that they knew for a fact that Bearded Armod had put six men
in wait for them in the wood, and it was likely that there would
be yet more in ambush in case the first lot missed. Thorfinn and
three others prepared themselves for the journey. Then Egil
spoke a verse:

> The fact is, if four men
> flank me in travel, then
> no six men would dare swing
> swords near where we're walking.
> But if I've eight brave men
> by me, I'll put to flight
> any twelve who turn up
> trying to stage a fight.[1]

Thorfinn and his men decided that they would go into the wood with Egil and then there were eight of them all told. When they came where an ambush lay ahead they saw the men there. But the men of Armod's household waiting there saw there were eight of them and did not bring themselves to attack. They disappeared into the wood. When Egil and his men came up where the spies had been they saw that things were not too safe. Egil said that Thorfinn's party should go back but they offered to go on. Egil would not have this and he told them to go home. They did so, turning back, while Egil and his men kept on their way, being now four, all told. When the day was well on, Egil and the others became aware that there were six men in the wood, and they had an idea that these must be the men of Armod's household. The spies ran up and attacked them, and they fought back, with the result that Egil brought down two men and the ones who were left ran off into the wood. Then Egil and his men went on their way, and there is nothing to tell until they emerged from the wood and took lodging beside it at the house of a farmer called Alf who was known as Alf the Rich. He was an old man, rich in possessions, but of a strange temper so that he could not maintain a household about him, only a few people. Egil was warmly welcomed there, and Alf talked to him openly. Egil asked in detail for news and Alf told whatever he knew. They spoke most about the earl and about the Norwegian king's messengers who had previously gone east to claim the tribute there. Alf's conversation showed him no friend to the earl.

74

Egil and his companions got ready for their journey early in the morning, and as they were leaving Egil gave Alf a fur jacket. Alf accepted the gift gratefully. 'This will make a coat for me'[1] and he asked Egil to visit him on his way back. They parted as friends and Egil went on his way, coming in the evening to the court of Earl Arnvid where he was most warmly welcomed. Seats were given to the travellers alongside the high seat. When Egil and his men had stayed there the night they put forward their errand to the earl, together with the Norwegian king's message that he wished to have all the tribute from Varmland which was in arrears since Arnvid had been put in charge. The earl said that he had paid all the tribute and handed it over to the king's messengers. 'But I do not know what they have done with it afterwards, whether taken it to the king or run off with it out of the country. However, since you carry the genuine tokens that the king has sent you, I will pay all that tribute which is due to him, putting it into your hands. But I will not take responsibility for what you do with it.' Egil and his men stayed there for a time, and before Egil left the earl paid them the tribute. Some of it was in silver, some in furs. Egil said to the earl as they parted, 'We shall now deliver to the king the tribute we have taken, but you are to know, Sir, that this is far less money than the king believes is due to him from here. Even then I have not taken into account that he will think you ought to pay compensation for his messengers whom, according to report, you have had killed.' The earl denied that this was true. They parted on this. When Egil had left, the earl called to him two brothers, both with the name Ulf, and he said, 'This big man, Egil, who was here for a time will, I suspect, not do us much good when he comes to the king. We can tell the way in which he will report our affairs to the king from the fact that he threw in my face such a matter as killing the king's men. Now you are to go after them and kill all of them to prevent their carrying this slander to the king. I think the best plan would be to ambush them in Eidskog forest. Have enough men with you to be certain that none of them escapes and that none of your men is killed by them.' The brothers got ready for the journey taking thirty men. They made for the wood where they knew every path. Then they kept a watch for Egil's journey. There were two ways through the wood. One went over a certain ridge, a stiff climb and a narrow path—that was the shorter route. The other was round the ridge where there were wide fens with tree trunks laid over them, and that was a narrow path to travel. Fifteen lay in wait at both places.

75

Egil went on until he arrived at Alf's house, and he was there for the night and well looked after. The next morning he got up before daylight and prepared for the journey. As they sat over breakfast the farmer Alf joined them. He said, 'You're getting ready early, Egil, but my advice would be not to hurry on your way. Rather keep a watch out for yourselves, for I think there are men lying in wait for you in the wood. I cannot supply men to go with you in strength, but I will make this offer. You can stay here with me until I am able to tell you that the wood is passable.' Egil said, 'This is mere nonsense. I will make my journey as already planned.' Egil and his men got ready to travel but Alf was against it, and told him to turn back if he found that the way had been trodden. He said that no-one had gone west through the wood since Egil went east 'unless those have gone whom I suspect are wanting to meet with you'. 'What do you think? How many will there be if it is as you say? We are not helpless even if there is some difference in numbers.' He said, 'I and men of mine went up into the wood and we found men's footprints. There must have been a lot of them all together, and the track went on into the wood. If you don't believe me go and look at the track, and turn back if it looks the way I say.' Egil went on his way. When they came to the road which led through the wood they saw the track of both men and horses. Then Egil's companions said that they should turn back. 'We will go on,' said Egil. 'It doesn't seem strange to me that men should have passed through Eidskog. It is a public road.' Then they went on and the track continued with a great number of footprints. When they came to where the roads separated the tracks split up as well, an equal number in each direction. Then Egil said, 'Perhaps Alf was right. We will get ourselves ready just as if we were expecting a confrontation.' Then Egil and his men threw off their cloaks and all loose clothing. They put these on the sledges. Egil had kept in his sledge a long coil of rope, for men who go on long journeys usually have extra rope with them, in case there should be a need for making harness. Egil took a large flat stone and put it in front of his chest and stomach. He made it fast there with the rope, winding it round and round right up to his shoulders. Then they went on their way.

Eidskog is like this: there is real forest right up to the settlements on both sides, but in the middle there are wide stretches of brushwood and scrub, and some places quite free of trees. Egil and his men took the shorter route which went over the ridge. They all had shields and helmets, and cutting and thrusting weapons. Egil went first. When they came to the ridge it was wooded lower down but treeless up on the rocks. When they reached the rocks seven men ran out of the wood and up to the rocks after them and shot at them. Egil and his men turned towards them and stood in a line across the path. Then others came down at them from the top of the ridge and threw stones at them from there, and that was by far more dangerous to them. Then Egil said, 'Now you get away among the rocks, and get what

shelter you can, and I will get up to the top.' They did so. When
Egil came up from the rocks there were eight men ahead of him
and they all went at him together and attacked. Yet there is
nothing to tell of this exchange, except that it ended in his killing
them all. Then he went on to the ridge and threw down stones.
Nothing could withstand that. Soon three Varmlanders lay
dead and four got away into the wood, and they were wounded
and battered. Then Egil and his men took their horses and
went on until they came over the ridge, but the Varmlanders
who had got away took the news to their company who were
beside the fen. They headed forward then by the lower path and
so were in front of Egil on the road. Ulf said to his companions,
'Now we must plan our attack on them, and trap them so that
they cannot run away.' He said, 'This is how things are. The path
runs alongside the ridge and the fen reaches up to it. Up above a
crag juts out and between crag and fen there is only the width of
the path. Some of us will go past the crag and attack them if they
press forward, and the rest shall be hidden here in the wood and
rush out after them as they come on round. We'll make sure
no-one gets away.' They did as Ulf said. Ulf and ten men with
him went forward round the rock. Egil and his men came
on their way knowing nothing of these plans until they reached
the narrow path. Then men with weapons ran out behind them.
Egil and his men turned round and defended themselves. Then
the others came out at them, the ones who had been beyond the
crag, and when Egil saw that he turned against them. There was
a quick exchange of blows and Egil felled some there on the path,
the others dropped back to where the ground was more level.
Egil followed, attacking. Ulf fell there, and in the end Egil
alone killed eleven men. Then he turned to where his companions
defended the path against eight men. Both sides were wounded.
When Egil came up the Varmlanders ran off at once, and the
wood was close by. Five of them got away, all badly wounded,
and three died there. Egil had many wounds, but only slight
ones. They continued now on their way. He bound up the
wounds of his companions and none of them was fatal. They
sat in their sledges and drove for what was left of the day. But
the Varmlanders who got away took their horses and made
east from the wood to the settlements where their wounds were
bandaged. They got an escort for themselves until they reached
the earl and reported their unlucky journey to him. They said
that both Ulfs had fallen and twenty-five men were dead.

'Only five got away alive, and even those are all wounded and battered.' The earl asked what the news was of Egil and his companions. They answered, 'We hardly know how much they were wounded, but they attacked us boldly enough. We retreated when we were eight and they were four. Five of us escaped into the wood and three perished. But as far as we could see Egil and his men were as fresh as ever.' The earl said that their journey had turned out disastrously. 'I could have stood the great loss of men if you had killed these Norwegians. But when they are west out of the wood and they tell this news to the king of Norway we can expect the harshest of terms from him.'

76

Egil went on until he came west out of the wood. They reached Thorfinn's house at evening and were warmly welcomed there. Egil's wounds and those of his companions were bandaged. They stayed there for several nights. Helga, the farmer's daughter, was on her feet and cured of her illness. She and all of them thanked Egil for that. They rested themselves and their horses there. The farmer's son who had carved runes for Helga lived not far away. It came out that he had asked for her in marriage but Thorfinn had not been willing to consent. Then he tried to seduce her but she was not willing. Then he thought he would carve love-runes for her, but he had not the skill, and what he had carved caused her illness. When Egil was ready for his journey Thorfinn and his son went with him on his way. There were ten or twelve of them in all. They stayed with them all that day on their guard against Armod and his men. But when the news spread that Egil and his company had fought and won against overwhelming odds in the wood, Armod did not think it likely that he could raise his shield against Egil. He sat at home and all his men with him. Egil and Thorfinn exchanged gifts at parting and promised each other friendship. Then Egil and his companions went on their way, and no news is reported of their journey before they reached Thorstein's home. Their wounds were healed by then. Egil stayed there till the spring, but Thorstein sent messengers to King Hakon taking the tribute to him which Egil had fetched from Varmland. When they came to the king they told him all the events which had taken place on Egil's journey, and handed over the tribute. The king thought he had evidence that what he had previously suspected must be true, that Earl Arnvid must have killed the two sets of messengers whom he had sent east. The king said that Thorstein might stay in the country and be at peace with him. The messengers took the road home and when they got back to Thorstein they told him that the king was pleased with the expedition and that Thorstein might now live in peace and friendship with the king.

King Hakon went east into Vik during the summer, and from there he set off on an expedition east into Varmland with many troops. Earl Arnvid fled, and the king took heavy payment from those farmers against whom he thought he had a case, judging from the reports of those who had gone for tribute. He put another earl in charge and took hostages from him and from the farmers. On that occasion King Hakon travelled widely throughout Vastergotland and subdued it, as his saga tells, and as we find in those poems that have been made about him. It is also told that he went to Denmark and made raids throughout the region. With his two ships he cleared twelve ships of the Danes. Then he gave the name of king and authority east in Vik to his nephew, Tryggvi Olafsson.

Egil got a merchant ship ready during the summer, and provided a crew for it. At their parting he gave to Thorstein the longship which he had brought from Denmark in the autumn. Thorstein gave fine gifts to Egil and they promised each other firm friendship. Egil sent messengers to Thord his kinsman in Aurland giving him authority to arrange about the properties Egil owned in Sogn and Hordaland, asking him to sell if there should be buyers. When Egil was ready for his journey and the wind was favourable they sailed out along the fjord and so took the northern route by Norway and then out to sea. They had very fair winds. They came from the open sea into Borgarfjord and Egil steered the ship in along the fjord and into harbour just below his farm. He had the cargo carried home and the ship brought ashore. Egil went home to his farm, and people were glad to see him. Egil stayed there that winter.

77

By the time Egil came back from his expedition the district had become fully settled. All the men who had taken land had died, but their sons or their grandsons were alive and were living in the area. Ketil Gufa came to Iceland when the land was already well-populated. He spent the first winter at Gufuskalar on

Rosmhvalanes. Ketil had come east across the sea from Ireland, and had a lot of Irish slaves with him. At that time all the lands on Rosmhvalanes were settled. Ketil decided to leave and go in to Nes, and he spent the second winter at Gufunes but did not settle there. Then he went in along Borgarfjord and spent the third winter at the place since called Gufuskalar, and the river where he kept his ship during the winter and which flows down to the sea there is called Gufua. Thord Lambason was living at Lambastadir. He was a married man with a son called Lambi, who had by this time grown to be a big and strong man among his contemporaries. The next summer when people were riding to the Assembly Lambi rode there also. At that time Ketil Gufa had gone west into Breidafjord to look there for a place to settle. In the meantime his slaves ran away. During the night they reached Thord's farm at Lambastadir, kindled fire in the buildings and burned Thord indoors together with his whole household. They broke into his stores and carried out goods and treasures. Then they drove up the horses, loaded them and went out to Alptanes. The next morning about the time of sunrise Lambi came home having seen the fire during the night. There were several of them together. He rode immediately in search of the slaves, and men from the farms rode to his support. When the slaves saw the pursuit they ran off leaving their loot unprotected. Some ran out into the Fens and some along by the sea until the fjord was ahead of them. Lambi and his companions pursued them and killed the one called Kori—which is why the place has since been called Koranes—but Skorri and Thormod and Svart dived in and swam from the land. Then Lambi and the others looked for boats and rowed in pursuit, finding Skorri on Skorraey and killing him there. Then they rowed out to Thormodssker and there they killed Thormod. The rock is named after him. They caught still more slaves whose names survive in the place-names. Afterwards Lambi settled at Lambastadir and was a good farmer. He was physically strong, but not an aggressive man. Ketil Gufa went west into Breidafjord, and settled in Thorskafjord. Gufudal and Gufufjord are named after him. He married Yr the daughter of Geirmund Blackskin. Vali was their son.

There was a man called Grim, the son of Sverting. He lived down below the Heath at Mosfell. He was rich and from a good family. His half-sister was Rannveig who was married to Thorodd Godi in Olfus. Their son was Skapti the Lawspeaker. Grim also

became lawspeaker later. He asked for Thordis in marriage, the
daughter of Thorolf, the niece and step-daughter of Egil. Egil
loved Thordis as deeply as he loved his own children. She was a
most beautiful woman. Since Egil knew that Grim was a man
of good birth and the match an excellent one, it was agreed on.
Thordis was married to Grim. Egil paid over on her behalf her
father's inheritance. She went home with Grim and they lived
at Mosfell for a long time.

78

There was a man called Olaf, the son of Hoskuld Dala-Kollsson
and of Melkorka, the daughter of the Irish king Myrkjartan.
Olaf lived at Hjardarholt in Laxardal in the Breidafjord dales
in the west. Olaf was an extremely wealthy man. He was the
most handsome in appearance of all the men then living in
Iceland, and a man of great quality. Olaf asked for Egil's
daughter Thorgerd in marriage. Thorgerd was beautiful, a very
tall woman, clever, rather proud, but usually equable. Egil knew
everything about Olaf and he recognized that this was a fine
match, so Thorgerd was married to Olaf. She went home with
him to Hjardarholt. Their children were Kjartan, Thorberg,
Halldor, Steindor, Thurid, Thorbjorg, and Bergthora who was
married to Thorhall Godi, the son of Oddi. Thorbjorg was
married first to Asgeir Knattarson and afterwards to Vermund
Thorgrimsson. Thurid married Gudmund Solmundarson. Their
sons were Hall and Bard the Fighter. Ozur Eyvindarson, the
brother of Thorodd in Olfus, married Egil's daughter Bera.
Egil's son Bodvar was by then fully grown. He was a young man
of great promise, handsome in looks, tall and strong just like
Egil or Thorolf had been at his age. Egil loved him very much,
and Bodvar was very attached to his father. One summer a ship
came into Hvita river and there was a great deal of trading there.
Egil bought a lot of wood and had it brought home by the men
of the household who made use of an eight-oared boat of
Egil's. On one occasion Bodvar asked if he could go with them,
and they let him do so. He made the journey to Vellir, with the
men, six of them all together on an eight-oared boat. When
they were ready to go back, high tide was late in the day, and
since they had to wait for it they set off late in the evening. A
violent south-westerly gale blew up and the ebbing tide flowed
against it. It became rough in the fjord as it often can. The end

came when the boat sank under them and they all perished. The
bodies were thrown up the next day. Bodvar's body came ashore
at Einarsnes, others came up on the south side of the fjord,
and the boat drifted there too. It was found near Reykjahamar.
Egil heard the news that day and rode at once to look for the
bodies. He found where Bodvar's corpse had been washed up,
lifted it, set it across his knees, and rode with it out to Digranes
to Skalla-Grim's mound. He had the mound opened, and he laid
Bodvar down there beside Skalla-Grim. Then the mound was
shut and this was not finished till sunset. Afterwards Egil rode
home to Borg and when he reached home he went immediately
to the locked room where he usually slept. He lay down and
bolted the door. No-one dared to speak to him. It is said that
when they put Bodvar down Egil was dressed like this: his
leggings were wound tightly round his legs, and he had on a red
fustian tunic, close-fitting at the top and laced at the sides. The
story goes that he swelled up so much that both tunic and
leggings tore apart. The next day Egil did not unlock his room.
He had taken no food nor drink. He lay there all that day and the
next night. No-one dared to speak to him. The third morning, as
soon as it was light, Asgerd sent a man on a horse—and he rode
as hard as he could west to Hjardarholt—to tell all of this news
to Thorgerd. He arrived in the middle of the afternoon, and told
Thorgerd also that Asgerd had sent word that she was to come
south to Borg as soon as she could. Thorgerd immediately had
a horse saddled for herself, and two men went with her. They
rode through the evening and the night until they reached Borg.
Thorgerd went into the hall at once. Asgerd greeted her and
asked whether they had eaten supper. Thorgerd said loudly, 'I
have not had supper, and I will have none till I am with Freyja.[1]
For myself I know no better plan than my father's. I will not live
after my father and my brother.' She went to the locked room and
called, 'Father, open the room. I want both of us to tread this
path.' Egil unlocked the door. Thorgerd went into the room and
let the door shut behind her. She lay down on the other bed which
was there. Then Egil said, 'My daughter, it is good that you wish
to go with your father. You have shown great love towards me.
Can it be expected that I should wish to live after such a grief?'
Then they were silent for a time. Egil said, 'Now, daughter, are
you chewing something?' 'I am chewing seaweed,' she said, 'in
the hope that it will make me worse. Otherwise I am afraid I
shall live too long.' 'Is it bad for you?' said Egil. 'Very bad,'

she said. 'Will you have some?' 'What does it matter?' he said.
A little later she called out asking for something to drink. She
was given a drink of water. Egil said, 'That is the effect of eating
seaweed, you grow more and more thirsty.' 'Do you want a
drink, Father?' she said. He accepted it and swallowed greedily.
It was in a horn. Thorgerd said, 'We have been cheated. It is
milk.' Egil bit a piece from the horn, all that he could get in his
teeth, and then threw the horn down. Thorgerd said, 'What plan
should we follow now? This purpose is foiled. Now, Father, I
should like us to live long enough for you to compose a dirge for
Bodvar, and I will carve it on wood, and after that we will die if
we think it right. I fear your son Thorstein will be slow to compose a poem for Bodvar, and it will not do for him to die un-
sung, since I am sure we shall not be sitting drinking at his wake.'
Egil said that it was unlikely he would be able to compose even
if he tried, 'but I will see,' he said. Egil had had a son called
Gunnar and he also had died a little earlier. This is how the
poem begins:

> My tongue, leaden with grief, lies
> Listless, will not stir to song.
> No poem moves in my mind,
> My heart is heavy with tears.
>
> So many tears! Such sadness!
> All my thoughts are dark with death.
> How can I breed song from such
> Blackness? How quicken the breath?
>
> Rain in my sad heart and rain
> Drenching the land. And the lash
> Of wind on water. On Nain's
> Rocks the sea splinters and howls.
>
> My lineage ends, like the storm-
> Felled maples of the forest.
> I have buried the bodies
> Of too many of my kin.
>
> I search for speech, for telling
> Praise of my long-dead parents.
> Words bud in my mind now, break,
> Blossom and blaze in green song.

The battering wave that broke
My father's line broke my life.
It smashed through as the wild sea
Breaches the widest sea-wall.

Ran, you have been hard on me.
My dearest friends are all dead.
And now you have slit that strand
Asgerd and I wove with love.

Oh, if a sword could heal my hurt,
Ægir would brew no more beer.
I'd fling myself at that fierce
Wave-raiser and his mate, Ran.

But it seems I have no strength
To kill my dear son's killer.
In the minds of men I move
A mere lonely, thwarted man.

The sea has stripped me of much.
Bad and bitter work, to count
Dead kin, since Bodvar stepped out
Of life and lit on new paths.

No stuff of evil there. Son,
You would have grown to goodness.
But Odin took you before
Your sapling strength was full-branched.

Others could say what they would,
To him my words mattered most.
At home my word was his law,
His support gave me new strength.

And then I think of the pain
A brother's death has brought me.
When the storms of battle swell
I think of him and think this:

Who now will stand by my side?
Who else will dare war's danger.
For without my friends I need
Planned flight when I fight hard men.

A hard task, to find much trust
In any man now, anywhere.
Brother betrays brother, buys
Rings with his bartered warm corpse.

Not thoughts of vengeance, but thoughts
Of gold goad men on these days.
Offer a man the money
And he'll lie, steal, slander, kill.

But nothing can now repay
Me for Bodvar's brutal death.
I can't sire another son
To stand for the son who's drowned.

And though men try to ease my
Pain, I prefer solitude.
Dear son, with Odin now, son
Of my wife, you've joined your kin.

But the cold and constant sea-
God has left me lonely, wrecked.
I cannot hold my head up
Such weariness drags it down.

When fever killed my first son
Bodvar had all my best love.
I watched him grow strong and straight,
And knew he was free of faults.

Such memories rise in my mind!
And then I think of Odin:
A branch was torn from my tree,
But Odin bore it away

To the high halls of the gods.
This god has been good to me.
Yet I trusted him too much
And more than was good for me,

For he did allow that death.
Still, I sacrifice to him—
Not eagerly, but because
He gave me my two great gifts

And they salve my heaviest hurts.
I owe my art to Odin,
So, too, my flaring temper,
Which makes sure foes of all frauds.

And though all things go hard now
And Hel stands on the headland,
I wait her coming calmly,
And gladly, and in good heart.[2]

Egil began to cheer up as the making of his poem progressed,
and when the poem was finished he recited it to Asgerd and
Thorgerd and his household. Then he got up from his bed and
sat in the high seat. He called that poem *Sonatorrek*, 'The
Wreck of Sons'. Afterwards Egil held a funeral feast for his
son according to the old custom. When Thorgerd went home
Egil sent her on her way with gifts. Egil lived at Borg for a long
time and became an old man. It is not recorded that he became
involved in litigation with anyone here in this country. Nor is
anything said about his fights or duels after he settled here in
Iceland. We are told that Egil did not leave Iceland after these
events which have just been spoken of, and the main reason was
that Egil could not go to Norway because of the charges which
the kings thought they had against him, as was told earlier. His
home was magnificent, for there was no shortage of money.
Besides he had the right temper for it.

King Hakon, Æthelstan's foster-son, ruled over Norway for a
long time, but in his later years the sons of Eirik came to Norway
and disputed the kingdom of Norway with King Hakon. They
fought battles against each other and Hakon always won. They
fought the last battle in Hordaland on the island of Stord at
Fitjar. King Hakon won the victory, and received too his death
wound. After that Eirik's sons took over the Norwegian kingdom. The chieftain Arinbjorn was with Harald Eiriksson and
became his counsellor, holding very great honours from him.
He was in control of the troops and the defence of the country.
Arinbjorn was a good leader and a victorious one. He had the
revenues from the Fjordane district. Egil Skalla-Grimsson heard
the news that there was a change of king in Norway, and that
Arinbjorn had gone to Norway, to his home, and was living in
great honour. Egil then made a poem about Arinbjorn and this
is how it begins:

My words leap to praise a prince,
Won't stir for the stingy ones.
There's much to say of great men,
Little to tell of liars.

For them I'm full of contempt.
I save my art for my friends.
I have gone from court to court,
Proud of being a poet.

Time was, I found myself faced
With a powerful king's keen rage.
I wrapped-up well in courage
And off I went to his home.

He kept *his* people wrapped-up
In fear of his fierce anger.
From his seat at York he ruled
Harshly over all his land.

You weren't safe looking him straight
In the eye. No kindness there!
It glittered like a snake's, grew
More snake-like the more you stared.

Yet I dared to deliver
My glittering gift from Odin
To him, poured out a poem
That all men there could drink down.

My prize for this looked far from
Fair to those who had heard me.
I got no gold from Eirik,
But my black-browed head for keeps—

Which I took, with its two eyes,
(Bright stones hidden by my brows!)
Plus my mouth, that cave of verse
Where I'd stored my ransom-song.

I had my two rows of teeth,
Tongue, even my ears. Not much,
Perhaps. But still, better
Than the gold that king could give.

But best of all, best of all
Men, my friend stood by my side.
Arinbjorn! Each act of his
Spells out his name, his nature.

It was this great man saved me
From Eirik's full enmity.
The king's friend he might be, but
He saw I came to no harm.

For I'd killed the king's son and
He hated me for that act.
Yet my friend found ways to heal
My hurt and the king's hurt, too.

I would be a faithless friend
And a poor poet were I
Not to speak out about so
Fine a friend as he has proved.

This cairn of words I construct
Must stand the test of the years:
A monument to my much-
Loved friend—this good and great man.

It's not hard to hew my thoughts
To words that will shape his fame.
They crowd my mind, while my tongue
Picks out the most polished ones.

And first let me praise my friend's
Great-souled, generous nature.
Yet most men know about this—
The news spreads wide as his hand.

And who'd not be struck by the way
His wealth's on offer to all?
For Frey and Njord, those friendly
Gods, gave him riches to spare.

Friends ride from the earth's far ends
Beneath the wide wind-scooped sky
To his house. And when they leave
They're laden with goods or gold.

For he draws all men to him,
This firm favourite among gods
And men, befriender of both
Strong and weak, silly and wise.

Few men can match his largesse
Though their wealth may well match his.
And since great men are so rare
They must meet many men's needs.

At Arinbjorn's house no man
Was spurned, or sneered at or mocked.
All men were safe there and all
Went away weighed down with gifts.

It's wealth alone that he won't
Give house-room to. No gold's safe
With him. Brooches, bracelets, rings—
Out they all go from his home!

And though his wealth's the harvest
Cropped from battle-fields, it takes
A great soldier to spoil his
Friends with his hard-earned spoils.

Such giving cannot go
Unanswered. My friend must take
Some payment for his friendship
Which was not wasted on me.

That is why I woke early
And set to work with my words,
And built a poem of praise,
A lasting gift for my friend.[3]

There was a man called Einar who was the son of Helgi, the son of Ottar, the son of Bjorn the Easterner who took land in Breidafjord. Einar was the brother of Osvif the Wise. While still young, Einar was tall and strong and an able man. He began to make up poems, even when he was young, and he was eager to learn. One summer at the General Assembly Einar went to the quarters of Egil Skalla-Grimsson and they began to talk. The conversation quickly turned to a discussion of poetry. Each of them found these discussions enjoyable. After that Einar got into the habit of often going for a talk with Egil, and a close friendship evolved. Einar had come back from his travels a short time before. Egil asked Einar a good deal about news from Norway and about his friends, also about those whom he thought he knew to be his enemies. He also asked in detail about the leading men. In his turn Einar asked Egil about those events which had happened earlier, Egil's journeys and his great deeds. Egil got pleasure from this talk and it ended well. Einar asked Egil what had been the occasion where he had been most severely tested and wanted him to tell the story. Egil said:

> Once I fought eight on my
> own. Eleven men, twice.
> We left the dead to wolves. I
> was the one man to kill.
> But they were bitter fights.
> Battering swords on shields
> we marred and split metal.
> My sword flickered flame-red.[4]

Egil and Einar promised friendship between them when they parted. Einar was abroad for a long time with notable men. Einar was a generous man and usually without money, but a fine man and of great quality. He was a retainer of Earl Hakon Sigurdarson. At that time in Norway there were constant hostilities and fighting between Earl Hakon and the sons of Eirik who fled alternately from the country. King Harald Eiriksson fell south in Denmark at Hals in Limfjord, and he had been betrayed. He was fighting against Harald Knutsson, known as Gold-Harald, and against Earl Hakon. The chieftain Arinbjorn, whose deeds were told earlier, also fell there with King Harald. When Egil learned of the death of Arinbjorn he said:

> The ranks dwindle, they die,
> these dear bright friends of mine
> who flared in fight and would
> fire my drink with delight.
> Where now to search for such
> silver-free men as those
> who beyond land-starred seas
> sweetened a poet's words?[5]

The poet Einar Helgason was called Skalaglam.[6] He composed
a long poem on Earl Hakon which is called *Vellekla* 'Lack of
Gold', and for a very long time the earl would not hear the
poem because he was angry with Einar. Then Einar said:

> While most men slept I made
> verses for this great prince.
> It was hard work and now I
> wish that I'd slept instead.
> Hakon seems to think that
> there's no verse worse than mine.
> To want his favour was
> wrong. I've wasted my time.[7]

And he also said:

> I'll seek out Sigvaldi
> since he won't turn me down.
> He's a fighter and he
> has time for fighting men.
> When I've found him he won't
> wave me away. I'll bring
> my shield to Sigvaldi's
> ship and fight on his side.[8]

The earl did not want Einar to go away, and he listened then to
the poem, and afterwards he gave Einar a shield which was a
very fine treasure. It depicted scenes from the old sagas, and
strips of gold framed the pictures, and it was set with gemstones.
Einar went to Iceland and to a lodging with his brother Osvif.
During the autumn Einar rode east, arriving at Borg and staying
there. Egil was not at home at the time, having gone into the
north of the district, but he was expected back. Einar waited
for him for three nights, but it was not usual to wait longer than
three nights on a visit. Einar got ready to leave, and when he
was ready he went to Egil's place and fastened above it the
precious shield, and told the household that he was giving the
shield to Egil. Then Einar rode away, and Egil arrived back the
same day. When he came up to his place he saw the shield and
asked who owned that fine thing. He was told that Einar Skalaglam had been there and had given him the shield. Then Egil
said, 'Damn him and his gifts! Does he want me to lie awake

making poems about his shield? Get my horse. I'll ride after
him and kill him.' He was told that Einar had ridden away early
in the morning: 'by now he will have come west to the Breidafjord dales.' Then Egil composed a long poem and this is how it
begins:

> It's time I found trim words
> to gloss this glittering shield.
> Now I've this gift, I need
> new-minted gifts of verse.
> But don't think that I'll lose
> the grip I keep on my
> would-be wandering wild
> words. They'll be on tight reins.[9]

Egil and Einar maintained their friendship while they both
lived. The story about the fate of the shield later on is that Egil
had it with him on a wedding visit when he went north into
Vidimyr with Thorkel Gunnvaldsson and Trefil and Helgi the
sons of Red-Bjorn. The shield was dropped into a whey-tub and
ruined. Egil had the mounts taken off later, and they contained
twelve ounces of gold.

79

Thorstein Egilsson when he grew up was more handsome in
appearance than anyone, with white hair and a fair skin. He
was tall and strong, but no match for his father. Thorstein was
wise and peaceable, gentle and the most controlled of men.
Egil was not very fond of him. Thorstein too was not greatly
attached to Egil, but Asgerd and Thorstein had a close affection
for each other. Egil was beginning to age very much by then.
One summer when Thorstein was riding to the General Assembly
Egil stayed at home. Before Thorstein left home he and Asgerd
watched for their opportunity and took from the chest Egil's
silk clothes, Arinbjorn's gift, and Thorstein took them to the
Assembly. When he wore them going in procession to the Law
Rock at the Assembly they trailed on the ground and became
soiled at the bottom. When he came home Asgerd put away the
robes where they had been before. Very much later when Egil
opened the chest he found that the robes were soiled, and tried

to find out from Asgerd how this had happened. She told him
the truth about it. Then Egil said:

> This milk-sop for my heir!
> My inheritor ought
> not to cheat or try to
> trick me while I live.
> He would have done well to
> wait until I was in
> the soil and a stone mound
> stood where my old bones lay.[1]

Thorstein married Jofrid the daughter of Gunnar Hlifarson.
Her mother was Helga, the daughter of Olaf Feilan, sister of
Thord Gellir. Jofrid had previously been married to Thorodd
the son of Tungu-Odd. Soon after this Asgerd died. After that
Egil left his home, handing it over to Thorstein, and he went
south to Mosfell to his kinsman Grim, for he loved his step-
daughter Thordis more than anyone else living.

One summer a ship came out to Leiruvag, and the man in
charge of it was called Thormod. He was a Norwegian, a man
of Thorstein Thoruson's household. He brought a shield which
Thorstein had sent to Egil Skalla-Grimsson, and it was a very
fine possession. Thormod brought the shield to Egil, and he
received it with gratitude. The next winter Egil made up a long
poem about the gift of the shield, which he called *Berudrapa*,
'Shield-Song'. It begins like this:

> Seafarer, may the sweet
> songs of the god of verse
> drench your mind, and may your
> men's lips be stilled by art.
> For in the far and rich
> fields of Norway the seeds
> my song sows will ripen,
> so men may taste its fruit.[2]

Thorstein Egilsson lived at Borg. He had two illegitimate sons
Hrifla and Hrafn, but when he was married he and Jofrid had
ten children. One of their daughters was Helga the Fair over
whom Hrafn the Poet and Gunnlaug Snake-Tongue quarrelled.
Their eldest son was Grim, the next Skuli, the third Thorgeir,

the fourth Kollsvein, the fifth Hjorleif, the sixth Halli, the seventh Egil, the eighth Thord. The daughter who married Thormod Kleppjarnsson was called Thora. From Thorstein's children are descended a great progeny and many notable men. All those who are descended from Skalla-Grim are called the family of the Myramen, the men of the Fens.

80

Onund Sjoni lived at Anabrekka while Egil was living at Borg. Onund Sjoni married Thorgerd the daughter of Bjorn the Fat from Snæfellsstrond. The children of Onund and his wife were Steinar and Dalla who married Ogmund Galtason. Their sons were Thorgils and Kormak. When Onund became old and his sight poor he handed over his farm. His son Steinar took it on. Father and son were very rich. Steinar was a big man, physically strong, ugly, hunch-backed, long of leg and short of body. He was a very quarrelsome and aggressive man, difficult, courageous, full of energy. When Thorstein Egilsson had the farm at Borg he and Steinar were soon on bad terms. South of Hafslœk lies a fen called Stakksmyr. Water covers it in winter, but in spring when the ice melts, there is such good grazing for cattle there that it was counted the equivalent of a stack of the best hay. In the old days Hafslœk set the land boundary there, but in the spring Steinar's cattle frequently went on Stakksmyr when they were driven over to Hafslœk, and Thorstein's servants complained about it. Steinar took no notice of this, and the first summer things went on without any disturbance. The next spring when Steinar kept on with the grazing, Thorstein had a discussion with him, nevertheless talking calmly, and asking Steinar to restrict his cattle-grazing to the old limits. Steinar said the cattle would go where they liked. He spoke about it all rather arrogantly and he and Thorstein had some hard words. Then Thorstein had the cattle driven back out to the fens beyond Hafslœk, and when Steinar knew of this he put his slave Grani to stay with the cattle on Stakksmyr, and he stayed there all the time. This was towards the end of the summer. All the meadowland south of Hafslœk was grazed over by then. One day Thorstein happened to have gone up on the great rock at Borg to look around. He saw where Steinar's cattle were. It was late in the day, and he went out into the fens. He saw that the cattle had come a long way up the valley-bottom. Thorstein ran out across the fens and when Grani saw this he drove the cattle ruthlessly until they got to the byre. Thorstein followed on, and he and Grani met in the gateway. Thorstein killed him there. The place is in the home-field enclosure, and has since been called Grana-hlid, Grani's gateway. Thorstein pulled part of the field wall down on Grani and in that way covered his corpse. Then Thorstein went home to Borg, and the women who went to the byre found Grani where he was lying. At that they went back to the house and told the news to Steinar. Steinar buried him up in the hills, and afterwards put another slave to go with the cattle. His name is not remembered. Thorstein behaved as if he did not know about the grazing for the rest of the summer. The next news about this was that Steinar went out to Snæfellsstrond for the first part of the winter, and stayed there for a time. He saw a slave called Thrand who was bigger and stronger than anyone. Steinar wanted to buy this slave, offering a great deal of money for him. The slave's owner valued him at three marks of silver, putting the price half as much again as that of an ordinary slave. The bargain was made and Steinar took Thrand home with him. When they reached home Steinar talked to Thrand. 'This is the way things are. I want you to work for me, but all the jobs are already assigned. I will give you a task which will be no bother to you. You are to watch over my cattle. I think it important that they are properly looked after for pasturing. I do not wish you to accept anyone's judgment but your own about the best pasture in the fens. If you have not the sense and the strength to stand up against any of Thorstein's servants, then I am no judge of men.' Steinar put an enormous axe into Thrand's hand, the edge measuring nearly half a yard, and razor-keen. 'I have the idea, Thrand,' said Steinar, 'that it's by no means clear how highly you'll respect Thorstein's rank if the two of you meet face to face.' Thrand answered, 'I don't know that I owe any duty to Thorstein, and I think I know what task you have given me. You will not think you made a great investment in me. Still I think I have a good chance whatever the circumstances if Thorstein and I are put to the test.' Then Thrand took over the care of the cattle. He understood, in spite of not being there long, where Steinar had had his cattle kept, and Thrand watched over the cattle on Stakksmyr. When Thorstein knew of this he sent a servant to see Thrand, with instructions to tell him the boundaries between Thorstein's land and Steinar's. When the servant met Thrand he gave him his message, telling him to keep the cattle somewhere else, and saying that where the cattle were now was the land of Thorstein Egilsson. Thrand said, 'I don't care whose land it is. I will take the cattle where I think is the best pasture.' Then they parted. The servant went home and told Thorstein the slave's answer. Thorstein made no further move, but Thrand began to stay with the cattle night and day.

81

One morning at daybreak Thorstein got up and went up on the rock. He saw where Steinar's cattle were, then went out on to the fens until he reached them. There is a wooded hillock near Hafslœk, and Thrand was sleeping up on this hillock. He had taken his shoes off. Thorstein, having a smallish axe in his hand and no other weapon, went up on the hillock. Thorstein poked at Thrand with the axe-haft, telling him to wake up. He leapt up quickly and ready, seized his axe with both hands, and swung it up. He asked what Thorstein wanted. He said, 'I wish to tell you that I own this land and that you have the grazing on the other side of the stream. It is not surprising that you don't know the boundary here.' Thrand said, 'It doesn't matter to me who owns the land. I will let the cattle go wherever they find best.' 'It seems probable,' said Thorstein, 'that I, rather than Steinar's slaves, will want to have the control of my land.' Thrand said, 'Thorstein, you are much more stupid than I thought, if you want to get your night's lodging under my axe, and will risk the shame of it. It looks to me as if it can be reckoned that I have twice your strength, and I am ready to use it. And my weapon is better than yours.' Thorstein said, 'I will take this risk if you do nothing about the grazing. I expect there is as much difference in our luck as there is in the justice of our causes.' Thrand said, 'Now, Thorstein, you can see whether I have any fear of your threats.' Whereupon Thrand sat down and tied on his shoe, and Thorstein swung up his axe with vigour and brought it down on Thrand's neck so that the head fell forward on to his breast. Thorstein piled stones over him and covered his corpse, then went home to Borg. That day Steinar's cattle took their time in coming home, and when they could no longer be expected, Steinar saddled his horse. He was fully armed. He rode south to Borg, and when he came there he found men to speak with. He asked where Thorstein was, and they told him he was indoors. Steinar asked if Thorstein would come out, saying he had business with him. When Thorstein heard this he picked up his weapons and went out to the door. He asked Steinar the reason for his visit. 'Have you killed my slave, Thrand?' said Steinar. 'Certainly,' said Thorstein. 'You need not think anyone else did.' 'Then I see that you must think you have a strong arm to defend your land, since you have killed two of my slaves. But I do not count it a great exploit. In future I will offer you a far finer opportunity if you want to defend your land so zealously. From now on I shall not rely on other men to drive the cattle, and you can be sure of this, that the cattle will be on your land both night and day.' 'Look,' said Thorstein. 'Last summer I killed your slave, the one you put to pasture the cattle on my land, and after that I let you have the grazing as you wanted up to the winter. Now I have killed another of your slaves for you, the case against him the same as against the first. Now you can have the grazing for this summer as you wish. But next summer if you graze my land, and put men on the job of driving your cattle here, then I will again kill for you every man that accompanies the cattle, even though you come yourself. I will do so every summer, so long as you keep on with this behaviour over the grazing.' Then Steinar rode away home to Anabrekka, and a little later he rode up to Stafaholt. At that time Einar was living there. He was a man of rank.[1] Steinar asked him for his support and offered him money for it. Einar said, 'My help will not be much use to you unless other important men support the case.' After that Steinar rode up into Reykjardal to find Tungu-Odd, asked him for help, and offered him money for it. Odd accepted the money and promised his help, namely that he would side with Steinar in effecting a lawsuit against Thorstein. After this Steinar rode home. In the spring Odd and Einar made the journey with Steinar to issue the summons, and they had a great body of men with them. Steinar summoned Thorstein for the killing of his slaves, declaring the penalty of three years' outlawry for each killing, which was accepted for the killing of a man's slaves when payment for the slave had not been made within three days. Two sentences of three year outlawry equalled a sentence of full outlawry.[2] Thorstein did not issue any return summons, and a little later he sent men south to Nes. They came to Grim at Mosfell and reported these events there. Egil did not show much interest, but in private he asked detailed questions about the dealings

between Thorstein and Steinar, and also about those men who
had given Steinar support in this suit. Then the messengers
went back, and Thorstein was pleased with their journey.
Thorstein Egilsson took a great crowd of men to the spring
Assembly. He arrived a day ahead of the others, and he and
those of his men who had shelters there put roofs over them.[3]
When they had done this Thorstein put his men to work building
big walls for further accommodation, and then he had that
roofed. It was far bigger than any other shelter there, but there
was no-one in it. Steinar rode to the Assembly with a large
following. Tungu-Odd was in control of the men, and a great
number it was. Einar from Stafaholt was also well-accompanied.
They roofed over their shelters. The Assembly was crowded.
Men were pleading their cases. Thorstein offered no compensation on his own behalf, but gave this answer to those men who
claimed compensation, that he intended to wait for a verdict.
He added that he found those suits trivial which Steinar brought
forward over the killing of his slaves. He held that Steinar's
slaves had given provocation enough. Steinar behaved arrogantly over his law-suits. To him his charges seemed legal, and
his support enough to implement the law. For this reason he was
prepared to push his case. That day people went to the Assembly
place and men stated their cases, and in the evening the courts
would be open for the law-suits. Thorstein was there with his
men. He had the most say in the conduct and procedure at the
Assembly because it had been so when Egil held the rank and the
authority. Both sides were fully-armed. People could see from
the Assembly that a band of men rode below along Gljufra
river with their shields gleaming. As they rode to the Assembly
a man was riding in front wearing a blue cloak. He had a gilded
helmet on his head, a shield ornamented with gold at his side,
in his hand a sharp spear, the socket inlaid with gold. He
was girded with a sword. Egil Skalla-Grimsson had arrived
with eighty men, all well-armed, just as if they were prepared for
battle. That company was a choice one. Egil had brought with
him the best farmers' sons from the Headlands in the south, the
ones whom he thought good fighters. Egil rode with his band
to that shelter which Thorstein had had roofed and which had
so far stood empty. They dismounted. When Thorstein knew
his father had come he went out to meet him with all his men
and welcomed him warmly. Egil and his men had their stuff
brought in to their quarters, and the horses turned out to graze.

When this was organized Egil and Thorstein went with their whole company up to the Assembly place, and sat where they usually did. Then Egil stood up and said loudly, 'Is Onund Sjoni here at the Assembly?' Onund said he was there, 'and I am delighted that you have come, Egil. Your arrival will greatly improve the situation in the cases brought by the men here.' 'Is it by your advice that your son Steinar brings a law-suit against my son Thorstein, and has brought together all these men to make Thorstein an outcast?' 'It is not of my choosing,' said Onund, 'that they are unreconciled. I have spoken much on the subject asking Steinar to be reconciled with Thorstein, for as far as I am concerned on every occasion your son Thorstein has been a man I would not wish to dishonour. The reason for that is the old and close friendship which has been between us, Egil, since we two were brought up here as neighbours.' Egil said, 'It will soon be clear whether you say this in sincerity or hypocrisy, though I think the second less likely. I remember the time when it would have seemed unlikely to either of us that we would be prosecuting law-suits against each other, and not preventing our sons from acting as stupidly as I have heard seems probable here. To me it seems advisable that while the two of us are alive and so closely concerned with their quarrels, that we ourselves take over this case and settle it, not letting these men Tungu-Odd and Einar urge on our sons like horses. From now on let them find some other way of increasing their income than this sort of thing.' Then Onund stood up and said, 'You speak rightly, Egil. It is not fitting for us to be at an Assembly where our sons are quarrelling. Neither must we have the shame of being so feeble as not to reconcile them. Now, Steinar, I wish you to hand this case over to me, and let me proceed with it as I like.' Steinar said, 'I am not sure whether I want to throw away my law-suits. I have already provided myself with the help of important men. The only outcome of my case that I wish for is one that contents Odd and Einar.' Then Odd and Steinar had a talk together. Odd said, 'Steinar, I will provide the help for you that I promised to give you, either in law, or to produce such a conclusion as you are willing to accept. How your case turns out if Egil is to judge it will be your own affair.' Then Onund said, 'I have no need of Odd's tongue-roots. From him I have received neither good nor ill, but Egil has done many good things for me. I trust him far more than the others, and I am going to take charge of this. It will be better

for you not to have us all against you. I have so far been in
control for both of us, and so it is going to be now.' 'You are
full of energy in this suit, Father, and I think that we shall
often be sorry for it.' Then Steinar handed over the case to
Onund, and then he was to prosecute or reconcile it as the laws
allowed. As soon as Onund had control of these suits, he went to
find father and son, Egil and Thorstein. He said, 'Now Egil, it
is my wish that only you shall have the say and the deciding
voice in this matter, just as you like, because I trust you the best
to take charge of these cases of mine and all others.' Then Onund
and Thorstein shook hands and named their witnesses, and
along with the naming of witnesses, that Egil Skalla-Grimsson
should by himself decide the outcome of this case as he wished,
without reservation, there at the Assembly, and that was the
end of these law-suits. Men went home to their shelters. Thorstein had three oxen taken to Egil's and had them slaughtered
for his food supplies during the Assembly. When Tungu-Odd
and Steinar came home to their shelters Odd said, 'Now Steinar,
you and your father have brought our suits to an end. I now
count myself free, Steinar, from that help which I promised you,
however Egil's settlement turns out for you, for it was agreed
between us that I should give you such help that either you
were successful in your suits, or the cases ended in a way to
satisfy you.' Steinar said that Odd had helped him fully and
honourably, and their friendship would in future be much
firmer than before. 'I will declare that you are free of me in
the matter where you had obligation.' In the evening the courts
went out, and there is no report of anything noteworthy
happening.

82

Egil Skalla-Grimsson went to the Assembly place the next day,
Thorstein and all their company with him. Onund and Steinar
also came there, and Einar had come with his men and Tungu-
Odd. When people had put forward their law-suits Egil stood up
and said this, 'Are Onund and Steinar, father and son, near
enough to know what I say?' Onund said that they were there.
'Then I will declare the settlement of terms between Steinar and
Thorstein. I begin the case at the point when Grim, my father,
came here to this land, and took here all the land round Myrar,
and widely throughout the district, himself settling at Borg and

determining the land-ownership attached to it. He gave land beyond to his friends where they subsequently settled. He gave to Ani a farm at Anabrekka where Onund and Steinar have lived up to now. We all know, Steinar, where the land boundaries are between Borg and Anabrekka, that Hafslœk divides them. You did not, Steinar, act out of ignorance when you used Thorstein's land for pasture, and brought his property under your control, and thought that he would be so weak a representative of his family that he would endure your infringements on his rights. You, Steinar, and you, Onund, both know that Ani received the land from my father Grim. Thorstein killed two slaves of yours. It is obvious to everyone that they have fallen through their own actions and they are not men to be atoned for. Indeed even if they were free men they would still not be men to be atoned for. And, Steinar, because you thought you would rob my son Thorstein of his land-rights, those which he took over with my authority, and I took as inheritance from my father, you shall lose your land at Anabrekka and not be paid for it. In addition you shall not have farm nor living-quarters south of the Langa river, and you shall be away from Anabrekka before the removal days[1] have passed. Immediately after these days you can be killed with impunity by any of those men who wish to give help to Thorstein, if you will not go away, or you refuse to do any part of that which I have stated.' When Egil sat down Thorstein named witnesses to his arbitration. Then Onund Sjoni said, 'Men will say, Egil, that this arbitration which you have laid down and declared is somewhat unfair. There is this to be said about me, that I have done my utmost to prevent their quarrels, but from now on I shall not hesitate to injure Thorstein in any way I can.' 'This is what I think,' said Egil, 'that things will be worse for both of you, father and son, the longer our dealings continue. I thought that you would know, Onund, that I have held my own against men such as you and your son. And Einar and Odd who have taken so much upon themselves in this case have received here due honours.'

83

Thorgeir Blund, Egil's nephew, was there at the Assembly and he had given considerable help to Thorstein in these law-suits. He asked Egil and Thorstein to give him some land out there in the Fens. Previously he had lived to the south of the Hvita river down below Blundsvatn. Egil took a favourable view of this and encouraged Thorstein to let him come there. They established Thorgeir at Anabrekka, and Steinar moved his farm out across the Langa river and settled at Leirulœk. Egil rode home south to Nes, father and son parting on friendly terms.

There was a man with Thorstein who was called Iri, a faster runner than anyone and with better eyesight than most. He was a foreigner and a freedman of Thorstein's, but still he had charge of the sheep, especially to take the barren sheep up on the high ground in the spring and down to the pens in the autumn. After the removal days Thorstein had the barren sheep collected, those still remaining in the spring, and intended to have them driven to the high ground. Iri was driving the sheep while Thorstein and his servants rode up to the hills, eight of them all together. Thorstein was having a wall built across Grisartunga between Langavatn and Gljufra river, and had many men there during the spring. When Thorstein had looked at his servants' work he rode home, and when he came past the Assembly place Iri came running to meet him, and said that he wished to speak to Thorstein alone. Thorstein said that his companions should ride on while they talked. Iri told Thorstein that he had gone up on Einkunnir that day to see to the sheep, 'and I saw,' he said, 'in the wood above the winter-route, the glitter of twelve spears and some shields'. Thorstein said loudly so that his companions heard him directly, 'Why is he so eager to see me that I can't ride home? Still, Olvald will think it unfair if I refuse to talk with him when he's ill.' Iri ran off as hard as he could to the hills. Thorstein said to his companions, 'I'm afraid it will lengthen our journey if first we have to ride south to Olvaldsstad. Olvald sends me word that I must see him. If the matter is of importance Olvald won't think my visit is over-rewarding him for the ox he gave me last autumn.' Then Thorstein and his men rode south across the fens beyond Stangarholt, and so south to the Gufua river and down along the river on the bridle-path. When he came down from Vatn they saw to the south of the river a lot of cattle and a man with them. He was one of Olvald's servants. Thorstein asked if things were well there. He said that things were well, and that Olvald was in the wood at the tree-cutting. 'Then,' said Thorstein, 'you are to tell him that he must come to Borg if he has important business with me. I am going to ride home.' And so he did. It was learned afterwards that Steinar Sjonason had been sitting up on Einkunnir that day with eleven men. Thorstein behaved as if he had not heard this, and things were quiet.

84

There was a man called Thorgeir, a kinsman and close friend of Thorstein's. At that time he was living at Alptanes. It was Thorgeir's habit each autumn to hold an autumn feast. Thorgeir went to see Thorstein Egilsson and invited him to visit him. Thorstein promised to come and Thorgeir went home. On the set day, still four weeks before winter, Thorstein got ready for the journey. Two of his household and a Norwegian went with Thorstein. Thorstein had a son called Grim who was then ten years old, and he also went with Thorstein. There were the five of them all together and they rode out to the waterfall and crossed the Langa river, then out, as the road took them, to Aurrida river. Beyond the river Steinar and Onund and servants of theirs were on a job, and when they recognized Thorstein they ran for their weapons, and then followed Thorstein and his men. When Thorstein saw Steinar was following, they rode out from Langaholt. There is a high narrow hill there. Thorstein's company dismounted and went up on the hill. Thorstein said that the boy Grim was to go into the wood and not be found with them. As soon as Steinar came to the hill they attacked Thorstein and a fight took place. Steinar's men were six adults, and as a seventh, Steinar's ten-year-old son. Men from other farms at work on the meadows saw all this and ran up to separate them. When they had been separated, both Thorstein's servants had fallen, and one of Steinar's men, others being wounded. When they were separated Thorstein looked to see where Grim was and found him. Grim was badly wounded, and Steinar's son lay dead beside him. When Thorstein got on his horse, Steinar called out to him saying, 'Are you running off, Thorstein the White?' Thorstein said, 'You will run further before a week has passed.' Then Thorstein rode out over the fens keeping with him the boy Grim, and when they came out to a hillock there the boy died, and they buried him there on that hillock. It is called Grimsholt, and the hill where they fought is called Orustuhvall, the hill of the battle. Thorstein rode to Alptanes in the evening as he had intended and stayed at the feast for three nights, then prepared for the journey home. Men offered to go with him but he did not want it. The two of them rode together. On the day when

Steinar expected Thorstein to be riding home he rode out along the coast. When he reached the sandy banks down below Lambastadir he stayed there on the slopes. He had the sword called Skrymir, the best of all weapons. He stood there in the sand-hills with drawn sword, and kept watch in the direction where he saw Thorstein riding out over the sands. Lambi lived at Lambastadir and saw how Steinar was acting. He left the house, went down to the bank, and when he reached Steinar, seized him from behind, under the arms. Steinar tried to throw him off. Lambi held on and they rolled down the sand-hill. At the same time Thorstein and his companion were riding along the lower road. Steinar had been riding his stallion, and now it galloped down by the sea. Thorstein and his friend saw it and were surprised, for they had not known about Steinar's journey. Then Steinar pulled across to the edge of the bank, for he did not see that Thorstein had ridden past. When they came to the edge Lambi pushed him down from the hill, a move for which Steinar was not prepared. He sprawled down on to the sand, and Lambi ran home. When Steinar got to his feet he ran after Lambi, but when Lambi reached the door he ran in and slammed the door shut. Steinar struck at him and the sword stuck fast in the edge-timbers.[1] They parted there. Steinar went off home on foot. But when Thorstein came home he sent a servant the next day out to Leirulœk to tell Steinar that he should move his farm to the far side of Borgarhraun, or, as an alternative, Thorstein would demonstrate against Steinar that he was the more powerful, 'and then the choice of escape will no longer be open'. Steinar got ready to go out to Snæfellsstrond and established his farm at a place called Ellidi, and in this way his dealings with Thorstein Egilsson ended.

Thorgeir Blund lived at Anabrekka. He was an aggressive neighbour to Thorstein in every way he could manage. One time when Egil and Thorstein met, they had a long discussion about their kinsman Thorgeir Blund, and all their talk went the same way. Then Egil said:

> It took a trick of words
> to get me Steinar's land.
> I thought then I'd worked for
> Thorgeir's needs, and was pleased.
> But my sister's son has
> spoilt the promise of his

fine youth. He does harm now.
How strange he should so change![2]

Thorgeir Blund left Anabrekka and went south into Flokadal, because Thorstein did not think he could get on with him though he tried to be tolerant. Thorstein was no trickster, but a just man, not encroaching on others. Still, he held his own if other men challenged him, and most men found it far from easy to contend against him. Odd was at that time a chieftain in Borgarfjord south of the Hvita river. He was the temple-priest and controlled the temple to which all men paid dues this side of Skardsheid heath.

85

Egil Skalla-Grimsson grew to be an old man, and in old age he found movement difficult, and both his hearing and sight failed him. His legs became stiff too. At that time Egil was at Mosfell with Grim and Thordis. One day Egil walked outside by the wall, and he tripped and fell. Some women seeing that laughed and said, 'There's no hope for you, Egil, now you fall by yourself.' Then the farmer Grim said, 'The women did not jeer at us so much when we were younger.' Then Egil said:

> I dodder, shake, fall down,
> dumped on my bald skull. My
> prick's like a lamb's tail, use-
> less as my dead-man's ears.[1]

Egil became completely blind. One day in winter when the weather was cold Egil went to the fire to get warm. The house-keeper went on about the great marvel it was that a man such as Egil had been should get under their feet, so that they could not do their work. 'Be reasonable,' said Egil, 'even if I am getting cooked by the fire, we can make room for both of us.' 'Get up,' she said, 'and go to your seat, and let us do our work.' Egil got up and went to his seat and said:

> Blind, I sat by the fire,
> begged that woman's pardon.
> To think that I've come to
> this grovelling, this end!

> Æthelstan gave me gold!
> Great men were my friends! Time
> was that an angry king
> approved my apt, skilled words.[2]

Another time when Egil went to the fire to get warm, a man asked him if his feet were cold, and told him not to put them too near the fire. 'As you say,' said Egil, 'but now that I cannot see, it is not so easy to steer my feet. Blindness is very dreary.' Then Egil said:

> I've lain here a
> long time now, old,
> cold and lacking
> a king's good care.
> My feet freeze up
> like widows' beds
> while these cold crones
> won't give me warmth.[3]

In the early days of Hakon the Great Egil Skalla-Grimsson was in his eighties, and at that time still strong, apart from his blindness. One summer when people were getting ready for the Assembly, Egil asked Grim if he could ride to the Assembly with him. Grim was reluctant. When Grim and Thordis had a talk with each other Grim told her what Egil had asked. 'I want you to get to know what is at the back of this request.' Thordis went to have a talk with her uncle Egil. Egil's greatest pleasure at this time was to talk with her. When she found him she asked, 'Is it true, Uncle, that you want to ride to the Assembly? I wish you would tell me what you are planning.' 'I will tell you,' he said, 'what I have thought. I intend to take with me to the Assembly those two chests which King Æthelstan gave me. They are both full of English silver. I intend to have the chests carried to the Law Rock at the time when it is most crowded. I intend to sow the silver, and I shall be very surprised if they all share it fairly between them. I hope that there will be kicking and punching, and it might turn out eventually that the whole of the Assembly is fighting.' Thordis said, 'It seems a splendid idea to me, and will be remembered as long as there are people in the land.' Then Thordis went to Grim and told him Egil's plan. 'We cannot let him carry out such a dreadful plot.' When Egil had a

talk with Grim about travelling to the Assembly Grim firmly
dissuaded him, and during the Assembly Egil stayed at home. He
was not pleased about this and frowned a lot. Mosfell had a
shieling for summer-pasture and Thordis was at the shieling
during the Assembly. One evening at Mosfell when people were
getting ready for bed, Egil called to him two of Grim's slaves.
He told them to get a horse for him. 'I wish to go to the baths.'
When Egil was ready he went out, and he had with him his
chests of silver. He mounted his horse and was last seen riding
down the meadow past a bank which was there. In the morning
when the men were getting up they saw that Egil was wandering
around the hill to the east of the farm and leading his horse.
They went and fetched him home. But there was no return of the
slaves nor the treasure-chests, and there are many guesses where
Egil has hidden his money. To the east of the farm at Mosfell a
ravine runs down the hill, and it has been noticed that in rapid
thaws the water comes flooding down, and afterwards when the
waters have subsided English coins have been found in the
ravine. Some men guess that Egil must have hidden his money
there. Below the meadow at Mosfell are wide fens, incredibly
deep. Many hold it for a fact that Egil will have thrown his
money in there. To the south of the river are hot springs, and not
far from them great pits in the earth, and some people think
that Egil will have hidden his money there, for grave-fire is often
seen in that direction. Egil said that he had killed Grim's slaves,
and also that he had hidden his money, but where he had hidden
it he told no-one. Egil became ill the next autumn, and his death
followed. When he was dead Grim had him dressed in good
clothes. Then he had him taken down to Tjaldanes and made a
mound there. Egil was laid in the mound with his weapons and
clothing.

86

Grim at Mosfell was baptized when Christianity became the
law in Iceland. He had a church built there. Men say that
Thordis had had Egil moved to the church, and an indication
of this is that when a church was built at Mosfell later, and that
church which Grim had built at Hrisbru was pulled down, the
churchyard was dug up. They found a man's bones under the
altar. They were bigger by far than the bones of other men.
People thought they could tell from the stories of old men that

these would be the bones of Egil. The priest Skapti Thorarinsson was present—an intelligent man. He picked up Egil's skull and put it in the churchyard. The skull was incredibly big, and the weight of it seemed even more unbelievable. The skull was all wrinkled outside like a harp-shell. Skapti next wished to discover the thickness of the skull. He picked up a good big hand-axe, swung it with one hand as hard as possible, and struck the skull with the back of the axe, intending to break it. Where it struck, the skull whitened but was neither dented nor broken. We can see from this that while flesh and skin covered it such a skull would not easily be injured by the blows of little men. The bones of Egil were laid down at the outer edge of the churchyard at Mosfell.

87

Thorstein Egilsson received baptism when Christianity came to Iceland, and had a church built at Borg. He was a firm believer and followed good customs. He became an old man, died of illness, and was buried at Borg in the church which he had built. A great kin is descended from Thorstein, many notable men and many poets. These are the Myramen, the men of the Fens, as are all those who are of Skalla-Grim's line. For a long time in that family the men continued to be strong and good fighters, some of them men of wisdom. The big difference is that into that family the finest-looking men in Iceland have been born—such were Thorstein Egilsson and Kjartan Olafsson, the son of Thorstein's sister, and Hall Gudmundarson, as well as Helga the Fair, Thorstein's daughter, over whom Gunnlaug Snake-Tongue and Hrafn the Poet quarrelled—but most of the Myramen were extremely ugly. Thorgeir, the son of Thorstein, was the strongest among his brothers, but Skuli was the biggest. He lived at Borg after the time of his father. Skuli spent a long time on viking raids. He was in the prow of Earl Eirik's ship Jarnbard, when King Olaf Tryggvason fell. Skuli fought in seven battles while on his viking expeditions (and he seemed to everyone a great and fearless champion. After that he went out to Iceland and settled in the farm at Borg, living there until old age, and many men are descended from him. There the saga ends). [1]

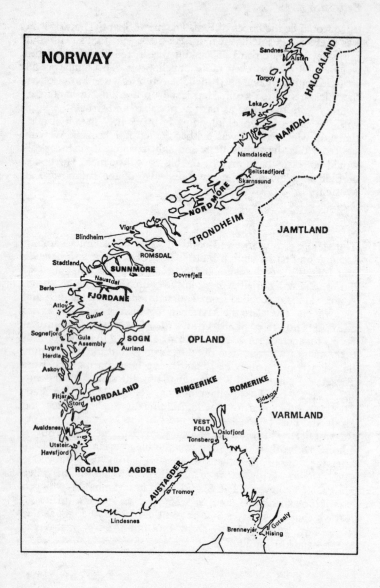

Areas of viking activity mentioned in *Egils saga*.

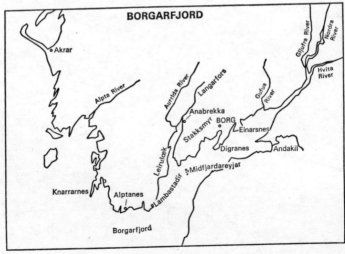

BORGARFJORD

Notes

1   **1**   The term berserk was used to describe a fighter believed to have greater strength than the norm, and to be impervious to iron. *Egils saga* itself provides descriptions of berserk symptoms: see ch. 27 (p. 39) where Kveld-Ulf becomes berserk and ch. 64 (p. 118) where Ljot's berserk characteristics are described. See further Foote and Wilson *The Viking Achievement*, p. 285.

2   ON *lendr maðr*. The main distinctions of rank among free men below the rank of earl or king are, in *Egils saga*, *lendr maðr*, *hersir*, *hǫlðr* and *bóndi* which I have translated respectively as nobleman, chieftain, freeholder and farmer. These distinctions are analysed in detail by Foote and Wilson, op. cit. pp. 84–5 and 129–30.

3   The name *Ulf* means 'wolf' and *Kveld-Ulf* means 'Night-Wolf' or literally 'Evening-Wolf'. Shape-changers were men and women who were believed to have the power to assume animal form. While the human body lay in sleep or a trance, the spirit ranged abroad in bird or animal guise.

3   **1**   He was called *Harald lúfa* until he redeemed his vow, after which he was called *Hárfagri*, 'Finehair'.

2   Literally 'rolled himself out of the kingdom'. *Heimskringla* explains: 'King Hrollaug went up on to the mound where the kings usually sat, and had the king's high seat made ready and sat down in it. Then he had cushions placed on the bench where the earls usually sat. Then King Hrollaug rolled himself from the king's high seat into the earl's seat and himself awarded himself the name of earl.' All the material about Harald's conquests is dealt with in more detail in *Haralds saga*, see Bjarni Aðalbjarnarson's edition of *Heimskringla* I (Reykjavík 1941).

3 ON *hamingja* originally signifying a man's guardian spirit comes to equal 'luck'. The concept 'luck' continues to indicate a man's personal share rather than the operation of chance. Kveld-Ulf points out elsewhere that Harald's luck is greater than that of other men, and tells Thorolf, ch. 19, that though he may have ability he has not the luck needed to match himself against Harald.

4 1 *Klofi:* 'Cleaver'. Sigurður Nordal points out in his note on this name that Thorfinn, Earl of the Orkneys, had a similar appellation—*hausakljúfr*, 'skull-cleaver'.

2 It was said in ch. 2 that Olvir had made many love-songs about Solveig. Such an action was considered a slur on family honour and could in Icelandic law be punished by the lesser outlawry. The attack on Olvir by Atli's sons, Solveig's brothers, is therefore a normal act of vengeance.

3 Only one poem and one fragment of Olvir's are preserved. The complete poem is in *Hauksbok*, the fragment in Snorri's *Edda*.

4 This refers to land inherited from one's ancestors, not given by grant from the king. For a full definition see Foote and Wilson, op. cit. pp. 81–2.

5 Iceland was almost certainly discovered by the Swede Gardar Svavarsson about A.D. 860, though there are conflicting accounts. The first settler was the Norwegian Ingolf Arnarson (see chs. 23 and 25 of *Egils saga*) who settled at Reykjavík circa A.D. 874.

7 1 ON *hálfbergrisi*. Nordal compares with the nickname 'Halftroll' in Kveld-Ulf's family, and says that such nicknames appear to have been used of men whose ancestry was part-Lapp.

2 ON *skúta*. Alan Binns comments: '*Skúta* is never as far as I know described as rowed by so many men a side, and only rarely by number of benches, usually just number of men. Both these systems would be consistent with a craft on which one man pulled two oars, implying a narrower, lighter, lower-sided boat than the *karfi*. This is what you

would expect from its frequent appearance in association with larger vessels, but in distinction from them. As long as warships did carry largish boats the usual term for them was "pinnace".'

3 The later quarrel over inheritance depends on whether this sum could properly be considered *mund*, the bridegroom's payment for the bride. Harek says in ch. 9 that they can provide witnesses that *mund* was paid. But Bjorgolf's use of the word *lausabrullaup* suggests payment for a slave rather than *mund*. Nordal's notes make it clear that in Norwegian law the ceremony described here did not make Hildirid Bjorgolf's legal wife, and her sons therefore do not have the inheritance rights that they subsequently claim.

4 ON *finnskattr*. In the account which Ohthere gives to King Alfred Lapp-tribute is described as follows: 'Their wealth is mostly in the tribute which the Lapps pay them. That tribute is in the skins of beasts, in the feathers of birds, in whale-bone, and in ship-ropes which are made from whale-hide and seal-hide. Each pays according to his rank. The highest in rank has to pay fifteen marten skins, five reindeer skins, one bear skin and ten measures of feathers, and a jacket of bearskin or otterskin, and two ship-ropes. Each of these must be sixty ells long, one made from whale-hide the other from seal.' (Translated from Sweet's *Anglo-Saxon Reader*, revised by Dorothy Whitelock (1967) p. 19.)

8 1 Audun got his nickname which literally is 'bad poet' because he stole a refrain from a poem composed by his kinsman Ulf Sebbason about King Harald.

2 Thorbjorn Hornklofi's poems are frequently quoted in *Haralds saga*. It is thought that his nickname derives from the fact that in one of his poems on Harald he adopts the persona of a raven, and *hornklofi* is a poetic word for 'raven'.

9 1 Thorolf, Bard etc. were *í stafni* and the king's berserks *í sǫxum*. Alan Binns comments: '*Sax* is the part aft of the stem where the hull is narrowing more sharply towards the bow, and therefore at the bulwark level flaring out from the waterline. Left to themselves the planks at this point would

tend to spring outwards and therefore had to be strengthened by the *saxbǫnd* which run from one bulwark to the other. The bows at Skuldelev are finished off with sections of dummy clinker planking carved out of one piece, and I have not seen any name suggested for this piece. I suspect myself that in ON it might well have been called *sax*. Presumably the berserks were there because, although behind those in the actual stem, they are not sheltered as these are by the up-raised prow, but are more exposed as the ship's side has swept down by the time it gets to them.' The men in the stem are called *stafnbúar* (sing. *stafnbúi*). This select band here are Thorolf, Bard, Eyvind and Olvir. The other occasions in the saga when the word *stafnbúi* is used are limited. Thorgils Gjallandi is Thorolf's *stafnbúi* (ch. 13). Thorfid the Strong, close kinsman of Bjorn the Freeholder, is Egil's *stafnbúi* (ch. 48). He subsequently marries Egil's sister. Skuli, Egil's grandson, achieves the distinction of being *stafnbúi* for Earl Eirik Hakonarson (ch. 87). Alan Binns comments: 'I am sure the implication "right hand man" or "trusty comrade" is the important one. "Was in charge of the bow" would overstress the rank, but it must have had connotations of rank, for *frambyggjar* were just in the fore-part of the ship and were not such a select band of trusted men as the *stafnbúar*.'

2 ON *tjalda* 'to pitch a tent'. This verb is regularly used of covering ships, and I have sometimes translated simply as 'cover' sometimes 'rig awnings'. Alan Binns prefers the second of these as more correct and specific: 'It brings out the important fact that these ships were scarcely livable-in without the tent up, hence the nights in harbour.'

10   1 Possibly representatives of the Swedish king, but more probably from the district round Novgorod, ON *Garðarikriki*.

2 The ON *hundrað* is actually 120. Wherever men are calculated by the *hundrað* I have tended to use the English 'hundred' as a translation on the assumption that round numbers rather than precise figures were intended. All translations of large numbers are therefore approximations.

3 ON *skreiðfisk*. Arnold Taylor comments: 'This refers mainly to fishing for cod, but also to haddock which would be split and dried for food.' See also ch. 17.

14 1 ON *Kvenir*. Cf. OE *Cwenas* in Ohthere's description:
'Beyond the mountains Sweden borders the southern part
of the land as far as the north, and the country of the Cwenas
borders the land in the north. Sometimes the Cwenas make
raids on the Norwegians across the mountains, and sometimes the Norwegians make raids on them. There are very
large fresh-water lakes throughout these mountains and the
Cwenas carry their boats overland on to the lakes and from
there make raids on the Norwegians; they have very small,
very light boats.' Sweet, op. cit. pp. 19–20.

2 ON *Kirjálar*. Karelia equals the east part of Finland and
the neighbouring districts of Russia.

3 ON *askraki*. The translation 'marten' is based on
Ohthere's statement that part of the Lapps' tribute was in
marten skins, see above ch. 7 note 4. The word *askraki* is
found only here, and the meaning is not known. Nordal
suggests that it is a loan-word into Norse from Finnish or
Russian. Pierre Naert in an article 'Askraka', *Arkiv för
Nordisk Filologi* 67 (1957) pp. 176–81, argues that this
must represent scribal corruption from *a. skraka* in a previous manuscript, the *a.* being a normal abbreviation for
alla 'all'. He derives *skraka* from a hypothetical Old Finnish form *skraha (modern Finnish *raha*) meaning 'skin'
or 'fur', the equivalent of ON 'grey wares'. A phrase meaning 'all furs' or 'all grey furs' was thus wrongly copied by
a scribe who did not know what it meant.

17 1 ON *Vágar*. Modern Ostvago and Vestvago. The ON
form simply means 'the bays'. Nordal comments that this
is the best fishing ground off Norway.

2 White goods and grey goods are distinguished. The grey
goods are furs, the white goods sheepskins and cloth, ON
vaðmál. Foote and Wilson point out (op. cit. p. 171) that
since the word *vaðmál* is found as a loan-word in Middle
English this is evidence that the material itself was exported.
They discuss further (p. 172) the types of cloth that were
imported into Scandinavia. That Thorolf was both exporting and importing cloth is explained by the fact that he
was exporting coarse stuff (twill?) and importing luxury
cloths (cf. Arinbjorn's gifts of clothes made from English
cloth in various colours, ch. 67). This is the point of Thorolf's

remark when he loses the return cargo that his household would not be so finely dressed as he had intended.

19   1   Nordal notes that the usual route along the Norwegian coast was the inshore one, but Thorolf takes the open sea route so that no news of his activities can circulate.

      2   ON *ármaðr*. See Foote and Wilson, op. cit. p. 131. *Egils saga* mentions various other men in charge of the king's farms. The comment on Atloy-Bard (ch. 43) that 'he was not a man from a great family, but King Eirik and Queen Gunnhild had a high regard for him' seems typical of saga attitude to these men.

20   1   The nick-name means 'Bald-Grim'.

21   1   i.e. make all possible speed away from the meeting with Thorolf.

22   1   The distinction is not really between 'slaves' and 'servants' but between two kinds of slaves ON *þrælar* and *mansmenn*. It may be between the slave born on the estate and the bought slave. It is normal in the sagas when men resorted to burning each other in their homes for only the fighting men of the household to be attacked in this manner. All those who because of sex, age or status were not considered able to bear arms were permitted to leave the building.

      2   When the king took part in a battle it was customary for him to be protected by a circle of men, shields overlapping.

      3   ON *bautasteinar*. Scholars disagree over the meaning of the first element. Nordal offers two interpretations both depending on the sense 'stab' for the first half: either 'a stone driven into the earth' or 'a stone in memory of a man killed by weapons'. The context however makes it clear that these were memorial stones. The Eddic poem *Hávamál* says that *bautasteinar* seldom stand by the roadside unless kinsmen raise them for kinsmen. The saga of Hákon the Good had the line 'Tall *bautasteinar* stand by the grave of Eirik Ullserk'.

23   1   ON *frændi skyldr*, literally 'an obliged kinsman', that is,

one sufficiently close to have an obligation to take vengeance.

2 The Icelandic *Landnámabók* ('Book of the Settlement') records full details of the first settlers, their background, their landholdings and their descendants.

3 ON *goði*. In the pre-Christian settlement of Iceland the word means 'priest' but always carried with it the sense of temporal power. Norwegian terms of rank such as *jarl* or *hersir* were not operative in Iceland. The general term for a free farmer, *bóndi*, is retained, and power in Iceland is vested among the *goðar*. See Foote and Wilson, op. cit. pp. 132–135.

24 1 'Now I have learned that Thorolf has perished north on the island. The Norns are harsh to me. The Thunderer chose the sword-swinger too early. Old age (Thor's weighty wrestling friend) prevents me from going to battle (the assembly of the goddess of metal). There will be no quick vengeance though my heart urges me.' [The kenning for 'old age' is a reference to the story in which Thor challenged his enemies to a wrestling-match and was invited to try his skill against an old woman. She turned out to be Old Age herself, and the moral is that old age can bring the best of men to their knees.]

25 1 The original here simply says 'Beigaldi was a coal-biter'. 'Coal-biter' is a popular term in the sagas for the lazy child spending his time by the fire, who later turns out to be a hero.

2 In fact only eleven are named. The same names recur in the descriptions of Skalla-Grim's gifts of land to his followers (chs. 28 and 29) with the exception of Grim the brother of Grimolf.

27 1 ON *bryntroll* literally 'troll' or 'enemy of the mailcoat'. It is sometimes described as a double-bladed axe. David Wilson comments: 'There is no such thing as a double-bladed axe.'

2 ON *lypting*, a raised section at the stern of the ship.

3 Skalla-Grim describes his poem as a *kviðling*, a 'little verse'. It is in popular rather than scaldic metre, the lines

have four syllables not six, and instead of the usual elaborate pattern of assonance and consonant echo, the lines are linked by alliteration and end rhyme:

> Nús hersis hefnd
> við hilmi efnd;

The word order is straightforward and there are no kennings.

28 1 Finnur Jónsson sees this as a reference to the quarrel between Thorstein Egilsson and Steinar, chs. 80–4. Nordal disagrees, suggesting that the quarrel referred to here is one otherwise unrecorded.

30 1 'The blacksmith (pole of iron) must rise very early who wishes to win silver from the wind-sucking bellows (clothing of the brother of the sea). I let sledge-hammers ring on the hot iron (gold of the fire) while the wind-eager bellows (stirring-cabin of the wind, i.e. that which sets the wind in motion) whistle.

31 1 'Still I have come to the hearth of Yngvar, he who gives to warriors gold (the bed of the gleaming thong of the heather). I was anxious to find him. You will not, giver of the twisted, shining gold (land of the snake) find a better three-year-old craftsman of poetry than I am.' [*Thong of the heather* is a snake, and the snake's *bed*, according to tradition, is gold.]

2 'The skilful sword-smith (pole that tempers the wound-gosling) gave to word-keen Egil three ever-silent snail-shells (dogs of the furious sea) as payment for his poem. The traveller (man who knows the horse of the sea-plain), he who knew how to delight Egil, gave a fourth gift, a duck's egg (bed-treasure of the brook-partridge).'

32 1 ON *borg* which I translate 'fort' in ch. 52, 'town' when it is used of York in ch. 59. The translation 'broch' here is because the only place on the island of Mousa which could possibly be described as *borg* 'fortified settlement' is the broch.

36 1 ON *karfi*. Alan Binns comments: '*Karfi* is always des-

cribed in texts I know as rowed by so many men on each side, which suggests that each man pulled a single oar. The boat was presumably too heavy, and the oars too long and heavy (because of a higher freeboard?) for one man to manage two. This suggests it was like a miniaturised longship, confirmed by reference in lawbooks to its later use for coast defence vessels, and by the fact that it usually seems to be an independent unit (i.e. not dependent on a larger vessel). I do not think there is any etymological justification for using "cutter" as a translation, but it does suggest a similar class of small official vessels, like Revenue cutters, pilot cutters etc.'

37 1 The area inhabited by the Biarmar (cf. OE Beormas) is the land round the White Sea. Ohthere says of the land on the far side of a river plausibly identified as the Varzuga: 'The Beormas had fully cultivated their land' and observes further that it seemed to him that 'the Lapps and the Beormas spoke nearly the same language.' The unlikely feature of the story is that Eirik won Gunnhild on this expedition, though it agrees with the version in *Haralds saga*, which gives a long description of how Gunnhild was found studying magic under Lapp tuition. The *Historia Norvegiae*, contradicting all the Icelandic sources, is probably right in saying that Gunnhild was the daughter of King Gorm of Denmark. This would account both for her sending Eyvind to Danish protection, and for her own return to Denmark after the death of Eirik Blood-Axe.

2 The name of the island in the viking age was *Fenhring* and the name of the farm *Askr*.

38 1 'Many flaws lie along the edge of the fierce axe (wound-wolf). I own a soft axe (wood-griever). There is deceit in the axe. Let the coward blade with its smoked shaft go back. There was no need for it to come here. That was a king's gift.' [*Wound-wolf* and *wood-griever* are normal kennings for axe.]

40 1 This is obviously a childish composition. The word order is simple and there are no kennings. Nordal points out that Egil uses the word *knǫrr*, literally a cargo ship,

and oars were rarely used on these. Also the place of the helmsman was not in the prow.

44 1 'You told the warrior (enemy of trolls) that there was a lack of drink, while you were sacrificing to the spirits. This is the reason, breaker of burial mounds, that I consider you subtle in trickery. Far too maliciously you concealed the evil in your mind from men unknown to you. You have played a bad trick, Bard.' [The *spirits*, ON *dísir*, are deities about whom very little is known. The evidence is summed up by Foote and Wilson, op. cit. p. 192.]

2 'I carve runes on the horn, redden the spells in blood. I put these words on the horn (wood from the root of a wild animal's ear). Let us drink as we wish the draught poured by cheerful maidservants. Let us know how the beer that Bard marked affects us.' [The *root of the ear* is the part of the head from which the ear grows, and its *wood* is the horn. The *wild animal*'s horn is the aurochs' horn.]

3 'I'm getting drunk, Olvir grows pale with drinking. I let the beer (rain from the aurochs' spear) pour through my lips. You manage your feet badly, warrior (inciter of the rain of the spear-cloud). It's beginning to rain poems (the rain of the thanes of the High One is beginning to rain).' [The *aurochs' spear* is the horn and its *rain* is beer. *Spear-clouds* are shields and their *rain* is battle. The *High One* is Odin, his servants (*thanes*) are poets, and their *rain* is poetry.]

45 1 'In such a way have I, valiant, freed myself from the house of Gunnhild and of Eirik (guardian of the land of Lister) that some three servants of Eirik (the valkyrie's champion) delay their journey, hellbound for the high halls of Hel.' [*Lister* is a district of Norway. ON *helgenginn* means dead, but a *double entendre* is clearly intended. *Hel* is the goddess of the dead.]

47 1 'We shall, warrior (painter of the wolf's tooth), make our swords glitter in the air. We have to perform our deeds in the summer (mild season of the valley-fish). Let everyone go as quickly as possible up to Lund. Let us make the harsh song of spears before sunset.' [*Valley-fish* are snakes.

Winter is referred to elsewhere as the death of snakes, so their *mild season* is evidently summer.]

48 1 ON *skaut*, translated as 'bag', is the corner of a piece of cloth or a cloak.

2 'What are you doing in my seat, child? You have seldom given corpses (warm bread) to the wolf. I should prefer to be on my own. You have not seen the raven in autumn hover over blood (milk of corpses). You were not there when edges of swords ran on shell-thin edges.'

3 'I have gone with bloody blade and screaming spear where the ravens (wound-partridges) followed. Vikings fought fiercely: raging we gave battle. Fire ran through men's houses. We let the bloody corpses sleep in town-gateways.'

4 Nordal's note points out that when kings or chieftains drank with their retainers to 'go on to the floor' was a great honour.

49 1 'Drinking in a group'. This was when the horn or other vessel was passed round from man to man until it was empty. When two shared a horn if they were man and woman (as Bjorgolf and Hildirid in ch. 7) the amount drunk was not measured. But if two men shared a horn quarrels could arise, as here, if one drank more than a fair share. Serious drinking took place when each man had a horn to himself. One might adduce here the episode when Utgarda-Loki offered Thor a full horn, with the challenge: 'To us it seems good drinking if the horn is emptied at one go, but some people take it in two drinks. Still there is no-one here who is such a poor drinking man that he cannot empty it in three.'

2 'We made a really fierce attack off Jutland's coast. The viking, he who guarded the kingdom of the Danes, fought well, until he, Eyvind the Braggart, quick-witted, leapt down from his ship (sea-steed), he and his troop of warriors, to swim east ashore.'

51 1 Hring and Adils are obviously Norse not Welsh names. They presumably represent fictional names attached to men

whose real names have been forgotten. The poem (ch. 55) in which their names occur is unlikely to be genuine.

52 1 'Olaf put to flight one earl and felled the other. Fighting was fierce. I have heard that the prince is bold in battle. Godrek trod a fool's path on the battle field. The oppressor of the English holds half of Alfgeir's land.'

2 Campbell thinks that the names Vinheid and Vinuskog in the prose are based entirely on a misunderstanding of the poem (ch. 55) which says that Thorolf fell by the Vina river. He argues that this poem must mean Thorolf fell on the Bjarmaland expedition mentioned earlier in the saga, and it is erroneously included in the English material, causing confusion in the saga and among scholars. See Campbell's edition of *The Battle of Brunanburh* pp. 68–80, and more recently, more briefly and more dogmatically his Dorothea Coke Memorial lecture *Skaldic Verse and Anglo-Saxon History* pp. 5–7. Jón Helgason's demonstration that the poem itself is probably late (see 'Höfuðlausnarhjal' in *Einarsbók*) removes a major premise from Campbell's theory.

55 1 'Earl's killer, he who feared nothing, went valiantly into Odin's great fight. Brave-hearted Thorolf fell. The earth will grow by Vina over my noble brother. It is death-bitter. But grief must be concealed.'

2 'In front of the standard pole I loaded with corpses the field west over the sea. The battle (storm) was furious when I attacked Adils with blue Adder. Young Olaf raised a steel-storm against the English. Hring held a weapon-council. The ravens are not hungry.'

3 ON *pallinn þann inn óæðra:* this is the only time in the saga that the word *pallr* is used of the seating arrangements (except for *þver-pallr* used in chs. 71 and 72 for the place where women are sitting). It might be a conscious attempt to distinguish English custom from Scandinavian.

4 On this verse see Note on the Translation, pp. xxiii–xxv.

5 'My downcast eyebrows (peaks of the eyelids) knew how to droop with grief. Now I have found that which levelled the furrows of my forehead. The prince has cleared from

my eyes my brows (fencing crags of the plain under the hood). He is hostile to armrings.'

The *plain under the hood* is the face. Poets frequently praise princes for hostility to gold, i.e. generosity with gold. Their duty is to distribute gold, not cherish or hoard it.

6 'Now the noble-born son of kings who towers over lands makes battles stern, has brought down three princes. The land fell under the race of Ella. Æthelstan did more. All bend low before that kin-famous king. This we swear to, prince (breaker of the fire of the wave).' *Refrain* 'Now the highest Scottish hill (reindeer road) lies under bold Æthelstan.' [*The fire of the wave* is gold, and the *breaker* or distributor of gold is a prince, here Æthelstan. To refer to England as the *land of Ella* and the English as *the race of Ella* is not uncommon in scaldic verse, and it is generally assumed that the Ella referred to must be Ella of Northumbria, killer of Ragnar Lodbrok. I find it improbable that the Scandinavians should assume this petty character loomed so large in English history, and think it more likely that tradition preserved the name of Ella, king of the south Saxons of whom Bede says (*Historia Ecclesiastica* II, 5): 'He [Ethelbert] was the third English king to hold sway over all the provinces south of the river Humber. . . . The first king to hold this position was Ælla King of the South Saxons'; or alternatively of that Ella of Deira instrumental in inspiring the missionary zeal of Pope Gregory.]

56 1 'The woman (goddess of the hawk-cliff) grows used to my discourtesy. Once, when young, I dared readily lift my eyebrows (cliffs across the forehead). Now I am obliged to thrust my nose (block between the brows) into a cloak when *gerd* (ON *gerðr*, 'headdress') of *as* (ON *áss*, 'ridge') comes into the poet's thought.' [*Hawk-cliff* is arm, and *goddess* of the arm is a normal kenning for woman. The pun whereby Egil conceals Asgerd's name is more complicated than the above translation indicates, since Egil, having split her name into two syllables, then substitutes for those syllables other words with a similar meaning.]

2 'I rarely conceal in poetry (the giants' drink) the name of the woman (goddess of the stone) related to me by marriage. The sorrow of the woman (town of the sea's fire)

subsides. Some warriors (rousers of the valkyrie's clash) dabble with fingers of poetry in Odin's mead.' [The second kenning for woman is an unusual one, but the word translated *town* is actually *borg* and Egil may have intended a reference to Borg his home—and the home of Asgerd's childhood. *Fire of the sea* is gold. *Clash of the valkyrie* is battle.]

3 'The legal organization of the country goes back to the time of Harald Finehair, when the west-coast legal federation known as Gulathing was created. Its central assembly was near the mouth of Sognefjord, and in time all the western provinces ... belonged to it.' Foote and Wilson, op. cit. p. 46. But the saga-writer evidently believes that at this period only three districts belonged, those of Fjordane, Sogn and Hordaland.

4 'Thorn, son of thorn, calls my wife (pourer of beer) slave-born. Onund is busy with his avarice. Warrior (spearshaker) I have a wife (goddess of the needle) entitled to her inheritance. Receive, son of kings, our untrammelled oaths.'

5 'The inheritance betrayer, heir of Thornfoot, destroyed my inheritance. I receive his threats and imprecations whenever I try to repay him for such unlawful seizure of my estates (sorrow of oxen). We have quarrelled about much gold (land of snakes).'

6 ON *stýrði* means steered rather than captained, but it is clearly Ketil who is at the steering when Egil hurls his spear.

7 'Now the valiant warrior (Odin of the clash of the warflame) has brought down ten of the thanes of our company. But I am to blame because the stout spear (flying-thorn of Freyja of the wound-salmon) sent from my hand, flew straight between the crooked ribs of Ketil.' [*War-flame* is sword and its *clash*, battle. *Wound-salmon* is sword. *Freyja* of the sword is a valkyrie. The *flying-thorn* of a valkyrie is a spear.]

8 'May the gods drive the king from the land. So shall the powers repay him his robbery of my wealth. Odin and the gods be roused against him. Frey and Njord make the people's tyrant fly the country. God of the land be angry towards the foe of men, the one who destroys sanctuaries.'

57   1 'Thor (landgod) the law-breaker has put a long road before me. The enemy of brothers deceives himself in his wife. I have to repay Gunnhild for being driven from the land. Her temper is ruthless. When young, I managed in a moment to pay back treachery and inflict hurt.' [Egil refers to his earlier rapid vengeance on Bard, when he first incurred Gunnhild's enmity.]

2 'Too long we have sat enduring injustice from this man (tree of the bright world of the fish of the fjord of the heather) —once I guarded my wealth better—before I let Berg-Onund in the sleep of death grow used to his wounds, then Hadd, then Frodi. I draped the earth (bedfellow of Odin) with blood.' [*Fjord of the heather* is the earth, its *fish* the snake, the snake's *bright world*, gold. *Tree* of gold is a normal kenning for man.]

3 'We fought and I did not care about feuds. I reddened my warflame in the blood of the son of the warlike Blood-Axe and Gunnhild. Now there have fallen thirteen men (fir-trees of the moon of the sea) on one cutter. The warrior has done his work.' [*Moon of the sea* is gold, *trees* of gold are men.]

4 It has been suggested that the runes carved on the pole would be the texts of Egil's two poems calling on the gods to drive Eirik from the land. Magnus Olsen, writing out Egil's poems in runes in tenth-century speech-forms, arrived at a total of 72 runes for each half of these two verses, the number 72 being three times the number of letters in the runic alphabet and therefore a number of power. The theory is attractive, even if that of a romantic rather than a sceptical runologist. Jón Helgason in 'Höfuðlausnarhjal' demonstrates that the first poem must be later than the tenth century.

5 'The furious wind (enemy of the mast) vigorously cuts a file with the chisel of storms into the level road of the ship, before the prow: and with it the cold wind (wolf of willows) merciless in its blasts, files down the sea-king's swan before the prow, over the figure-head.'

58   1 David Wilson suggests that this description is based on thirteenth-century houses, and must be a late addition to the tale.

2   This action was taken so that if Skalla-Grim should walk after death, his steps should lead him back to wall not door.

59   1   Manuscript variants here offer the alternative readings 'against the vikings' and 'against the vikings and the Scots'.

2   ON *seiðr*, a form of magic regarded with some awe and some distaste. It was not a magic necessarily put to evil purpose. The one performing it fell into a trance, and his or her spirit was then free to do good or evil to another person, or to learn about the future.

3   'I have come a long journey sailing into cross-winds on the wave-way, riding the horse of the sea-king, to visit the ruler of English fields. Now the ready warrior (wielder of the wound-flame) has found, with his overabundant courage, the strongest thread in the race of Harald.'

4   Killings done by night or in secret are murders. The translation 'shameful suggestions' does not indicate how loaded the term is that Arinbjorn has used, ON *níðingsverk*.

5   ON *drápa*, a formal poem of praise including a refrain. In *Gunnlaugs saga* Gunnlaug tries to discredit a fellow-poet by saying: 'Why did you only compose a *flokkr* about the king? Didn't he seem to you worth a *drápa*?'

6   Gunnhild.

60   1   'I went west over the sea and I carried poetry (the sea of Odin's mind-shore). That was my voyage. At the ice-breaking I drew the oak afloat. I loaded the cabin of my ship with a cargo of praise.

I offer myself to the prince's hospitality (*or* the prince offers me hospitality). I have a duty to praise him. I carried my poem (mead of Odin) to the fields of England. I have achieved praise of the prince. Certainly I praise him. I ask for a hearing because I have brought praise.

Prince, think on this—it is fitting—how, if I have silence, I recite my song. Most of mankind have heard what battles the king has fought, and Odin saw where the dead lay.

The din of swords on the rim of shields increased. War grew round the prince. The prince advanced. Then there was heard the river of swords resounding, flowing mightily, the chant of battle (the storm of metal). [*River of swords* ought to be a blood kenning, but here since the emphasis is on noise, it must be another battle kenning.]

The web of spears was never out of place before the king's merry rows of shields (spear-plains). There the sea (plain of seals) lay in blood, resounded in anger under the banners.

Men fell to the ground at the flight of arrows. Eirik got great renown from that.

If people are silent, I have more to say. We have learned more about their courage. Wounds increased at the meeting of princes. Swords broke on blue edges. [*Meeting of princes* could be a general term or a specific reference to Eirik's battle with his brothers.]

Sword (saddle of the whetstone) clashed on sword (glory of battle). The sword (wound-engraver) bit. That was the blood-snake. I learned that men (Odin's oaks) fell before the sword (ice of the belt) in battle (the game of iron).

There was thrusting of spear points and clashing of sword edges. Eirik got great renown from that.

The prince reddened the blade. There was food for the ravens. Arrows took life. Bloody spears flew. The destroyer of Scots fed the wolf (horse of the giantess). The sister of Nar (Hel, or Death, goddess of the dead), trod supper for the eagles.

Eagles (battle-cranes) flew over the rows of corpses. The beaks of the ravens (wound-mews) did not lack blood. The wolf tore at wounds while blood (the wave from the spear-point) splashed up towards the beaks of ravens.

The end of hunger came for the wolf (steed of the giantess). Eirik offered corpses to the wolf by the sea.

The warrior woke the valkyrie of battle (*or* the valkyrie woke the warrior) and caused the shields (ski-fence of Haki's rock) to rattle. Points broke. Points bit. Bow-strings carried arrows from bows. [*Haki* is a sea-king, and his *rock* therefore is the sea. The *ski* of the sea is a ship, and the *fence* of the ship, shields, hung round the side of the ship when at anchor.]

The flying arrow bit. Peace was ended. The elm was drawn, the wolf was glad. The people's protector withstood death. The yew-bow twanged at the battle (drawing of edges).

The prince drew the yew-bow. Arrows (wound-bees) flew. Eirik offered corpses to the wolf by the sea.

Still I wish to make clear to men the disposition of the prince. I shall hasten with my praise. He throws out gold (river-fire) but the prince holds his land in a horn-grip. He is most to be praised. [No-one is sure what *horn-grip* ON *hornklofi* means, but the general sense is clear, that Eirik is generous with gold but keeps a hold on his lands. This is so inappropriate, though part of the conventions of praising a king, that it is difficult not to suspect irony if the poem is Egil's, incompetence if an interpolator's.]

He breaks gold (arm-fire), he offers gold (the wrist-stone). The distributor of rings does not expect praise for thrift. He spends much gold (gravel of the hawk-strand), he gladdens seafaring men with gold (Frodi's flour).

He swings the shield (field of spear-points) with the arm (seat of rings). His fame increases here as everywhere—I speak what I have thought—Eirik's deeds are known east over the sea. [The last part of this also suggests irony or incompetence. In Norway it would be conventional praise to say that a king's fame had spread west over the sea, but there is little tact in indicating that Eirik is known in Norway or even Iceland.]

Prince consider what I have composed. It is good that I had silence. I stirred with my mouth from the depths of my mind the poem (Odin's flood) about Eirik (the artist of battle).

I carried the praise of the prince to the breaking of silence. I know the measure of words in the company of men. From the mind (home of laughter) I brought praise for the prince. It has progressed so that most have heard it.'

This poem known as *Hǫfuðlausn* 'Head-Ransome' is composed in the metrical form *runhenda*. The pattern links full alliteration with end-rhyme:

> lofat vísa vann
> víst mærik þann
> hljóðs biðjum hann
> því at hroðr of fann.

If authentic it must have made its impression largely because of the use of end-rhyme, unfamiliar to a viking audience, see Stefán Einarsson's 'The Origin of Egill Skallagrímsson's Runhenda'. In the original, stanzas 6, 9, 12 and 15 represent the refrain and consist of four lines only, not the usual eight. It is not found in *Möðruvallabók*, the chief manuscript, and Jon Helgason has indicated the possibility of its being a later interpolation, not a genuine Egil poem.

61   1   'I am not unwilling to receive this head (helmet-crag) from the prince, ugly though it is. Where is the man who got a finer gift from a generous son of an all-powerful king.'

This is another 'little verse' in popular metre:

> Erumka leitt
> þott ljótr séi, . . .

2   'The unjust warrior (provider of blood for ravens) allowed Egil to rejoice in the sight of his black-browed eyes. The courage of my kinsman helped me. I am able to control, now as earlier, my well-born head (seat of the helmet) before the warrior (god of the war-snake).' [John Lucas's version of this expands the hint offered by *unjust* into a more dramatically emotional statement.]

64   1   In the original the island is called *Höð*, but the farm of Blindheim is actually on the island Vigra.

2   'I disliked the ugly anger of the king (land-demander). The cuckoo does not perch if it knows the eagle (vulture of battle) hovers over him. There I made use again as so often of Arinbjorn (the bear of the eagle's seat). He is not all defenceless who boasts of loyal helpers on his travels.' [Arinbjorn's name is concealed. His name divides into two syllables, *björn*, meaning bear, and *arinn*, hearth-stone. By substituting the word *arinn* for the phrase *eagle's seat* the name can be found.]

3   Nordal notes that *Ljótr* is a traditional name of villains, not surprisingly since it means 'ugly'.

4   'Let us on to the duel, men. We will forbid the girl to this man. Fridgeir cannot raise battle against this warrior (rouser of the valkyrie's storm) who bites the rim of his shield and sacrifices to gods. Our enemy glares at us with the eyes of the doomed.'

5 'It is not right to refuse Ljot's little requests. I play against the pale one with the darting sword (twig of the mailcoat). We will get ready for battle, and I will not let him have hope of mercy. We will, warrior, shape a fight in More for the poet.'

6 'We will strike with polished swords (hilt-wands), aim at shield with blade, test the sword (shield-moon), redden the sword in blood; I will cut Ljot off from life, play hard with the pale one, calm with iron the bold one, may the eagle come to the corpse.' [In the original no word for 'sword' is used more than once.]

7 'To me the warrior (propeller of spear-fire) seems to move away somewhat from attack. The luckless hoard-demander is afraid. The warrior (pole of arrow-dew) delays his blows, does not stand firm. The evil one treads widely round the field before the hairless head.' [*Spear-fire* is a kenning for sword. *Arrow-dew* is blood. The *hairless head* is Egil.]

8 'The warrior (wolf-feeder) fell, he who had accomplished most evils. The poet cut off Ljot's leg. I gave peace to Fridgeir. I did not look for a reward for this from the warrior (distributor of the sea-flame). For me it was a fitting game with the pale one in the fight (clash of spears).' [*Sea-flame* is gold.]

65 1 'Blue Dragvandil did not bite the shield when I wielded it, because Atli the Short blunted its edges continually. I used strength against the speech-hasty sword-user. I let my teeth destroy at need. I carried out the sacrifice.'

67 1 Æthelstan died c. A.D. 939, Eirik Blood-Axe in A.D. 954. In fact Æthelstan had already died before Egil's visit to York which is assumed to have taken place c. A.D. 948.

2 'The warrior gave freely to the poet a silk robe with gold clasps. I shall never have a better friend. Arinbjorn has not spared himself. He has gained power alongside chieftains. It will be long before another such man is born.' [In his version John Lucas has abandoned scaldic metre, finding it inadequate for conveying the genuine feeling in the poem, and has substituted for it the Yeatsian trochaic tetrameter line.]

68 1 On this proverb see an article by Bo Almqvist, 'Er konungsgarðr rúmr inngangs, en þrǫngr brottfarar: et fornisländskt ordspråk och dess iriska motstycke', in *Arv* 22 (1966) pp. 173–93.

71 1 'My mother sent me to you for this purpose, to bear word to Egil that you should be wary. The woman (goddess of the horn) said this: arrange so your stomachs that you, our guests, may in time have better provisions.'

2 'I am eager to bear witness to your food with my vomit (cheek-fluid). I bear weighty testimony that I ventured on this walk. Many a guest chooses better payment for his lodging. We do not often meet. The vomit (beer-dregs) lies in Armod's beard.' [The point of this whole revolting episode appears to be that Armod had the idea of murdering his guests, and the women's warning prevented it.]

3 'I drain off every cup though the man (rider of the sea-king's horse) frequently carries beer (the sea of the horn) to the hand of the poet (god of poetry). I leave no ale (pool of malt) in the horn, though the warrior (rouser of the sword-storm) brings me the horn till morning.' [The *sea-king's horse* is a ship, and his *rider* a seafarer. This is a general kenning for man.]

72 1 'The ill-speaking man (giver of the arm-snake) makes use of his wife and daughter. I am not afraid of the warrior (sharpener of battle). You will not seem to yourself to have deserved for your drink, to be happy, as things are, in your dealings with the poet. We'll be off on our long journey.' [The *arm-snake* is gold.]

2 'A man shall not carve runes unless he fully understands how to control/interpret them. It happens to many a man that he is led astray through a dark stave. I saw on the shaped whalebone ten hidden runes carved. That has brought the woman (linden-tree of leeks) great injury for a long time.' [A *stave* means a letter of the runic alphabet.]

73 1 'Know, if I travel with four there are not six who are able to meet me in fight with red swords (the battle-god of the shield's cutting knives). But if I journey with eight there are not those twelve who can terrify the heart of me, dark-

browed one, at the fight (drawing of edges).' [The *battle-god of the shield* is Odin, and his *cutting knives* are swords.]

74   1   Egil gave Alf a *loðólpa* and Alf claimed he would get a *loðkápa* from it. Nordal's note points out that the two words appear to have been used interchangeably for a top garment (the first syllable *loð* means 'fur') but the *ólpa* may have been wider, and the *kápa* of a more elaborate cut, in which case an *ólpa* that fitted Egil might well make a *kápa* for Alf.

78   1   Thorgerd's reference to the goddess Freyja means, of course, that she will eat her supper not in this world but in the next.

2   'There is great heaviness in moving the tongue, or in lifting the tool (steelyard) of song. There is not much hope of poetry (Odin's theft) nor is it easy to carry from the cavern of thought.

Heavy sobbing causes heaviness, and it is not easy to cause a flow of poetry (that happy discovery of the sons of Frigg formerly carried from Jotunheim) from the mind (place of thought). [References to poetry as Odin's theft, *the discovery of the sons of Frigg*, etc. are to a legend in which Odin obtained from the giants the mead of poetry.]

Which lived without reproach on the boat of Nokkver. [This is corrupt and no-one is clear what it means.] The sea (wounds of the neck of the giant) howls, down before the doors of the boat-house of Nain. [*Nain* is a dwarf name, his *boat-house* is the rocks, and here the reference is probably to Skalla-Grim's mound.]

For my race comes to an end, like storm-felled maples of the forest. The man is not brisk who carries the broken joints of a kinsman's corpse down from the floor [i.e. of the hall].

Yet first I will count the corpse of my mother and the death of my father. This I bear out from the mind (word-temple), the timber of praise, leafy with speech.

Grim to me was the gap which the wave broke in the kin-stronghold of my father. Incomplete and open stands the gap in my line which the sea wrought for me.

Ran [goddess of the sea] has dealt most roughly with me.

I am stripped of close friends. The sea has slit the bonds of my race, a strand twisted into the rope of myself.

Know if I could avenge the injury with sword, time would be at an end for the alesmith. If I could fight the brother of the wind (wave-troubler) I would match myself and against Ran (Ægir's moon). [The god of the sea, *Ægir*, is also the brewer for the gods, therefore *alesmith*. His mate or *moon* is *Ran*.]

But I do not seem to myself to have strength in this cause against the slayer of my son. Clear to the eyes of everyone are the unsupported footsteps of an old man.

The sea has robbed me of much. It is bitter to count the death of kin, since Bodvar (the shield of my race) turned lifeless on the paths of joy.

I know myself that in my son was not grown the stuff of an evil man. If that man (shield-wood) had reached full ripeness before Odin took him to himself (*or* until he had become a full-grown warrior).

Always he valued most the words of his father, though all men spoke otherwise. He upheld me in the home (?) and of my strength was the chief support.

A brother's loss often comes into my thought (wind of the moon-bear). I think about him when battle increases look out for him and think on this: [The *moon-bear* (or moon-enemy) is a giant, and *wind* of the giant means thought.]

Who is minded to stand by my side, what other man will be there in danger. Often I need this against stubborn men, I become cautious in flight when friends diminish.

It is very difficult to find one whom I can trust among all the peoples of the worlds (gallows of Odin). For evil betrays his kin, selling for rings the corpse of his brother. [i.e. accepting financial compensation instead of taking vengeance.]

I find that often when money is offered . . . [rest of stanza lost, but presumably continuing the theme of the preceding stanza.]

It is also said that no-one may get recompense for a son, unless one's self begets yet a son to be seen by others as a man born in his brother's place.

I take no pleasure in the company of men, though each keeps peace with me. My son is come to Odin's home, the son of my wife to visit his kin.

But against me stands with unshakable mind Ægir (the lord of the fen of mixed malt). I cannot hold upright my head (earth of the hood) my head (wagon of thought). [*The fen of mixed malt* is beer.]

Since the furious fire of illness took from home my son, I know that one who avoided blame, was wary of faults. [Gunnar, Egil's second son, was the first to die, presumably of a fever.]

I remember that still that Odin (the speech-friend of the Gauts) raised up into the home of the gods the ash-tree of my race, that which grew from me, the kin-branch of my wife.

I had good things from Odin (the lord of the spear). I became ready to trust in him, before the victory-lord, Odin (friend of chariots) broke friendship with me.

I make no sacrifice to Odin (the brother of Vilir) the foremost of the gods out of eagerness. Yet Odin (Mimir's friend) has provided for me recompense for injuries if I make a better count.

Odin (the wolf's adversary), used to fights, gave to me poetry (a flawless art) and that temper which made known enemies out of tricksters.

Now things are hard for me. Hel (the sister of Odin's foe) stands on the headland. Yet I shall gladly, with good courage, unconcerned wait for my death.'

The metre of this poem, *Sonatorrek*, is *kviðuháttr* in which the odd lines have three syllables, the even lines four:

> lastalauss
> es lifnaði . . .

There are two stresses to each line, and each pair of lines is linked by alliteration, preferably on both stressed syllables in the first line, and one in the second, but sometimes only one in each. The main manuscript of the saga *Mǫðruvalla-bók* preserves only the first stanza of this poem, the rest is added from another manuscript.

3 'I am swift of word to praise a prince, but short of speech towards the niggardly, outspoken about the deeds of a lord, but silent about people's lies.

Full of contempt for tellers of tales, I am singing the praises of my friends. I have, with the flawless mind of a poet, sought many a seat of princes.

Formerly I had gained the anger of a powerful king a son of the Ynglings. I drew the hat of daring over my dark head and made my way to the chieftain's home.

Where, under the helmet of terror, the all-powerful lord of the people sat in the land. The king ruled in York with harsh thought for his sea-washed shores.

It was not safe, nor without terror, to look at the light of Eirik's eye (moon of the brow), when serpent keen the eye (forehead moon) of the all-powerful, shone with terrifying light.

Yet I dared to bring my poem (bolster-price of the snake) before the lord of the forest, so that the poem (cup of Odin) came frothing to every man's ear-mouth. [*Odin*, in the likeness of a snake, went to Gunnlod and slept with her. In return she gave him the gift of poetry.]

My poet's reward did not seem fair to look at, to men in the prince's house. I received from the chieftain for my poem (mead of Odin) this wolf-grey head (hill of the hat).

This I accepted and two went with it, the black treasures under my drooping brows, and that mouth which took my head-ransom to the prince's feet.

With that I received my rows of teeth and the tongue, and my ear-lids endowed with hearing, and that gift of the glorious king was counted better than gold.

There stood by me on the other side, better than many lords (enemies of gold) my true friend, he whom I could trust, whose honour increases in every action.

Arinbjorn who alone, first of men, brought me from the king's enmity, friend of the prince who in no way betrayed me in the court of the warlike prince.

And let the great furtherer of my deeds ... of Halfdan that there might be injury to his race. [The manuscript is illegible for part of this stanza. Nordal suggests that it contained a reference to the quarrel between Egil and Eirik, and that 'injury to his race' is a reference to the killing of Rognvald.]

I will be called a friend-thief, disappointing hopes in my poetry (drink of Odin), unworthy of praise and promise-breaker, unless I make payment for this gain.

Now it is seen where, with the poet's feet on a steep path, I shall set before all men, in the sight of many, the fame of the mighty kin of chieftains.

The stuff of fame is easily shaped with the plane of my voice for my friend Thorir's kinsman. For two or three ideas lie chosen on my tongue.

I tell that first which most know, which seeks out the ears of all people, how liberal Arinbjorn (the bear of the table of the terror of the birch) seemed to men. [*The terror of the birch* is fire, *the table* of fire, the hearth-stone (*arinn*), *the bear* of the hearth-stone (*bjǫrn arins*) is Arinbjorn.]

To everyone it is a wonder how he endows men with riches, but Frey and Njord have bestowed on Arinbjorn (the Stone-Bear) money as his strength.

For at the home of the chief descendant of Hroald goods in abundance stream to all. One sees friends riding from all directions across the wide earth (base of the wind-bowl). [*The wind-bowl* is heaven, its *base* is the earth.]

He had a draw-rope to men's ears like a prince. He was dear to the gods among the multitude of men, friend of Vethorm, the help of the weak/the Veklings. [*Vethorm* is unknown, and the last phrase is not clear.]

He does that which most men will fail to do though their money does not fail them. I do not say it is a short distance between the houses of princes, and it is not easy to shaft the spears of all. [Nordal interprets: 'Because such men are rare, so much rests on them.']

At Arinbjorn's no man went from the longship of the bed treated with mockery or with hard words, with his hand (spear-home) empty.

He is fierce to wealth, he who lives in Fjordane, he is bitter enemy to gold rings (the race of Draupnir), he is the foe of rings (the thief of Son) dangerous to rings, a treasure-killer.

He has got his life's field well-sown with wealth (the breaking of peace). [The rest of the stanza is missing. Presumably the *breaking of peace* means wealth because it refers to loot won by fighting.]

It would not be right if the gold-diminisher had thrown on the sea (mew-path) hard-ridden by sea-horses (stud of Rokkvi i.e. ships) the many gains he gave to me.

I was early awake. I put words together as the morning work of the tongue (speech-servant). I built a pile of praise which long will stand not readily broken, in the hedged field of poetry.'

Arinbjarnarkviða is in the same metre as *Sonatorrek*.

4 'I fought alone against eight, twice against eleven, so we gave the dead to the wolf, I alone was their killer. We had a hard exchange in fighting with swords (knives that terrify shields/make shields shake). I let the sword (fire of the foreign sheath?) be wielded by the arm (ash-tree of the sleeve?)' [The text is corrupt and the last two kennings are based on Nordal's emendations.]

5 'They decrease now, the bright men of battle (the assembly of the god) they who diminished gold (daylight of the meadgiver). Where am I to look for open-handed men, those who on the far side of the island-studded sea (belt of the earth) hailed silver (dripping snow of the hawk's high hill) on me for my words.' [The *meadgiver* is the horn, and its *light* is gold, because gold was often used in the decoration of drinking horns. The *hawk's hill* is the hand, and its *snow* is silver.]

6 Einar's nickname which means 'tinkling-scales' is explained in *Jómsvíkinga saga*: 'The earl took a fine pair of scales made of burnished silver and gilt all over. With it were two weights, one of gold, the other of silver, on each of which the figure of a man was engraved. They were called lots. The peculiarity of the weights was this, that when the earl put them on the scales and said what they were to signify, if that one came up which he wanted, then it trembled in the bowl so that it gave off a tinkling sound. The earl gave the scales to Einar who was delighted with the gift.' *The Saga of the Jomsvikings* trans. N. F. Blake (1962) p. 33.

7 'While others were sleeping I generously made poems (the drink of Odin) about the defender of men who rules over the land. I repent this. I think further that to the breaker of gold, the valiant leader, no poet seems worse than I am. Too eagerly I sought out the prince here.'

8 'I shall seek the earl, the one who dared with his sword to make food for the wolf. I shall line with ring-shields Sigvaldi's ship which has double rows of oars. The one who swings the sword (wound-snake) will not wave me away, when we find that lord. I shall bear my shield out to the ship (sea-king's ski).' [This poem is also quoted in *Jómsvíkinga saga*.]

9   'It is time to illumine with my praise the bright shield
(fence of ships) which I have received. The message of the
treasure-sender came home to my hand. I shall not lose
control of the reins of my poem (dwarf's sea-horse). Listen
to my words.' [*Sea-horse* is ship, and the *dwarf's* ship is
poetry.]

79   1   'I have not the heir, the inheritance possessor, I need.
My son has cheated me while I'm alive. I count this cheating.
The man (rider of the steed of the waters) could well have
waited until men (users of sea-skis) had piled stones over
me.' [*Steed of the waters* and *sea-skis* are both kennings for
ships. The *rider* of the one and *user* of the other is seafarer
or just man. To *pile stones over* someone is to build his
burial mound.]

2   'Seafarer, may the king's thane hear my poem (waterfall
of the long-haired friend of the altar-fire). May your retainers concentrate on silence. Often shall good be heard of
my poetry (seed of the eagle's beak) in Hordaland pastures.
[*Sea-farer* is Nordal's interpretation of a complex and probably corrupt kenning. The *friend of altar-fire* is Odin, and
his *waterfall*, poetry. *Seed of the eagle's beak* is also poetry,
the reference again being to an episode in Odin's adventures
when obtaining it.]

81   1   The rank of *goði*. See ch. 23, note 3.

2   On outlawry see Foote and Wilson, op. cit. pp. 381–3.

3   Men owned temporary accommodation at the Assembly
which they tented over—the verb is *tjalda*, the same one
used for covering ships, see ch. 9, note 2.

82   1   Four days in spring usually at the end of May.

84   1   ON *vindskeið*, the edge-board at a gable-end.

2   'With words I drew the land from the hand of Steinar.
Then I thought I was working for the need of Geir's son.
My sister's son failed me. At that time he promised fair.
Blund could not refrain from harm. At such things I wonder.'

85   1   'My head wobbles (I have a wavering gait of the steed
of the neckband). I am tottering on to my bald head. The

borer of the hill of the legs is soft. Hearing decreases.'
[ON *borr bergis fótar* must be the penis in spite of the efforts
of some early scholars to read the kenning differently. This
is a half-poem, four lines instead of the usual eight.]

2 'Blind I went to sit by the fire. I asked the woman
(goddess of the skirt) for compassion. I carry hurt in my
eyes (fields of the eyelids) I whom a land-glorious king
honoured with gold (the word of the giant). An angry king
formerly had pleasure in my words.' [The first king referred
to must be Æthelstan, the second Eirik.]

3 'It seems to me a long time that I lie by myself, an old
man, too old, without protection of a king. I have heels
(widows) two very cold ones, and these women need the
flame.' [Egil puns on ON *ekkja* which means *widow*.
Another word for widow is *hæll* which also means *heel*.
This is another 'little poem' in popular metre:

> Langt þykki mér
> ligg einn saman . . .]

87 1 The main manuscript *Mǫðruvallabók*, AM 132 fol. ends
with 'expeditions'. The part in brackets is added from
MS AM 453 4to.

Egil's Family

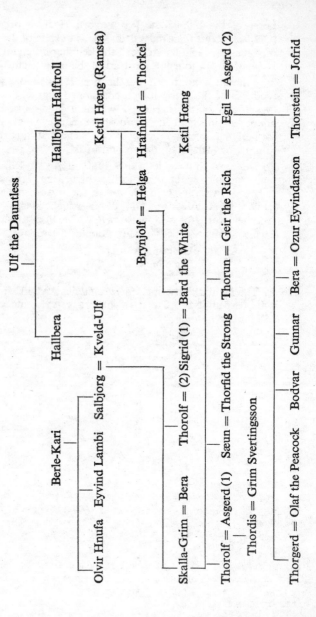

Select Bibliography

EDITION

Sigurður Nordal, *Egils saga Skalla-Grímssonar* (*Íslenzk Fornrit* II, Reykjavík 1933; reprint 1955).

FACSIMILE EDITIONS

Einar Ól. Sveinsson, *Möðruvallabók* (*Codex Möðruvallensis*). *MS. No. 132 fol. in the Arnamagnæan Collection* . . . (*Corpus codicum Islandicorum medii aevi* V; Copenhagen 1933).

Jón Helgason, *The Saga Manuscript 9.10. Aug 4to in the Herzog August Library Wolfenbüttel* (*Manuscripta Islandica* III; Copenhagen 1956).

TRANSLATIONS

W. C. Green, *The Story of Egil Skallagrimsson* . . . (London 1893). E. R. Eddison, *Egil's Saga* (Cambridge 1930; reprint 1968). Gwyn Jones, *Egil's Saga* (Syracuse 1960; reprint 1970).

TRANSLATION OF EGIL'S POEMS

Lee M. Hollander, *The Skalds. A Selection of their Poems, with Introductions and Notes* (New York 1945).

BIBLIOGRAPHY

Halldór Hermannsson, *Bibliography of the Icelandic Sagas and Minor Tales* (*Islandica* I; Ithaca, N.Y. 1908); and *The Sagas of Icelanders* (*Islandica* XXIV; 1935).

Jóhann S. Hanneson, *The Sagas of Icelanders* . . . (*Islandica* XXXVIII; Ithaca, N.Y. 1957).

Lee M. Hollander, *A Bibliography of Skaldic Studies* (Copenhagen 1958).

Hans Bekker-Nielsen, *Old Norse-Icelandic Studies: A Select Bibliography* (Toronto 1967).

Hans Bekker-Nielsen and Thorkil Damsgaard Olsen, *Bibliography of Old Norse-Icelandic Studies*. Annual bibliography. 1963 ff. (Copenhagen 1964 ff.).

SELECTED READING IN LANGUAGES OTHER THAN ENGLISH

Per Wieselgren, *Författerskapet til Eigla* (Lund 1927).

Ólafur Lárusson, *Ætt Egils Halldórssonar og Egils saga* (*Studia Islandica* II; Reykjavík 1937).

Sigurður Nordal, *Íslenzk Menning* I (Reykjavík 1942).

Jón Helgason, 'Athuganir um nokkur handrit Egils sögu.' *Nordæla. Afmæliskveðja til Sigurðar Nordals* (Reykjavík 1956) 110–48.

Odd Nordland, *Hǫfuðlausn i Egils saga: Ein tradisjonisk studie* (Oslo 1956).

Peter Hallberg, *Snorri Sturluson och Egils saga Skallagrímssonar. Ett försök til språklig författerbestamning* (*Studia Islandica* XX; Reykjavík 1962).

Vésteinn Ólason, 'Er Snorri höfundur Egils sögu?' *Skírnir* 142 (Reykjavík 1968) 48–67.

Jón Helgason, 'Hǫfuðlausnarhjal.' *Einarsbók. Afmæliskveðja til Einars Ól. Sveinssonar* (Reykjavík 1969) 156–76.

Anne Holtsmark, 'Skallagrims heimamenn.' *Maal og Minne* (Oslo 1971) 97–105.

Bjarni Einarsson, *Litterære forudsætninger for Egils saga* (Reykjavík 1975).

FURTHER READING IN ENGLISH

A. H. Smith, 'The site of the Battle of Brunanburgh.' *London Mediaeval Studies* I (1937) 56–9.

Alistair Campbell (ed.) *The Battle of Brunanburh* (London 1938).

Alistair Campbell, 'The opponents of Haraldr hárfagri at Hafrsfjǫrðr.' *Saga-book of the Viking Society* 12 (1942) 232–237.

B. J. Whiting, 'Óhthere (Óttar) and Egils saga.' *Philological Quarterly* 24 (1945) 218–26.

Stefán Einarsson, 'The origin of Egil Skallagrímsson's Runhenda.' *Scandinavica et Fenno-Ugrica. Studier tillägnade Björn Collinder* (1954) 54–60.

Theodore M. Andersson, *The Icelandic Family Saga: an analytic reading* (Cambridge, Mass. 1967).

A. L. Binns, 'The navigation of viking ships round the British Isles in Old English and Old Norse sources.' *The Fifth Viking Congress* (Tórshavn 1968) 103–17.

Anne Holtsmark, 'On the werewolf motif in Egil's saga Skalla-grímssonar.' *Scientia Islandica—Science in Iceland* 1 (1968) 7–9.

Gwyn Jones, 'Egil Skallagrímsson in England.' (Sir Israel Gollancz Memorial Lecture.) *Proceedings of the British Academy* 38 (1952) 127–44.

Gwyn Jones, 'The Angry Old Men.' *Scandinavian Studies. Essays presented to Dr. Henry Goddard Leach* ... (1965) 54–62.

P. G. Foote and D. M. Wilson, *The Viking Achievement* (London 1970).

Alistair Campbell, *Skaldic Verse and Anglo-Saxon History* (The Dorothea Coke Memorial Lecture in Northern Studies, London 1971).

P. M. Mitchell, 'Höfuðlausn: Erik's izzat.' *Mediaeval Scandinavia* 5 (1972) 45–8.

Michael L. Bell, 'Oral allusion in *Egils saga Skalla-Grimssonar*. A computer-aided approach.' *Arkiv for nordisk filologi* 91 (1976) 51–65.

Kaaren Grimstad, 'The giant as a heroic model: the case of Egill and Starkaðr.' *Scandinavian Studies* 48 (1976) 284–98.

E. O. G. Turville-Petre, *Scaldic Poetry* (Oxford 1976).

Donald K. Fry, 'Polyphemus in Iceland.' *Acta* 4 (1977) 65–86.

Margaret Clunies Ross, 'The art of poetry and the figure of the poet in *Egils Saga*.' *Parergon* 22 (1978) 3–12.

Roberta Frank, *Old Norse Court Poetry* ... (Islandica XLII; Cornell University Press 1978).

Michael L. Bell, 'Fighting words in *Egils saga*: lexical pattern as standard bearer.' *Arkiv for nordisk filologi* 95 (1980) 89–112.

Ralph West, 'Snorri Sturluson and *Egils saga*: statistics of style.' *Scandinavian Studies* 52 (1980) 163–93.

Melissa A. Berman, '*Egils saga* and *Heimskringla*.' *Scandinavian Studies* 54 (1982) 21–50.

R. I. Page, 'A Tale of Two Cities.' *Peritia* 1 (1982) 335–51.

Index of Personal Names

Names of people who play no part in the saga but occur only in genealogies, etc., are in lower case

209

Index of Place-Names

217